Art Since 1945

Harry N. Abrams Inc., New York

Art Since 1945

Art Since 1945

60 color plates

120 gravure plates

Marcel Brion, Paris

Sam Hunter, New York

Giulio Carlo Argan and Nello Ponente, Rome

Umbro Apollonio, Venice

Otto Bihalij-Merin, Belgrade

Will Grohmann, Berlin

Herbert Read, London

H. L. C. Jaffé, Amsterdam

J. P. Hodin, London

Library of Congress Catalog Card Number: 58 - 13480
Milton S. Fox, Editor
Printed in Germany by M.DuMont Schauberg, Cologne

Contents

France (School of Paris) · *Marcel Brion* 11

Belgium · *Marcel Brion* 53

Italy · *Giulio Carlo Argan and Nello Ponente* 85

Spain · *Umbro Apollonio* 121

Poland, Yugoslavia · *Otto Bihalij-Merin* 125

Germany, Austria, Switzerland · *Will Grohmann* 155

Great Britain · *Herbert Read* 221

Holland · *H. L. C. Jaffé* 251

Scandinavia · *J. P. Hodin* 255

USA · *Sam Hunter* 283

Notes 332

Bibliography 349

List of Plates 351

Index 367

Preface

Painting in the years since 1945 has reached so high a level of accomplishment, style, and assurance, on both sides of the Atlantic, that it invites a preliminary stock-taking and an attempt to summarize dominant creative ideas. This should be of particular interest to us on this side of the water, since at no other time in our history has American art been so highly regarded abroad, and its influence on current work so readily acknowledged.

In art today, most people will recognize a community of concepts, a linkage between leading personalities not only within a given country, but also among nations and between Europe and America. Yet, the widespread notion that modern art suffers from complete uniformity is wrong. Indeed, it is evident to anyone seriously concerned with contemporary artists and their ideas that—despite lively international relations, despite international exhibitions and competitions, despite the numerous publications on modern art in every language and the diffusion of modern works through reproductions, despite exchanges of all sorts—enough regional qualities are left to make it difficult for any single individual to evaluate the entire variety of the contemporary creative effort. We must, after all, view the work of art as arising from some particular human situation and not merely as a detached aesthetic phenomenon. We want to know not only where good pictures are being painted but also why they look the way they do.

It was decided therefore to distribute the text and the choice of illustrations for this book among a number of authors who know the art of their own or another country from long and intense experience. It was hoped in this way to assure that no essential achievements would be overlooked and no extraneous judgments would intrude. Needless to say, the criteria of what makes a great work of art (and who today can be sure of what has a claim to greatness, since we lack the necessary distance from our own creations?) are independent of national yardsticks. Still, what cannot be readily classified needs to be observed from day to day in order to be properly diagnosed and placed in its own proper context.

The art of France is better known than that of any other country and has for a long time been in universal demand. In recent years French art has experienced another remarkable expansion through resident foreign artists who, under the name of School of Paris, are enriching and modifying the physiognomy of French art; thus, understandably enough, this chapter is larger than the one dealing with England. The latter includes consideration of a number of sculptors, since in England modern sculpture occupies a leading position and has become indispensable to any account of England's contribution to modern art. In Italy the situation is different, insofar as, since the emergence of Futurism about half a century ago, contemporary painting has pursued its own fairly steady course. Still, the Italian authors felt it advisable to cast at least a passing glance at the situation of architecture and sculpture, and their links with modern Italian painting.

The American author, on the other hand, had to take account of the fact that in his country the modern movement has had a fitful development, and that the decisive forces of current modern American painting did not emerge or begin to assume their present shape until the time of the Second World War. Although the existence of a native American tradition is often denied, and although many American artists have spent profitable years of study in Europe, it is clear that today, at least, there exists an authentic American school which has already cast ist influence over European art.

In Germany, finally, the present situation has been very largely conditioned by the fact that for twelve years the country was cut off from the international artistic scene, so that the resumption of this link in 1945 was a sudden, almost violent one. The smaller areas of creativity have been treated in shorter supplementary chapters.

We have not attempted any conclusions from a comparison of the various countries here discussed. They would not only be premature; they might very well be entirely misleading. Every author has been given all necessary leeway so that he would not be obliged to express the specific qualities of his area through some predetermined pattern of approach. Any such schematization would have distorted the approach which might be appropriate to the art of each particular nation. We have preferred to run the risk of incongruity among the various chapters rather than to enforce an arbitrary conformity.

The reproductions have been treated in much the same free fashion. A given artist or movement may have a certain degree of importance with the outsider, and quite another in native minds. Also, a color plate sometimes carries more weight than a page of text, while a black-and-white reproduction may seem to imply that the work shown is of lesser importance. For such reasons we believed it essential to leave responsibility for the choice and distribution of illustrations to the authors. Let us concede, however, that the decision of what to reproduce in color has not been entirely a matter of artistic evaluation. Ideally, all the illustrations ought to be in color, but the cost of such a book would be prohibitive.

Although much has been written about the art of the past decade, we are still too close to the events themselves to play historian. We all are part of the contemporary scene and are thus not in a position to judge it dispassionately. The best that any of us can do is to try to be as objective as possible, without surrendering our own considered personal judgments and responses. This has been the goal of our authors.

The Publishers

In conformity with the plan of this collective work, our subject is French painting, particularly the School of Paris, as it has generally been called for the last few decades. This term is vague: for this is no "school" in the usual sense of the word (School of Barbizon, School of Worpswede, School of Laethem-Saint-Martin), and any painter of any nationality can belong to it, provided he live in Paris, or at least in France. Indeed, the term is almost meaningless for another reason: because the pictorial vocabulary of our epoch is more universal, more international than ever before. This is especially true of abstract art, which has been the general language of two generations of painters, all of them vigorously individualistic, yet all painting in a style that ranges from Milan to San Francisco, from London to Buenos Aires, and from Berlin to Tokyo. Incidentally, this internationalism is one of the things the partisans of nationalism in art hold against the nonfigurative painters, forgetting that such a blurring of national particularities (to the extent that Impressionism, Neue Sachlichkeit, Pittura Metafisica can be said to have been national phenomena) is highly favorable to the development of individuality. Moreover, contacts between artists of nationalities as widely differing as those gathered under the label "Ecole de Paris" result in fruitful interaction. Since we have no absolute yardstick for determining whether a given foreign artist living in Paris belongs to this School of Paris, it is possible that the reader will find mentioned, in the following pages, more than one painter whom he would regard as rightfully belonging in a chapter dealing with his own nation, or conversely, he may be surprised by omissions.

Whereas the geographical definition of the School of Paris is only approximately accurate, the period covered by our analysis seems to be more clearly delimited. Studying the evolution of painting from 1945 to this day, we shall inevitably have to deal with both artists whose fame dates from the preceding period, and artists whose individuality is in process of forming. For the last ten years the art historian and the critic have witnessed prodigious rocket-like starts, slow maturations, examples of genuine and patient organic development, or cases of forced growth in which the deepening of the inner being does not keep pace with advantages in technique. Premature success has harmed certain painters as much as late and stinting recognition has harmed others. Recognition is not always determined exclusively by merit, and the art historian must beware of the infatuations of others. He must maintain a wait-and-see attitude, which the art lover or even the critic may not share.

This essay will deal primarily with the painters who fully matured after 1945, whose evolution has most clearly asserted their originality, vigor, and authenticity, and the "young painters," whose exceptional gifts and individuality have marked their very debuts as exceptional. However, it may be of interest to inquire whether "the masters" whose fame had long been established and undisputed, have not revealed new characteristics in their works executed after 1945. A "new period" of a famous artist is just as important and deserving of scrutiny as the aesthetics of the young generations. Generally speaking, the greater an artist, the more fruitful is his capacity for renewal. Whether this renewal bears on his subject matter or on his technique, whether he deepens spiritually or expands spatially, producing works that are more serious or more imaginative, we find that his conception of art and his manner of expression have never become stabilized or frozen. Thus we must take into account the more complete conquest of space evidenced in George Braque's paintings (plate 15) which he composed after 1948 on the theme of the Bird, symbolizing extreme openness, and after 1949 on the theme of the Studio, an enclosed space within which space is perpetually created by the breathing forms and the intense inner life of the objects. We must also mention the several series in which Fernand Léger introduced familiar and naturalistic figures into a formal architecture of volumes which are dynamic and joyous and at the same time characterized by great compactness; for instance, the series of the Cyclists, painted in the United States between 1945 and 1948, and permeated with the atmosphere of that country where he lived for several years. The numerous variations on *Country Outing*, *Grand Parade* (1952–1954), and *Builders* (1950) which he executed after his return to France disclose the emergence and development of conceptions that may have been latent in his earlier works, but which had never been carried out so brilliantly. The refinement of the "crystalline state" in Jacques Villon's paintings, the fluidity of his color bathing the architecture of the forms, is also a new phenomenon which must not be underestimated; the same may be said of the analogous development toward transparency and lightness in the paintings that Matisse executed in 1953 in the church of Vence, which may be regarded as his aesthetic and spiritual testament.

A similar tendency will be noted in Chagall's preference for gouaches over the last few years. A great variety of techniques has always been one of the essential features of Max Ernst, and this variety has considerably increased since 1945; at the same time his landscapes of Arizona and Colorado, where he spent several years after 1946, disclose a more direct perception and a more inclusive vision of nature, which may also have become deeper through the artist's contact with the Indian world. In the course of the last few years, André Masson, by his own admission, has developed a new depth, both optical and emotional. As for Picasso, forever committed to change, his variations on Delacroix' *Women of Algiers* composed between December 1954 and February 1955, are a good example of the metamorphosis of a formal style, which has also been stimulated by his ceramics and "concrete" sculptures; the latter are structures developed out of the formal features of ordinary objects (such as a shovel or a bicycle handlebar). Here the renewal of technique and of aesthetics benefit from unusual chance encounters skillfully integrated

1　Edouard Pignon. 1947　(*Ecole de Paris*)

into the formal structure. And as though 1945 really had the significance of a fateful date, it was then that Auguste Herbin (b. 1882), who had combined esoteric symbolism and plastic figures reduced to primal elements, was led to compositions whose geometrical and chromatic simplicity serves as the vehicle of a mystic conception of Being and Time. Previously, his long explorations of form and color—he had begun as a figurative artist and then turned to Cubism—had resulted in his definitive formulation of "a nonfigurative, nonobjective art," which he also presented in the book he published under this title in 1949. Like Herbin, André Beaudin (b. 1895) is by no means a "young" painter. But those who have followed the development of his art over the last thirty years will discover that around 1948 his formal script was transformed, and since then it has given rise to a certain abstract quality, which without destroying the object reduces it to the function of a magic incantation.

This quality also makes its appearance in the works of Geer van Velde (b. 1898). Composed in accordance with the spirit of the Dutch interiors of the seventeenth century, they carry to their ultimate conclusion the explorations of Samuel van Hoogstraeten, Carel Fabritius, Pieter de Hooch, Emmanuel de Witte, and Vermeer of Delft. In the works of these old masters, the sense for abstract form was clothed in the natural appearance of the object, but the geometric structure and the crystal-clear construction of space were the essential elements, and could be recognized in the objects represented. In Geer van Velde's paintings these objects lose their predominance but are not eliminated, for, having become essences, they continue to live their secret life.

Studying the impact of the Second World War on the evolution of contemporary painting conceived of as a social, economic, political, and spiritual phenomenon, we find that it has not been affected in an obvious and direct way, but that there is nonetheless an incontestable parallelism between the great currents of thought and the currents of artistic creation, a parallelism that characterizes all periods in the history of art. It is a natural, biological, unconscious, and spontaneous parallelism: in most cases the artists had no personal acquaintance with the books or philosophical theories that had changed the direction of thought, but they were influenced by them because they lived in the climate determined by that thought, because, by virtue of their sensibility, they are interpreters of their epoch at least to the same extent as writers and philosophers. It will also be noted that Existentialism, which is truly the system of thought most characteristic of our epoch, corresponds to two very different tendencies of contemporary art. One is dramatic realism, whose subject is the spectacle of human misery, most strongly expressed in absurd situations, of which human suffering is most often the consequence; the other is abstraction, by means of which modern man escapes from the uncertainty and insecurity of the modern world,

2   Nicolaes de Staël. 1947 *(Ecole de Paris)*

creating an absolute and absolutely new reality, freed from the precariousness and irreality of the objectively real. It can also be conjectured that scientific progress may have influenced art, that the unique beauty of some unusual representations (photographs of nebulae, of crystals, of microscopic sections) discloses a new visual world to the artist, in which he finds not models, but creative stimulus. In short, new aspects of nature, rarer, more surprising, more varied, testifying to the majestic beauty of cosmic life, arouse the painter's emotions even though he may have no scientific training and may merely come across such powerfully inspiring images in popular magazines. By making such vicarious use of the microscope or telescope, the artist becomes intimately acquainted with a nature different from the one known by his predecessors.

Just as philosophical theories influence the artist, not dialectically, but atmospherically, as it were, so scientific insights into the structure of the universe reach him as images, and whether or not he is aware of them, become part of the complex of plastic forms that strikes his senses and help to determine the character of his creations.

Three principal tendencies share between them the post-1945 pictorial art. That year cannot be regarded as an absolute starting point, for the formation, maturation, and evolution of aesthetic currents do not manifest themselves suddenly any more than they vanish suddenly and forever. As is always the case, the new currents (which alone concern us here, for the lazy repetition of obsolete forms and loyalty to a lifeless academicism, however legitimate and perhaps indispensable for the gratification of some aspects of taste, must be excluded from this essay) contain an element of tradition, whether because this tradition is inseparable from a particular aesthetic of a given country, or because it unavoidably determines a given artist's creative life. The Impressionist tradition, and the love of vibrant colors as autonomous factors of emotion, sometimes independently of the form, are still continued by artists of a refined sensibility and a very sure taste, giving rise to a graceful and delightful realism. Such artists are Maurice Brianchon (b. 1899), Jules Cavaillès (b. 1901), Roland Oudot, Yves Brayer, Roger Chapelain-Midy (b. 1904), and Legueult and André Planson (b. 1898). Their works dating from after 1945 do not mark a stylistic break, nor even an essential transformation in relation to paintings executed before that date, for these artists had by then reached the age of forty or more, and their aesthetic conceptions and personal techniques had become stabilized. They brilliantly continue a French tradition of sensitive and sensual gracefulness, which often seems a normal development of Impressionism, whereas in Despierre, Souverbie, Pelayo, and Desnoyer an underlying will to form, which might even reach the point of a relative geometric purity, suggests a remote influence of Cubism, and to an even greater extent of derivative styles, where complete divorce from the living figure is avoided—for instance, the painting of André Lhote.

There is a great ambiguity inherent in the very notion of reality. The old problem of the relations between objective and pictorial reality became urgent in 1945, because the ever-growing importance of abstract art had led the "realists" to stiffen their resistance; to this we may add the political success of historical materialism which, in art, corresponds to naturalism that strives to be social, an art for man, as contrasted with the doctrine of art for art's sake. Many artists were attracted by Marxist materialism; Picasso rallied to it, as well as others, but unconditional obedience to the party line is not favorable to an artist's development. Nor has it been proved that an anecdotal, sentimental, or historical art is more "social" than another kind of art. In France only one artist, André Fougeron (b. 1912), illustrator of the misery and humiliations of the proletariat, has really adhered to naturalistic aesthetics, truthful in the sense we say a photograph is "true," and sentimental, since its function is to arouse social emotions.

Outside of party discipline and of any social doctrine, various realistic currents came into being after the horrors of the war. In some of theses, episodes of the war were illustrated in a narrative style, while others represented the general atmosphere of moral and material suffering, the cruelty, discouragement, rage, and despair which characterized the time. "Every period must have its artists who express and represent it for the future," says Bernard Buffet (b. 1928; plate 29). Everything depends on how you interpret the word "represent": abstract art is, at bottom, probably more representative of our epoch than descriptions of physical and spiritual misery. There are talented artists among these Neo-Realists, many of whom are conscious of continuing the old French tradition of the *maîtres de la réalité*. To react against an art that they looked upon as dehumanized, some of them as early as 1935 had formed a group called Forces Nouvelles: this included Lasne (b. 1940), Humblot (b. 1907), Jannot (b. 1909), Rohner (b. 1913), Vénard (b. 1913). Repudiating art for art's sake and the tendency to pure pictorialism at the expense of the subject, these painters strive toward an art of human emotion, in which the subject has the important function of recording the emotion. From the very beginning this austere goal required the use of somber, drab, depressing colors, which we find today in Humblot's leaden skies and Buffet's gloomy grisailles. The ascetic realism of Minaux (b. 1923), the sober objectivity of Vénard, in whose works, however, the pictorial and structural problem usually gets the better of human emotion, the violent colorism of Lorjou (b. 1908), whose impetuous Expressionism often inspired by current events aims at condemnation of social wrongs, come to supplement the poetic vision of misery we find in the paintings by Francis Gruber (1912–1949) and some of the works by André Marchand (b. 1907) in the period 1940–1945.

Among the artists belonging to a younger generation, special mention will go to Guerrier (b. 1920) who first evoked everyday life in a sober and vigorous art, later turned to a Neo-Realistic religious art, and more recently has produced warm and richly colored landscapes rising far above objective truth in lyrical flights of sensibility and imagination.

The realistic tendencies reflected the striving to bring the artist and his art back to social life, to counteract the divorce that had occurred between the painter and his public when Cubism made painting an art for initiates. This striving took concrete shape with the creation of the movement called *Peintres témoins de leur temps* ("Painters, Witnesses of Their Epoch") with an annual Salon, whose purpose is to induce artists of various tendencies to resume their role as interpreters of their age. Visits to plants and other enterprises were organized to bring painters into contact with workers, in the hope that the workers would inspire a social art. The instinct impelling the artist to produce a work that is first and foremost pictorial whatever its subject, and regardless of whether the subject is present or absent, burst the walls of narrowminded realism; the problem of reality was formulated at a new level. The paintings of Anton Clavé (b. 1913) and Aizpiri go so far as to transform the natural appearance into a kind of fairyland. The artists treat reality lyrically and plastically because the picture is first and foremost "painting," and all other considerations are secondary; while nature is never tamed to the point of being a purely formal structure, painted reality is the only reality that matters aesthetically. Objective reality is transposed into subjective reality in many different ways by painters who have abandoned traditional representation but who do not go so far as to abandon figures. A figurative art of the created, not the natural, figure stimulates the interpretation of the inner image which remains connected with visible nature.

This evolution ist very pronounced in André Marchand, who moved from the dramatic realism of 1945 to a somewhat arbitrary and sometimes geometrical structural transcription of natural objects *(Bulls, Women of Arles)*, and finally to subtle and graceful bouquets of colors, in which the sparkling sea and the air traversed by birds are delicately unreal, and yet refer to presences, the night, the waves, the sun. For the object can "be there" in the picture in various ways—as a suggestion of essential forms, an evocation of sensory qualities, a reference to a sensation or an emotion. The object can be picturesquely descriptive, though it is reduced to curious relationships of volumes and tones, as in the works of Francis Tailleux (b. 1913); or serve as a theme for a more or less eloquently plastic narrative, as in the works of Rebeyrolle. An energetic and vigorous talent, such as that of Edouard Pignon (b. 1905, color plate 1), solidly rooted in vegetal life, in communion with the rhythms of the earth and the rising of sap, abolishes all distinctions between subject and object. As a result of the powerful creative inspiration, and the irresistible movement of forms, the scene—olive picking, for example — is merely a motif, a focal

3   Maria Elena Vieira da Silva. 1955   *(Ecole de Paris)*

point of lines around which the volumes and colors are organized in accordance with the requirements of the canvas. As for Francisco Borès (b. 1898), who began as a Cubist when he was a friend of Juan Gris, he cares little whether the object represents or does not represent. His still-life compositions, his beaches with reclining figures as undulant as the waves themselves, are governed by a single concern—that for the pictorial quality which balances the delicate and solid tones, and the transparency that produces form instead of abolishing it. The plastic construction follows the color relations, so intense in their delicacy that they are sufficient to uphold the whole architecture of the painting.

Thus objective and subjective reality can be recorded in various ways, very different from one another, under the single label of reality, and lead to abstraction. To what extent is objective reality inseparable from the object? Can the object be treated as a merely formal element without forcing the artist to return to the world of nature? Will pure and free invention, which is the privilege of nonfigurative art, resign itself to a possible return of the form of the object, however evasive and ghostlike this form may be? Such was the dilemma of Nicolaes de Staël (1914–1955, color plate 2), who was unable to free himself from the conflict inherent in nonfigurative composition. He loved objects, and at the same time feared their tyranny. However peaceful his last marines of 1954–1955 may appear to be, the conflict remained unresolved. The possible incorporation of the figure—often a mere aura of a figure, an astral body so to speak, an element freed from the heaviness and opacity of crude matter—into a composition without material substance, without weight, was for him an insurmountable problem. He died from having dreamed too much of a spiritual medium, in which the world would still be present and recognizable, both as matter and as spirit.

In other artists, reality, at first obsessive, breaks up, rids itself of its compact and heavy mass, and is transposed into inverted sensory perceptions. Architecture turns into an unstable, imponderable, vacillating substance, walls are constructed with trembling iridescences, marble borrows the nature of water, and the human figure becomes ghostlike. The cities painted by Vieira da Silva (b. 1908, color plate 3), turn into mirages. These mysterious transformations, begun in 1940, continue to this day. Tending to a space which is all depth and displaying a minimum of matter, these works are comparable to physical changes of solids into gases. Da Silva eliminates the haunting vision of the big city by reducing it to the consistency of the stuff "that dreams are made on." Here, the fata morgana reflects a victory of poetry over anguish, of light over opacity.

Charles Lapicque (b. 1898), who has thoroughly explored the principles of plastic and chromatic organization, seems to aim at harmonizing a keen and picturesque love of life with the desire to achieve a formal architecture, which would contain life without loss of its often capricious dynamism, its sinuous mobility. Lapicque came close to abstraction between

1944 and 1950, but he remains too attached to the figure as a pretext for fairylike colors to succumb to the temptation of geometrical or nonfigurative pathos; even the remotely allusive figure provides an initial reference to life. Not so Zoran Music (b. 1909), a Dalmatian painter of the School of Paris, in whose works life separates from the objects that originally carried it—the boats, horses, shepherds' cabins of his native country—and is embodied in canvases which are progressively divested of any reference to material things. The object is neither stylized nor distorted, but reduced to a sign, almost a hieroglyph. The figure become abstract is only remotely similar to what it was originally, and most often the beholder is unaware of the similarity to a motif. The manner in which the painter's recollection of the fishermen's nets at Chioggia is metamorphosed into a kind of wreath—which, however, preserves the sensation of weight of the water-drenched net, the tactile value of the glass balls and the cork ring—shows that nature is present in Music's paintings, even the abstract ones, thanks to a strong source in reality.

Music's method of reducing the living form to an abstract sign is comparable to that employed in the series of *Métiers* ("Trades") by Maurice Estéve (b. 1904, color plate 4), which marked this artist's adherence to abstract art. Betweens Estéve's figurative paintings and his recent purely abstract compositions, there intervenes a period (c. 1948) characterized by a logical organization of sensation, which derives from an Impressionist sensibility directed by a strong will to order and a very personal treatment of nature. Estéve possesses the kind of warmth that comes from contact with nature, and from the fact that not intellectual operation, but only sensory transference, takes place between perception and expression. This particular "school" of nonfigurative art, instead of obliterating natural appearance, preserves an intimacy with elemental forces. Its basic problem consists in the development of the sensation (or the recollection of the sensation) into a plastic idea that often is far removed from the original object.

The titles of Roger Chastel's paintings, and particularly their characteristic atmosphere, still echo natural appearance. Chastel's art, which is both harmonious and melodious, receives and contains this music emanating from the landscape which might be transposed, by other means and in a different way, into symphonic music. He would certainly reject the epithet of "abstract" if it were applied to him, although in his works the object vanishes in its own vibration, the radiance in which the outlines of things are abolished. And what is E. de Kermadec's "syntax" (cf. *Syntactic Landscape* of 1953 and *Song of Hope* of 1957) if not the will to replace the formal vocabulary by a language born of forms but benefiting from the sovereign freedom enjoyed by the artist who has given up natural figures? Moreover, syntax, i. e., the articulation of the vocabulary, matters more than the vocabulary itself, or, at least, can alone give the vocabulary its full effectiveness. It happens, in such a case, that the artist's great lyrical plan is condensed in a form both tormented and lucid, because passion and reason have had an equal share in developing it. The works of Atlan (b. 1913), are good examples of this tormented, painful, convulsive creation, which condenses and hardens into streaks of petrified lava, in the midst of which the original fire continues to smoulder. In Serge Poliakoff (color plate 5), on the other hand, the emotion is slack—in the sense of a slack sea or tide—spread out in large simple surfaces, stable and appeased, revealing color relations that are very frank and refined. The same may be said of younger painters, such as Bernard Dufour, whose plastic sensibility and coloristic sobriety are a faithful reflection of his inner life.

The vastness and diversity of the problems confronting a painter when he departs from traditional representation of figures result in as many different solutions as there are artists, and all of these solutions are equally valid. It is up to each painter to choose a discipline corresponding to his temperament. The one adopted by Léon Gischia (b. 1903, plate 16) is unambiguous. It reflects the work he did in proximity to Léger as well as his own many stage sets. We can also discern in him a remnant of the Cubist heritage, but his predilection for vivid and pure colors, and for clear-cut volumes treated as flat planes is indisputably personal. Likewise, the stages followed by Théo Kerg after his meeting with Paul Klee culminate in a nonfigurative art. At first it was that of the Abstraction-Creation group to which he belonged for some time: and then, as he evolved farther, it became a poetic colorism.

Thus also, from the rocky world of the quarries of Jacques Busse (b. 1922), there emerge noble and vigorously structural forms, still vibrant with mineral energies, which the artist's sensory intelligence builds up into solid abstractions; these are not intellectual, for they are permeated with the elementary virtues that presided over their birth. Reason and instinct, combined in correct proportions, make it possible to preserve contact with nature without dominating it or becoming enslaved by it: this accounts for the immense and massive "celestial bodies," enigmatic in substance and impressive in their majestic simplicity that Anna Eva Bergmann (b. 1909) sets within an unknown space, at once indisputable and mysterious.

Jean Bazaine (b. 1904, color plate 6), responding to nature, creates paintings inspired by a cosmic feeling, in which the elements live their independent lives and are transposed into plastic and pictorial constructions; natural forms shed their surface aspects and become pure energy and dynamism. The organization of the color tones neither describes nor suggests appearances, but directly discloses essences. It is by discovering these formal essences in tree trunks, rocks, rivers, and by reducing them to their lines of force that Bazaine has achieved that abstract quality which emanates directly from nature and preserves deep energies.

Works on slate, its difficulties and its attractions, reflect in Raoul Ubac (plate 34) a union

4 Maurice Estève. 1956 (*Ecole de Paris*)

between the artist and nature, comparable to that which we observe in Bazaine. The gravity of the clearcut forms, his preference for dull, sober, and somber colors, show that in nature Ubac seeks a harsh, rebellious support, in the image and likeness of his world which is "rough and rugged, secret and strong." In the works of Palazuelo, a Spaniard of the School of Paris, nature reappears in a similar fashion in his successions of horizontal rocky layers, reminiscent of highland strata, with preference given to earthy browns and rocky ochers. Here, too, nature, instead of displaying itself, shuts itself in, withdrawing into the haughty silence of the medium.

It is these allusions to nature—whether in the recognizability of the object, or in some implication in the title—that cause some of these painters to be denied the right to call themselves abstract. But such epithets have little meaning or value. The revitalization of the external reality of things by injections of the artist's inner reality has also marked the evolution of Camille Singier (b. 1909, plate 17), who aims primarily at expressing the pure object, then reduces this object to its luminous and transparent form, and finally to a musical chord, a plastic harmony between the qualities of the colors and vibration of light in a given atmosphere, as illustrated by his "Dutch landscapes" of 1956. If the term "landscape" is understood as a lyrical nonobjective transcription, perceived as an image, assimilated as an emotion, and transcended in a distinctly melodious and harmonious representation, Jean le Moal (b. 1909) may be likened to Singier (plate 17), and Manessier, of whom more later. The structural values of Le Moal's forms, which he reduces to their essential plasticity, and his need to transcend the forms in order not to be imprisoned in closed and opaque volumes, endow his paintings with a wholly personal vibration and a transparency that offers a glimpse into the secret and elementary nucleus of the object. In Le Moal, as in Singier and in the early works of Manessier (b. 1911), we perceive the strong influence of Bissière (b. 1888, plate 18), whose pupils they were. Bissière's art, intensely internalized, remains in close contact with nature. With reference to him, too, we may say that abstraction does not distort nature, but that it invents a vocabulary of colors and forms in which nature reflects its invisible substance. The image of the tree or of the bird sometimes remains in the paintings of this profound and subtle artist as a summons to the beholder not to confine himself to the formal data, but to look forward to a fairylike world, full of rustling leaves and singing nightingales.

Tal Coat (b. 1905, plate 19), who was a figurative painter until about 1945, has also evolved toward intimacy with things, and then toward exploration of their secret nature, in a quest for "signs," abridgements, and hieroglyphs of the structure of matter. After a perilous attempt to "pass to the other side," to liberate himself from forms and rid himself completely of appearance, he has adopted the mysterious ways of the Taoist sages who mastered the forces of nature by reducing them to signs. He has entered the domain of the ineffable; he seeks to express the great stream of cosmic energies not in order to dematerialize nature but to penetrate to the secret root of matter and to explore the ways of *natura naturans*. In a spirit akin to that of Tal Coat, a younger painter, Bellegarde, too, seems to apply himself to the exploration of that which man perceives simultaneously with his senses, his emotions, and his imagination; and Jean Villeri (b. 1898)—though he began his career (c. 1936) under the auspices of the Abstraction-Creation group, thus seemingly entering on the path of geometric abstraction—has chosen to endow his paintings with harmony and calm attuned to the elements.

This attempt to arrive at the very soul of the universe through inner emotion and plastic expression, without representing the objects in which it was traditionally contained, leads to an art which may be called religious, in the sense of a pantheistic communion. Non-figurative art also contributes extraordinarily rich and varied means to religious art in the narrower sense. Renunciation of the powerful emotional factor inherent in the figure and the anecdote makes for more intense spirituality, which no longer interposes objects between emotion and its expression. The abstract form expresses the sacred, the divine, all the more completely because it has shed its material garb, the weight of the body, the opaqueness of faces. Stimulated by the rebirth of religious architecture, painting has adjusted itself to the simplicity of the volumes. Ensembles such as the Vence chapel decorated by Matisse between 1949 and 1951; churches such as that of Assy, in which —despite the diversity of the artists who worked in them—the total inspiration remains harmonious; Manessier's stained-glass windows at Les Bréseux; Bazaine's mosaics at Audincourt; Leon Zack's (b. 1892) stained-glass windows at Notre Dame des Pauvres d'Issy les Moulineaux, to quote only a few examples, show the possible directions open today to an art that has rejected the help, and the constraints, of traditional figurative art.

Seeking its way between Neo-Realism and Symbolism, both of which led to blind alleys, religious art has discovered, in abstract painting, forms freed from all attachment to the letter, forms which have become pure vehicles of the spirit. Alfred Manessier (color plate 7) said that it is to the extent that the artist bases himself on his own essential, spiritual reality, that he arrives at and "revitalizes" the external reality of the world. He treats primarily scenes of the Passion, in which the Man-God bleeds and suffers, the nocturnal mystery of ceremonies in which great spiritual clarity is revealed in a darkness punctured by luminous lines. At the source of these paintings there is an emotion all the more powerful because it dominates the senses, the heart, and the mind simultaneously. Since the liturgy of religious services is constituted by a succession of moments in which an intimate contact is established between the worshipper and the sacrament, between man and God, the plastic projection of the emotional states determines Manessier's forms and colors. He chooses these instinctively and then orders them by his disciplined and constructive mind; they represent for him, who is their creator, but also for the beholder, a kind of epiphany, a supernatural revelation. Because Manessier is deeply religious, the problem of faith that has been raised in relation to various contemporary artists who contributed to collective religious projects does not concern him. His works completely realize the accord between matter and spirit, their unshakable harmony.

The refusal to eliminate natural reference, in conjunction with an obvious aversion for the intellectual stylizations which are always detrimental to life, are found in different forms in the paintings by Jacques Lagrange (b. 1917), Hélène de Beauvoir, Paul Berçot (b. 1896), and Arpad Szenes (b. 1897). These artists illustrate, each in his own way, the striving to introduce into abstract art the breath of nature, without reducing nature to a mere phenomenon. Jacques Lagrange's landscapes preserve the vibration of light which models and transforms the objects, sometimes accenting their inner architecture. Hélène de Beauvoir's paintings aim at a synthesis of movement in an arabesque that extends the gesture and goes beyond its limits by surrounding it with new temporal and spatial dimensions. Her art is based on a rigorous discipline and a refined sensibility. Its major goal is to integrate movement with form, to endow all the living energies with firm structures, to order the relationships between the object and the mind that perceives it in accordance with a dynamism expressing the basic laws of being, and to discover the compact stream of the essential within the whirlpool of appearances.

In the works of Paul Berçot, the poetic content of the image determines the development of the form, and the colors determine their harmonic overtones, somewhat as the tonal qualities of the various instruments create overtones in a chamber music ensemble. Reality is disclosed in the depths of the objects rather than in their contours; and formal likeness can be dispensed with all the more easily because the visible and the invisible are brought together and elucidated by the intimate palpitation of the object's essential being.

Arpad Szenes has long been tempted by abstract construction, yet has always striven to organize this construction around a group of allusive figures, products of an imagination that discovered essential rhythms in human motion. Szenes was fascinated by a higher level of abstraction, which is not hieratic stylization (as exemplified in Elamite ceramics of the third millennium B. C.), nor Cubist elimination of nature, but which reflects the need to preserve a reference to the human world, however arbitrary, as a support and inspiration of form as such. Thus the demarcation line between figurative painting and abstract painting becomes meaningless in many painters who refuse to confine themselves to either one of the two branches of art that are commonly regarded as absolutely opposed and incompatible. A very great number of contemporary painters believe that the problem of the real object and its relations with the purely pictorial object cannot be solved by

5   Serge Poliakoff. 1954   *(Ecole de Paris)*

summary method, nor by blind adherence to one aesthetic system or another. To postulate an irreducible antinomy between figurative and nonfigurative art is to oversimplify the problem, to see only one, and possible the least important, aspect of a question that involves the very concepts of thing and form, of existence and representation.

The sense of objective reality is today being renovated by the contribution of two aesthetic theories, which start from very different premises, but which are often similar in their formulations: the aesthetics of the so-called "Primitives," and the aesthetics of the Surrealists. Since the days when the vogue of the "Primitive" painters began with the success of Henri Rousseau—he partly owed this success to Guillaume Apollinaire who promoted him half in sincere admiration and half in joke—an ever growing interest was shown in the form of poetic reality or magic reality that is embodied also in the naive works of the so-called "Sunday painters." These workers, small shopkeepers or modest officials, often waited till their age of retirement to devote themselves to their hobby, which they practiced in all humility, with patience and diligence. Before becoming the objects of curiosity on the part of critics and collectors, they lived in happy obscurity, and painting was for them something sacred, as well as a diversion. No doubt many such artists died in obscurity, their works lost, before naive painting was elevated to the important place it occupies today. Usually self-taught, these painters laboriously learned a technique that aims at a faithful, accurate representation of everyday life; they have the ingenuous minds and hearts of the Primitives. They rediscovered a technique that is both simple and intricate, that has not been contaminated by the recipes or "gimmicks" of the various "schools." Their pictorial works are as sincere and as imbued with emotions as themselves.

The entry of the naive painters into the Musée d'Art Moderne in Paris, with the inauguration, in 1948, of the Wilhelm Uhde room reserved for them (Uhde was one of the first and most fervent discoverers of this art) marks their official recognition by museum curators. The special quality of passion and humility that makes the works of the "naives" so deeply moving clearly shows that they are not necessarily clumsy; by dint of painting, and thanks to their talent, the Sunday painters often display a fine personal technique which prevents the careful beholder from confusing them with the works of their imitators.

In the case of these masters—as in the case of those before 1945, Vivin, Bauchant, Bombois Eve, Peyronnet—painting is not a trade. Van Hyfte is a butcher, Léon Greffe a concierge, Schnubel a tobacco dealer, Demonchy a railroad employee, Crépin a plumber, Lagru a miner. Most of them became known at a fairly advanced age. Jean Fous had his first show at the age of 43, in 1944, and Déchelette at 48 in the same year; but Blondel did not exhibit his work until he was 57 (in 1950), Greffe showed at the age of 64, Van Hyfte at 61. Even more unusual is the case of Lagru who won fame with his extraordinary exotic and prehistoric landscapes only at the age of 80. These figures confirm the fact that the Primitive painters are little interested in success; painting, for them, is not a profession that is supposed to be remunerative and they are too ingenuous to seek fame. For almost all of the Sunday painters the ideal is exact and even meticulous transcription of reality, particularly in landscapes and scenes of humble life. They are poets, but their poetry, instead of seeking escape from what others would regard as humdrum banality, aims at the sublimation, through attention and love, of the humblest objects and insignificant events; these acquire, as a result of such intense treatment, a kind of super-reality. This is true of Blondel, a bus driver, who imagines an immense Paris, with, as is proper, buses in the foreground, but jutting into the sea, like a peninsula, with sailboats (*Tableau de ma vie*, "Picture of My Life," 1953). The same is also true of Jean Fous, a small shopkeeper, interpreter of bustling streets with throngs of people merrily jostling one another among open stands, with the almost miraculous surprises of the Flea Market and the Scrap-Iron Fair. The butcher Van Hyfte loves well appointed groceries or butcher shops like his own, their display windows shimmering with glowing colors. The shepherd Caillaud, who listened to Pan's messages in nature, accidentally found a box of watercolors when he was a prisoner during the Second World War, and discovered how to use them. In the organization of the forms in space he comes close to the Italians of the Trecento and the Persian miniaturists.

The discovery of the "naive" painters began, paradoxically, with the collection assembled by the humorist George Courteline, who did not realize the beauty of the works he bought, seeking merely to build up a "museum of horrors" to amuse or shock his visitors. Wilhelm Uhde, motivated, on the contrary, by admiration, enthusiastically collected and in 1928 exhibited a group of artists whom he designated as "the painters of the Sacred Heart." Today art dealers eagerly buy and show the works of the Primitives, and the Salons, which were stubbornly closed to them when they most needed to be encouraged and supported, welcome them generously. The Sunday painters have remained uncontaminated by the neighborhood of "learned" painting—they probably ignore it—and their work preserves its bonds with the great tradition of popular art, as it once manifested itself in religious images, ex-votos, and shop decorations.

The Surrealists who start from the magic conception of the world at which the Primitives arrive, often practice the same meticulous art of exact detail, of a tactile and spatial illusionism. They are not motivated by a taste for faithful reproduction, but rather by the surprise which such a manner arouses today in a public accustomed to free transcriptions of reality, to capricious brushwork, and to viewing with suspicion any academic objective representation. The recent works by Delvaux and Magritte (plate 35) in Belgium, and Carzou's *Apocalypse* (1956–1957) testify to the importance attached to an almost photographic precision by painters who seek to express the secret life of things. Carzou's painting is probably meant as such an evocation of the mystery contained in trivial objects; we are reminded of American photographers—so unlike Man Ray whose Surrealist photographs were the result of intricate elaborations and curious laboratory experiments. Formerly, all the artists who took their inspiration from the Book of Revelations had found in this text an inexhaustible source of fantasy in describing an unreal world. For Carzou, on the contrary, the apocalypse is the world of today, the real world with its technology that enslaves and poisons man with its soul-destroying machinism, its materialistic pleasures and comforts, which entrap him as in a spider's net, making him dependent and becoming the masters of his life. In relation to Carzou's last manner, all distinctions between naturalism and Surrealism are arbitrary, for here it is reality itself that becomes the interpreter, the prophet of the invisible powers that reside in the things created by man and not foreseen by the Creator.

The tendency not to look for the fantastic in the supernatural, but in a meticulous naturalism, also characterizes Pierre Roy, J.P. Allaux, and Stanislao Lepri. Roy creates a fairy-like atmosphere with unusual combinations of objects; these objects are not fairylike in themselves, they are everyday objects, but in entering into contact with each other they acquire a strangeness that pervades the painting, endowing it with a rare poetic quality. J.P. Allaux is almost a full-fledged naturalist; the kind of aura that surrounds the objects in his paintings comes from their being saturated with essential truth. Lepri, on the other hand, deliberately seeks and finds strangeness, incongruity, by exploring the secret life of individuals, trees, stones. His ability to perceive dangerous and disquieting traits in a seemingly innocent figure, in things that no one would imagine to be full of hidden dangers, partakes of clairvoyance; it is an ability to penetrate effortlessly into the "zone of shadows" which veils the world of appearance.

We should hesitate to call these painters Surrealists, and yet it would be wrong to class them as Realists since they differ from the latter in certain features that are precisely their most original and most vigorous. Furthermore, there is no agreement as to what is a Surrealist and the boundary line between Surrealism and non-Surrealism is as uncertain as that between abstract and nonabstract art.

Seemingly moving ever further away form contemplation and love of objective reality for its own sake, contemporary painting reaches the extreme positions of Surrealism and Abstraction. Surrealism retains only that part of the object which it can use for its fantastic constructions. Abstractionism repudiates the object as the principle and mode of representation. Both reduce reality to something inessential. Because dreams and visions

6   Jean Bazaine. 1955   *(Ecole de Paris)*

can be formulated only in terms of sensations produced by (seemingly) familiar objects, Surrealism seeks to reveal the magic nature of the trivial object; actually, there is no trivial object that does not acquire a striking individuality once it has become part of a system of unexpected relationships.

This is exemplified in the technique of *collage* and "exquisite corpses" which provide some of the most significant expressions of this latter-day supernaturalism. In these, the object is used as the starting point for a footloose imagination; it submits to every whim of an absolute subjectivity. In the end, it is stripped of its very nature as an object, acquiring a magic aura, a visionary unreality, or merely losing its natural functions. It is because Surrealist painting cultivated the techniques of hallucination and automatism, because it readily and even passionately obeyed all the promptings of the irrational, and succumbed to all the temptations of the dream, that it exerted a tremendous influence between 1920 and 1939. The adversaries of Surrealism were too rash in announcing that it had vanished, become banal or declined; actually its inexhaustible vitality was confirmed, after the war, by the great Surrealist Exhibition of 1947.

Comparing this exhibition with similar events which mark important dates in the history of the movement, for instance, the international Surrealist exhibitions (London in 1936, Paris in 1938, New York in 1942), we are struck by the growth of the movement, as shown by the number and fame of the exhibitors. In 1947 Surrealism sought to prove that it was not a small, exclusive group, but a vast complex of currents united in their rejection of all doctrinaire formulas. However, despite the brilliance of the Exhibition of 1947, Surrealism does not seem to have followed a clear-cut path of development. More particularly, it does not seem to have produced new artists equal to those who had revealed their talent before 1945.

We have already said that the use of pictorial methods fostering the operation of the mechanisms of hallucination, and the influence of the Arizona desert account for Max Ernst's new manner; nevertheless, the change is not decisive. Unlike Max Ernst, Léonore Fini, since 1950, has entered on a new path, exploring the mysterious domain of *peinture alchimique*, with images of "guardians" keeping watch over the "Philosophers' Egg." Fini's landscapes of imaginary countries, dreamlike and poetic in their aridity, provide still another domain for the explorations of this visionary artist. Coutaud, for his part, incorporates almost naturalistic forms into a paradoxical mixture of eroticism and the absurd; naturalistic forms also appear in Félix Labisse, whose brilliantly colored obsessive visions are bathed in a light without shadows.

The capital event in the transformations of Surrealist aesthetics during the last ten years is the pictorial oeuvre of the sculptor Alberto Giacometti (b. 1901, plate 28). His drawings and paintings (the latter in grisaille, with rare appearances of color) show ghostlike forms,

32

extraordinarily present, endowed with the reality of prophetic visions or dreams in which a haunted man encounters his *Doppelgänger*, his "double." The figure of the solitary passerby in Giacometti's paintings—astral body, ectoplasm, specter—is an emanation of the mysterious soul, its creator, as well as a messenger from the beyond.

Matta (b. 1912) peints ghostlike creatures suggesting larvae-men, or crossbreeds between humans and insects. He boldly and passionately explores invisible continents, which require new senses to be perceived, and where new mythologies are being elaborated. Since 1945, Victor Brauner (b. 1903) has sought to formulate other such new mythologies. Previously, he had been a Surrealist, and had also been active as a "fantastic" painter. His tendency to express the mysterious chronicles of his personal universe in hieroglyphics—those signs used by the Mayas as well as by the Egyptians—relates him to Wolfgang Paalen and to Toyen, who were also well known before 1945, and who now explore enigmatic domains of their own.

Among the poets of painting, special mention must go to Roger Brielle, whose imaginary realms are so convincingly graceful and seductive that the beholder is reluctant to acknowledge that they exist only in the artist's imagination. On intimate terms with the unknowable to which we are sometimes led by our anticipations, Brielle conjures up the most beautiful dreams, transforming them into a pictorial reality of rare excellence. The fantastic landscapes by Bona (b. 1926) and Dorothea Tanning open similarly immense, endless vistas into a world beyond reality, which make it directly accessible to our senses. Finally, we must mention in this context Oscar Dominguez, master of irony and pathos, always magical, who so often seemed to be but playing, but whose games, as is always the case with the Spanish, bore the imprint of the tragic conflict which led to his death.

The young painters are turning increasingly toward abstraction, because it affords greater and more varied possibilities of liberation than figurative Surrealism (which is more gratifying instinctually), automatism, visionary imagination, and the pure dream. The endless variety of expressive means available to abstract painting, the emotional directness of its forms that have no reference to material reality, make nonobjective art the ideal language of the supernatural, the spiritual.

Some artists saw in nonfigurative painting a liberation from whatever "literary" elements may have remained in figurative Surrealism. This is what induced Pavel Tchelitchev, famous for his Surrealist painting *Hide and Seek* (in the Museum of Modern Art, New York) to atttempt, in the last years of his life (he died in 1957), an abstract transcription of the lines of force of universal energy, the essential forms that are the abode of the principle of Life. Gérard Vulliamy (b. 1909), whose *Trojan Horse* was one of the most striking creations of Surrealist painting, has also gone over to abstract art. With his genuine poetic temperament, and talent of a colorist, he strives to translate the anguish that characterized his fantastic monsters into a nonfigurative color organization, and to replace the former restlessness by a solid, stable harmony. Mario Prassinos (b. 1915, plate 20) has also achieved complete independence in an eloquent graphic style, whose violence records rhythms of secret earthquakes.

Abstract art began as an austere, rigorous movement, based essentially upon "the sound and rich geometric requirement" (Fontené). It opposed the formal vagueness of Impressionism, and the pictorial disorder of Expressionism. "The picturesque is superseded by mathematics," Mondrian said. Delaunay died in 1941, Mondrian and Kandinsky in 1944; Malevich had died ten years earlier; Kupka lived until 1957. Whether coming from naturalism, Cubism or Expressionism, only those masters who presented abstraction as the rule of formal rigor had followers. This is why a new large group of artists with geometric and mathematical tendencies—the Salon des Réalités Nouvelles, founded in 1947—has revived New-Plasticism. Severity (some called it "sectarianism") long held sway in this movement, which admitted only the strictly formal, essentially geometrical, expressions of abstract art, rejecting the painters influenced by Impressionism or Expressionism, or not fully converted to pure geometry. Les Réalités Nouvelles introduced into abstract art an austerity and discipline that appealed to the mind more than to the senses. It subscribed to the principles that had been advanced as early as 1937 by the Abstraction-Creation group, which acquainted the School of Paris with non-French abstract art, and injected into it a strong dose of Constructivism and Neo-Plasticism. It was also believed that this abstract geometry was the natural and absolute conclusion of the Cubist explorations.

Three former Cubists—Auguste Herbin, Alberto Magnelli (b. 1888, plate 23), and Jean Deyrolle (b. 1911, plate 21)— declared that they had gone over to abstraction when they realized that they did not want to retain, in their plastic constructions, the references to objects which the Cubists had not wanted or dared to eliminate, and which they themselves justly regarded as superfluous. Strongly marked by Cubist aesthetics which Réalités Nouvelles pushed to the ultimate, this group struggled for ten years to uphold its ideal of rigor and purity. During those ten years, the epithet 'abstract' was indignantly rejected by the nonfigurative painters themselves, some of whom wanted to confine it to rigidly formal artists. They refused to regard as abstract artists those in whose paintings it was possible to recognize a reflection, an impression, or a recollection of nature.

Few terms in the history of art have been the object of more controversies; whereas we know exactly what is called Futurism, Cubism, or Fauvism, works described as "concrete art" by some were described and "abstract art" by others, and it would seem that both descriptions are equally correct or incorrect, depending on the meaning given to those terms. It

34

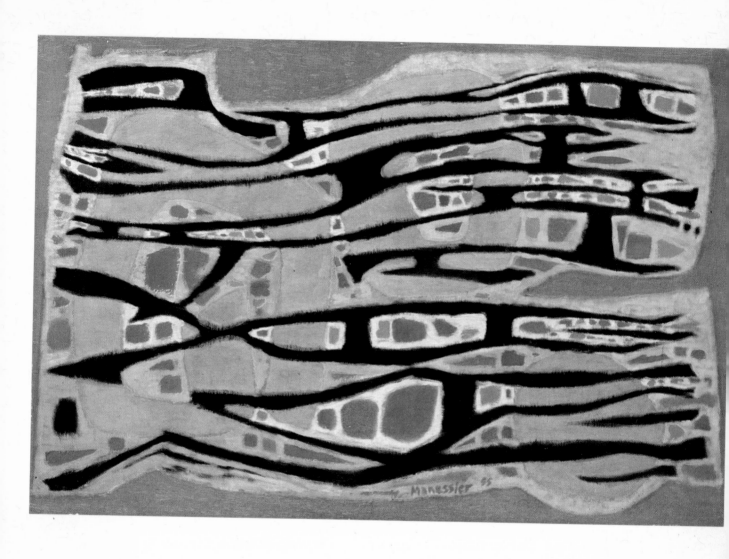

7   Alfred Manessier. 1956 (*Ecole de Paris*)

might be said, however, that in current usage, a "purely" abstract painting is uniformly flat, excluding all spatial illusion—a surface composed of forms as simple and rational as possible, i.e., geometric or nearly geometric, filled with flat pure colors, without concern for texture or brushstroke. Though seemingly poverty-stricken, this technique which repudiates plastic and pictorial effects, that is to say, effects deriving from the suggestion of depth and chromatic vibration, has proved capable of expressing a true symbolism of forms and colors in the works of Auguste Herbin. This painter remains uncompromisingly geometric, although, between his Cubist period and conversion to abstraction in 1926, he was figurative; at the same time he endows his forms and colors with esoteric meaning, so that the painting is transformed into a kind of coded message which can be deciphered only if one has the key. "By sacrificing the object we have rediscovered the Word and creative action."

A group of abstract painters, called Musicalists, of whom Henri Valensi is the most interesting, explores the potentialities of a kind of melodic or contrapuntal script. The nonfigurative constructions of these painters are inspired by music and often contain esoteric allusions. For even in the most geometric-minded abstract works, form has no true and full life unless it expresses the artist's inwardness. For this reason, as well as because the Salon des Réalités Nouvelles realized the danger of "aesthetic Jacobinism" and of excluding everything that did not absolutely adhere to its doctrine, abstract artists whose tendencies were not of the group were invited to send in their exhibits. The new broader spirit animating this group is expressed in the name it adopted in 1957—Réalités Nouvelles-Nouvelles Réalités. This marks an important date in the history of abstract art; Réalités Nouvelles recognizes that it is no longer the only orthodox group, and that the saying "in my father's house are many mansions" also applies to abstract art. Thus it came about that many artists who usually exhibit at the Salon de Mai (which also admits figurative painters and Surrealists) now show their works at the Salon des Réalités Nouvelles; formerly the two salons were regarded as opposed to each other. It is also significant that René Fontené, president of Réalités Nouvelles, paints works full of emotion and sensibility, in a manner that is a far cry from the rigorous geometry that characterized the group at its beginnings.

The strict abstractionist's ideal was to reduce the pictorial phenomenon to its purest expression, and at the same time to reintegrate art into society—the latter was the explicit ideal of the Neo-Plasticists Mondrian and Van Doesburg, and of the Constructivists Pevsner and Gabo. By its very nature the abstract work of art was no longer to be an item in a collection or even a museum, but an integral element of collective life. This was the idea that inspired the architects, sculptors and painters Schöffer, Gorin, Del Marle, André Bloc, and Edgard Pillet who founded the Groupe Espace. According to them, the work of art was to be conceived as a dwelling, a city quarter, a whole city, which would be raised to the rank of art by virtue of its forms and colors. This conception repudiates individualism as no longer suited to modern societies, and strives for a social art, not in the sense of the champions of a politically committed art, serving only to illustrate a given political myth, but a truly collective art: the work of art would no longer confront man as something external, special, but be part of his everyday existence.

At the same time aesthetic and technological novelties came to enrich this new conception, particularly as regards the utilization of movement. The idea is not absolutely new, for it had already been advanced by Marcel Duchamp, Mortensen (b. 1910), and Moholy-Nagy, among others. Schöffer's projections of changing colored forms, and Soto's, Bury's and Agam's *œuvre transformable* may also be compared to Calder's mobiles. The Swiss Tinguely who explores such harmonies involving form, color, and motion, and who strives to include also sounds, in 1957 showed *"tableaux"* in black and white; by means of a motor, the mobile elements are made to perform intricate rhythmic motions on intersecting planes. It may be expected that such new explorations which are still at a "primitive" stage will lead to interesting results. The integration of movement into sculpture is an accomplished fact; its integration into painting, which is more complex and difficult, seems to be pregnant with rich possibilities.

To what extent can we still speak here of painting? Can we apply the term "paintings" to César Domela's (b. 1900) *tableaux-objets* consisting of various materials, woods, metallic stems, plastics arranged into an ensemble of forms and colors that are spatially independent, organically powerful and at the same time refined? The association of color with sculpture, and new conceptions of space, put in question the radical distinction between painting and sculpture. Contemporary expression tends increasingly to do away with such arbitrary categories and separations. Since Domela invented his very personal technique after abandoning Neo-Plasticism to which he had adhered for several years, he has not been producing paintings in the proper sense of the term; but are we to regard him as a sculptor on the ground that he disposes his forms in space rather than on the surface? Once again we discover that all definitions are artificial, and unsatisfactory in relation to reality.

Except for Réalités Nouvelles, which advanced a clearcut program, the Groupe Espace which is related to it, and a few other shortlived groups, no full-fledged "schools" have formed. Every artist belonging to the so-called School of Paris, which gathers all nationalities and the most diverse tendencies, preserves his own vigorous individuality.

Richard Mortensen (b. 1910, color plate 8) who founded the Linie movement in Copenhagen in 1931, was one of the pioneers of abstract art. For some time he had followed Kandinsky's aesthetics, but around 1930 he devoted himself to geometric abstraction, and enriched the School of Paris with his clean, cheerful colors, and vigorous, somber forms. A great purity characterizes these works inspired by an ideal of authentic greatness and based on a rigorous economy of means. The fairylike poetry of his early paintings has yielded to a lyricism of dynamic forms in conflict, an intensely vital lyricism bursting with creative joy and expressing complete harmony between the artist's inwardness and the thing created.

Victor Vasarely (b. in Hungary, 1908, plate 22) has been a member of the School of Paris since 1930. His technique is called "plastic cinetics" *(cinétique plastique)* he goes beyond painting as such, and makes use of superimposed surfaces, transparent and mobile. Thoroughly familiar with optics, he believes that visual sensation can be renewed with the help of this science; his contribution is the discovery of a pure plastic language, which makes all extraplastic elements in the work superfluous. He is hostile to "subjectivity" and to the survivals of Impressionism and Expressionism in what he calls "the immense stagnant pool of nonfigurative art." He champions absolute objectivity: the work must completely eclipse the artist who creates it. This is also the ideal of Edgard Pillet.

For Dewasne (b. 1921), reason and will to construction are the basic elements of creation; everything that does not reflect the plastic feeling is excluded. Subordinating the elemental to the intellectual and to the logic of form and color, Dewasne is an excellent teacher. In his courses on abstract art he methodically analyzes the sensory functions and optical properties of colors and forms, and displays a great concern for formal purity and sobriety in his use of colors, brilliant, laid on flat, and as though varnished.

Jean Deyrolle (b. 1911, plate 21) began as a Cubist; around 1943, when he decided that figures were useless, he was converted to geometric abstraction, which he regarded as the logical conclusion of Cubism. But even though he eliminates the object, he does not renounce the emotional and suggestive richness that nonfigurative art can express more fully than any other. The plastic phenomenon, as he interprets it, is seen against the background of an emotion accorded with nature (though nature is not represented), and reflecting the mysterious bonds linking the individual to the cosmic soul. Deyrolle is not a dialectician of geometry; he is too much a poet for this, and the rigorous discipline to which he submits is self-imposed; it is thanks to this rigor that his interpretation of space which aims at depth rather than the three-dimensional illusion, is so original and effective.

One of the abstract painters who came from Cubism and has preserved its rigorous spirit, the Florentine Alberto Magnelli (b. 1888, plate 23) has belonged to the School of Paris since 1931. Nonfigurative painting is for him a point of arrival, not of departure. For some time he practiced figurative art, seeking to reduce forms to their essential expression and at the same time to organize their sensory functions; his balanced approach was in the tradition of the old Tuscan masters. In his series of *Stones*, executed around 1946, the

8   Richard Mortensen. 1957 (*Ecole de Paris*)

problem of space is solved in almost illusionistic terms; however, Magnelli's art as a whole rests upon a balance between intelligence and sensibility. His calm, sumptuous colors and the rhythmic movements of his volumes create an atmosphere of their own.

In abstract painting the very conception of space, its expression, and its representation raise problems that did not exist in figurative art, when the object, however distorted or stylized, was connected by a number of unambiguous relations with its internal space and the external space around it. The solution consisting in the elimination of this spatial problem by making the work strictly two-dimensional, a pure surface, a plane divested of reality and of the illusion of depth, marks a natural and legitimate reaction against the various solutions adopted in figurative painting. The fact remains, however, that the spatial problem is a spiritual and human one as well as a plastic one. The idea of giving the object a space of its own is based one a complex theory, almost a philosophical system. The object's movement and rhythms are communicated to the air surrounding it. The resulting conflict or harmony between the forms will assume the dramatic features it had in Expressionism, with this difference that Expressionism emphasized the individual's struggle against his intangible surroundings, while nonfigurative, nonrepresentational art emphasizes the artist's own inner drama. The way of expressing the atmosphere in which the forms live, and the space with which they communicate or from which they isolate themselves, are essential characteristics of the artist who, intuitively or dialectically, achieves a modus vivendi *in* space and with space.

Take, for instance the paintings by Hans Hartung (b. 1904, color plate 9). The extreme transparency of the forms cut by clusters of lines of force suggests a nonresisting space, a space that is refined, almost dematerialized; whereas the forms created by Bram van Velde (b. 1895) are convulsive and self-contained; kept in a state of perpetual metamorphosis by an internal chaos, they cannot isolate themselves from the surrounding atmosphere. The sovereign freedom enjoyed by Hartung's forms, in a space that tends to be more and more spiritualized, and thereby increasingly imponderable, is the freedom of spirit in relation to heavy and opaque matter. These forms are not definitively closed; the very violence of their movement has transformed them; incapable of rest, of fixity, they change continually. The economy of the pictorial means, the seeming simplicity—for none of these colors is simple, but, on the contrary, of a highly refined complexity—of a chromatism based primarily on the contrast between the transparency of the ground and the substantial vigor of the active forms, add further brilliance to this domination of space.

Total occupation of space and its division into a series of zones of energy completely filled up by tone vibrations and mobile formal elements characterize the paintings of André Lanskoy (b. 1902, color plate 10). He has achieved this result by gradual stages, gaining

9   Hans Hartung. 1957 (*Ecole de Paris*)

his insight into spatial problems in the course of the constructions that precede the composition of each painting. This excellent colorist whose geometric structures are flawless imposes a well-balanced, harmonious plastic order on his forms, taming their anarchistic ambitions for self-determination. It was against similarly anarchistic ambitions that Chapoval (1919-1951) fought desperately; he died young, without fully developing his potentialities. For this figurative painter, abstraction would have been an arduous conquest. Attracted by purely geometric forms, but dominated by his tragic temperament and the drama of his life, he, too, anxiously explored the nature of space and the relations between space and form.

Dmitrienko's forms are no longer enslaved by subject matter; his impetuous and restless temperament tends toward a monumentalism of striking originality and force. Michel Debré whose personality is very different, is engaged in a curious attempt to reintroduce form into content, to achieve a harmonious homogeneity between the elements in space and space itself. To carry this attempt to a successful conclusion he has developed a pictorial vocabulary that combines subtlety with vigor; its austerity often enhances his painterly values. A technique involving scratchings which lighten the forms has enabled Breuil to avoid the transformation of geometry into an a priori principle; his sensibility and the ease with which he produces volumes that are both solid and light prove that the problem of space can receive a solution in which the plastic sense and intelligence go hand in hand without contradicting each other.

Studying the development of Gérard Schneider (b. 1896, color plate 11) during the ten years when, after many experiments that had brought him close to Cubism and Surrealism, he became completely abstract, we see to what extent this development is governed by an increasingly vigorous and lyrical appropriation of space. The effort to delimit and isolate the form in the atmosphere yields gradually to a new conception: the object is dissolved with a view to increasing its power by vital and cosmic energies drawn from a space which is increasingly "open"—open in the formal sense of the term, as well as in the sense given it by Klee and Rilke. The purpose is not to abolish the outlines of the form, but to make it permeable to the great currents of energy that flow from one plastic element to another. Similarly, in the recent works of Pierre Soulages (b. 1919, color plate 12) the fluid air flows around the somber masses suspended in space by their own volume, and penetrates them; the structures are flexible having lost their original rigidity and purity deriving from Chinese calligraphy, and they evolve with greater freedom, their weight and substance no longer opposed to the imponderability of the atmosphere. The monumental architecture of large compact volumes does not prevent the painting from breathing calmly in unison with the universal.

Whereas figurative painting confined the Dionysiac sense to a fragment of the visual

10   André Lanskoy (*Ecole de Paris*)

world, which bore witness to the presence of the invisible, serving as its representation or symbol, the abolition of the figure with its limits and limitations gives the form more room for expansion, enabling it to fill the totality of space and to be totally filled by it. The full harmony, both warm and restrained, characterizing the paintings of Kolos-Vary (b. 1899) expresses the repose of matter saturated and illumined by the spirit, the accord of reason and instinct, and a subtle intimacy with real Being beyond appearance, which restores its reality to appearance itself.

The artistic and spiritual development of Jean Piaubert and Anita de Caro moves toward greater freedom and flexibility. While Piaubert "materializes" a thick and compact atmosphere around graphic figures, striving for monumentalism and a spiritual synthesis, Anita de Caro, on the contrary, seeks the imponderable. Her luminous forms clearly identify themselves; at the same time, being permeable to all currents, they display a capacity for mutation which is particularly striking in her recent paintings.

In the works of Kallos, the difficult problem of achieving unity between form and the inner and outer pressures that continually tend to modify form, has received a solution that is satisfactory both for sensibility and for intelligence, a solution that is characterized by a harmonious balance between the plastic and the pictorial elements. Hosiasson, on the other hand, seems to question the possibility of such an accord by his restlessness, by his hesitation, as it were, to realize the union between matter and spirit, a union which is always dramatically precarious. The temptation of the "formless" is, for this artist, a means to escape from the anguish aroused in him by the conflict with a tyrannical matter, which he must continually master without suppressing its volcanic vehemence. The works of Lagage, who is younger and less tormented, achieve more often, if not more easily, the balance in which the spiritual, plastic, and pictorial requirements are equally fulfilled. The colored elements in their freedom and strength can be integrated with the architecture of the painting in various ways: examples of such formal solutions, which illustrate various currents of nonfigurative art, can be found in the paintings of Carrade, Duthoo, Barré, and Gillet.

The term "Tachisme" was coined by the critic Michel Tapié to characterize paintings consisting of dabs or splotches of color ("*taches*"), whose arrangement at first sight seems to be governed by no constructive idea, to be determined by caprice or chance. Pure chance may serve as a legitimate means of expression: Chinese painters and Leonardo da Vinci studied designs formed by cracks in old walls or drifting clouds, but their purpose was to discover in such designs fortuitous similarities to man-created forms or figures. Chance arrangements of spots may thus be of interest either by their mimetic properties, or by stimulating certain techniques to which the fantastic painters and the Surrealists

11   Gérard Schneider. 1957 (*Ecole de Paris*)

resorted a great deal following in the footsteps of the Chinese and Leonardo. For the Tachiste painters, however, the splotch of color is a direct projection of emotion, without the intervention of reason, constructive ideas, or meanings; the dabs of color have an autonomous value, are something like the cry uttered by a man or an animal under the impact of an emotion. The artist's rational activity is reduced to a minimum; the uninformed viewer has the illusion that the painter has flung his colors on the canvas at random, and then linked them by sweeping brushstrokes.

This Tachiste technique is similar to a technique much favored in the United States, where it is sometimes called "action art." Completely spontaneous, instinctive, repudiating all closed forms, Tachisme strives not to *express*, but to *be* a dramatic state of mind. This "other art," as Michel Tapié called it in order to stress its total break not only with tradition but with all aesthetic theories and techniques prior to 1952, is the focal point of all the tendencies that oppose the "formless" to form. Such tendencies might be traced back as far as Impressionism; Monet's series of *Nymphéas*, if we disregard their subject—but has not the subject come to be regarded as unimportant?—seem to anticipate Tachisme. However, though these spots of color may start from the "formless," once they are on the canvas they inevitably become form, whatever this form may be. It is understandable that the striving for total freedom in conception and execution, which won so many adherents to abstract aesthetics, should have led to the extreme license of Tachisme; in fact, Tachisme is an Expressionism carried to its extreme consequences, such as might have been drawn by some of the artists of the German Brücke group, who however, were not bold enough to dissociate the spot of color from the object.

Clearly, such absolute independence of the creative elan, which no longer recognizes any subordination to formal elements, makes possible the development of a lyricism such as characterizes the works of Camille Bryen (plate 24). This painter, whose art is remarkably sure and whose poetic inspiration is subtly attuned to flexible, musical constructions, so light that they seem almost devoid of matter, does not yield to unconscious impulses. The magic of his art is accounted for by an inner responsiveness, an intricate color sense that orders the effusions of tone into an oriental bouquet, as it were, which by virtue of being both matter and spirit, reveals a mystic state. Bryen comes from the world of poetry; and in his indefinable suggestions of the "formless" he remains a poet of painting, with a clearly marked aspiration toward transcendence.

It was this aspiration that led him, in 1947, to found, with Georges Mathieu (plate 32 a), a movement called "Non-Figuration Psychique." However, Mathieu's position is different: in his works the spot of color tends to become a flourish, a dramatic stroke, a partly deliberate und partly instinctive recording of emotion. This dramatic stroke often has epic accents, and even though Mathieu uses titles referring to historical events, his paintings must not be interpreted as attempts to restore the value of the subject matter. Nevertheless, they do suggest feeling tones which should not be ignored. Mathieu's references to Charlemagne and the Capetian kings have no more "significance" than titles such as *The Crossing of the Beresina* or *Masked Knights* used by another Tachiste, Arnal (b. 1924), whose works have been described as reflecting "an ambiguous humanism."

"Action art," as we have said, an art that is pure instinct, pure utterance, no longer tries to express or to represent, but only to *be*: the painting is a pure being. The supreme exponent of this explosive art, which repudiates even the abstract forms that supplanted the figurative forms, is Wols, in whose works a conflict-torn inwardness is projected onto the canvas in a splash of tragic violence. Like the German Romantics Novalis and Kleist he was a precocious genius; he died in 1951, at the age of thirty-eight, but explosions of anger or despair are subject to conditions of time and space different from those of slow creative maturation. Nevertheless a certain internal order, poetic rather than plastic, characterizes the works of Wols (and Bryen as well), though it is not obvious; this order, and the construction it determines, are not imposed by the painter's will (which is neutralized by the very violence of his creative act), but by an unformulated inner law which governs both instinct and chance.

It would be wrong to regard Tachisme as a facile technique. No doubt some painters will use it as a means to escape from themselves, or from the obligations of structural formulation. But artists who do not seek facile expedients but have adopted this manner of painting for the sake of its dramatic qualities, will discover that its extreme freedom imposes new laws on them and the duty not to resort to trickery either in relation to themselves or their work. And even though it is not always easy to distinguish between genuinely inspired creators and clever fakers, the inner resonance of the painting will provide us with a clue as to which of these two categories a given artist belongs. Painters who are carried away by an elemental force comparable to the forces of nature, irresistible and uncontrollable, will discover in this method a means for complete personal expression.

A striving to become a part of the forces of nature; "a cosmic fulcrum," as Klee used to say, to vibrate in unison with the soul of the universe — such a striving seems to inspire the works of the Canadian painter Jean-Paul Riopelle (color plate 13). The name of the group he founded with Paul Emile Borduas at Montreal, Les Automatistes (1940), probably refers to the method of poetic invention that the Surrealists called "automatic writing." But for all its automatic features, Riopelle's art, which is related to "action art" or instinctive art, discloses an unconscious will to construction, a will that ends up by gaining the upper hand. There is no such thing as art based only on instinct. Sometimes it is the material itself that determines the character of the work. This is the case of Fautrier (plate 25): after painting a number of still-life compositions in which the objects were reduced to ghosts of objects, he has embarked on a venture that has been described as "the boldest in contemporary painting." His forms are thickly modeled, clotted, of an austere, economical color, and the artist's conscious intervention is reduced to a minimum. These forms are not rough sketches—we know that they are complete—and they move us because they combine a great refinement of color with a taste for the raw material— a material that we might regard as raw, if we did not realize the high intricacy of this art. Fautrier (plate 25) is as intricate as Dubuffet (plate 26), who uses every conceivable material in order to achieve elements of surprise for our tactile and visual sensibility, and to suggest incongruous analogies of the kind favored by the Surrealists. Reacting against traditional painting, in rebellion against art and "good taste," provocatively and skillfully anti-aesthetic, Dubuffet gives us a mixture of "raw art" and humor, and sometimes, poetry. Similarly, Robert Lapoujade (b. 1921) has found himself thrown back on his inner restlessness, in a region of contemporary painting neighboring that of the "formless"; he is motivated by his unwillingness to remain a prisoner of a tempting and perfect linear style, as well as by the need, felt by all true artists, to question everything, to embark on the unpredictable adventure of creation.

Opposed to the aesthetics based on the spot of color, but occasionally coming close to it (for the spot of color can become a sign, and vice versa), is the aesthetics of the "sign," which reduces form to its most concentrated graphic expression. The transformation of the painting into an arrangement of such signs or schemas, a "written text" that remains alive, is similar to the gradual transformation, within the realm of writing, of the pictogram into the ideogram, and the ideogram into the completely abstract alphabetic character. This art of the sign or the hieroglyph is practiced primarily by Western painters who studied the calligraphy of the Far East, for example the Belgian Alechinsky (b. 1927; plate 33), or by Japanese and Chinese painters who have introduced the plastic script traditional in their native countries into the School of Paris. We shall first mention Kami Sugai (b. 1919) whose large austere and moving forms, in red and black, are built around monumental solemn characters endowed with the clarity and magic powers that legend ascribes to writing.

Zao-Wou-Ki (b. 1920, plate 27), a Chinese artist of the School of Paris, has also cultivated the expressive sign, the suggestive line creative of life, in the tradition of the Sung dynasty draftsmen, but he has not confined himself to a graphic art that excludes his love for fairy-like landscapes. While "going back into the Chinese age" (Claude Roy), he kept painting misty mountain scenes with angular figures and trees which expressed an alliance, so to speak, between calligraphy and the "formless." His great dramatic canvases of 1956–57 combine the calligraphic and the "formless"; at present he strives for an imageless painting, characterized by what we might call a disciplined explosion, the romantic effusion

48

12   Pierre Soulages. 1954 *(Ecole de Paris)*

being subjected to the rules of self-mastery and mastery of form that jointly govern Far Eastern art. We witness similar explosions, of great chromatic subtlety behind their seeming violence, in the paintings of Sato.

We have tried to be as complete and as fair as possible in this brief panoramic survey. In conclusion we may say that while all the tendencies of contemporary painting remain active and fruitful—as is only to be expected, since each painter is faithful to his inner impulse and his personal aesthetics—the development of a nonfigurative art appears to be the major phenomenon of our epoch. This is not to say that this development involves no dangers, for it may lead to technical complacency, to an attainment of purely decorative effects even though the greatest profundity is the goal, or, as a result of a legitimate reaction, to rationalist and intellectualist aridity. Today, as always, the valid work of art is the one expressing an intense inner life. This inner life, authentic and focused above all on creative contemplation, leaves room for gratuitous fantasies and games of the brush, but whether an art is figurative or not, it translates the spirit of the epoch and the genius of the artist only if it is perfectly integrated, and brings the painter into accord with the forces of matter and the forces of spirit.

Contemporary painting is richer in "explorations" than any painting that preceded it, and these explorations, whatever their end result, are extremely fascinating in themselves. They demonstrate a renewal of form and means of expression vaster and more diversified than the art of the preceding centuries—and by the same token they are more complex, and more difficult to analyze or to describe. They bear witness to the fact that despite two world wars and the resulting economic and political crises, the aesthetic factor is still essential, and is becoming steadily more essential as the century grows older.

13   Jean-Paul Riopelle. 1956 *(Ecole de Paris)*

understand its differences from Flemish painting (we must not, however ascribe an absolute value to these differences). "The Flemings are more influenced by their sky, by their soil. Though steeped in Greek, Latin, French learning, at least in the past, they have always lived in the climate of Nordic civilizations. This accounts for the unity, the physical and spiritual continuity of their art in its opulent spendors, in its ever-renewed brilliance. The works of the Walloons are usually characterized by a certain intellectualism, a basic classicism, a formalism acquired by study, a sensibility restrained by a vigilant consciousness. We are inclined to say that they reflect a collective humanism." In fact, however, each artist has his own style, the plastic and pictorial language he invents for his own use, and this is what matters most in an appreciation of Camus' sensibility and his chromatic vibration. Like the other Walloon and Flemish Expressionists, he seeks to go beyond his restlessness and instability, in order to express, as Brussens said of Floris Jespers (b. 1889), the peaceful aspects of man and the static aspects of the object.

Jespers underwent a radical transformation when, at the age of sixty, he went to the Congo, and his works became impregnated with the solemn, secret, and somber magic of African forms. His paintings executed after 1950 reflect a genuine metamorphosis, as well as an enrichment of his individuality which needed this shock to achieve a new flowering. For Jespers today is the "painter of the Congo," just as Henri Victor Wolvens (b. 1896) is the "painter of the penitents of Furnes." He treated this subject several times, attracted by the tragic appearance of this procession, which is medieval in its severe and fierce gravity, and by the curious geometric effect produced by the pilgrims' crosses. Similarly, the Spanish landscape, with the fierce ramparts of Avila and the barren sierras, provided War van Overstraeten (b. 1891) with an opportunity to express himself in his characteristically austere style; this style has become increasingly severe since 1950, without losing its dreaminess. This latter characteristic is part of the artist's Flemish tradition, but it harmonizes well with the contours of Provence which he visits frequently.

A suggestion or a possibility of the fantastic always lurks in Expressionism, which discovers and "expresses" hidden aspects of reality, its secret soul. This fantastic element, on the other hand, is strongly asserted and displayed in Surrealism which has been a constant feature of the art of the Netherlands since Bruegel, Swanenburgh, Mandyn, Bosch, and so many others. The modern forms of this Flemish-Walloon Surrealism tend toward an exploration of the unusual, of the obscure regions of the visible world in which the invisible manifests itself as transparency, shadows, or reflections. Several exhibitions, in particular the one entitled L'Apport wallon au surréalisme (The Walloon Contribution to Surrealism; Liége, 1955), have demonstrated the richness and diversity of this art of the fantastic, which, outside of Belgium, is known chiefly from the works of Paul Delvaux (b. 1897) and René Margritte (b. 1898). This exhibition, which aroused considerable interest, made it

54

14   Gaston Bertrand. 1951 *(Belgique)*

possible to gain a better insight into, and revealed the works of, a number of young painters —
René Lambert (b. 1925), François Marlier (b. 1918), Alexis Keunen (b. 1921), Jacques
Lacomblez (b. 1934), Max Michotte (b. 1916), and Remy van den Abeele (b. 1918). The
method of these painters is to transpose dream experiences, spontaneous or provoked by
the techniques of hallucination, such as the French Surrealists have made use of.

The basic feature of the works of Maxime van de Woestijne (b. 1911) is that in them the
boundary between the so-called "real" world and the world of dreams is abolished.
Woestijne's pictorial language discovers and invents symbols expressing the individual and
collective anxiety of an age that has lost its spiritual balance. Frightening fantasies haunt
his paintings, in which the real objects are as disquieting as they were in the works of
Hieronymus Bosch. Likewise, in the art of Paul Renotte (b. 1906), everyday things hint at
suspicious complicities, and both their individual formulations and their interrelationships
disclose their strangeness; here the very objectivity and banality of a stone or a tree trunk
start us on a "Descent to the Impossible", which is the title to one of his best paintings.
The magic forests painted by Louis van de Spiegele (b. 1912), and the subterranean galleries in *Arabian Nights* (1954) by Jane Graverol (b. 1910) are matched by Jean Ransy
(b. 1910) in his "metaphysical landscapes," which are related to Giorgio de Chirico's paintings and to Italian *pittura metafisica*.

The Belgian Surrealists have used the collage—adopting the techniques of Man Ray and
Max Ernst rather than those of Schwitters—as a vehicle for the surprising event and the
incongruous association. Raoul Ubac (b. 1910), who later was converted to abstract painting, had composed some very interesting ones around 1940, but the most original and suggestive ones are the photographic *montages* of Marcel Lefrancq (b. 1916) and José Delhaye
(b. 1921). Another Surrealist who turned to abstract painting is Pol Bury (b. 1922), noted
today for his bold experiments with mobile forms; about 1945 he had produced Surrealist
works inspired by a subtle poetic sense, and intensely magical.

Deserving of special mention is Armand Simon (b. 1905), who is little known, for he has
been working in silence and solitude for many years. Inspired by certain books, above all
those of Nerval, Rimbaud, and Lautréamont, he has produced many compositions showing
a strange and disquieting world of larvae, monstrous agglomerations of germs, alarming
metamorphoses, a world teeming with formless creatures that are materializations of fear,
hatred, anguish, and a desperate urge to destroy. The dramatic authenticity of these night-
mares endows them with a frightening reality, comparable to that of the elementary organ-
isms created by Auvin Pasque (b. 1903) who represents the world at its beginning, the
epoch when Chaos tried its hand at differentiating forms. Jean Duboscq's petrified forests,
inextricable and hallucinating entanglements of vegetation (*The Roads of Death*, 1954)

originate in the same fantastic inspiration which seeks to discover in abstract shapes the face of those "possible worlds" which Klee spoke about.

Discussing Suzanne van Damme (b. 1901), Roger Bodart characterizes her art by the terms *rêve éveillé* (waking dream) and *rêve surveillé* (controlled dream) which are very apt, for this painter introduced into the absurdity of the dream a logic of her own, and occasionally even a playful spirit: her method of controlling the dream elements involves the danger of making them seem less authentic.

As for the two most famous Belgian Surrealists, Delvaux and Margritte, we may say that their works have shown no essential transformations since 1945. Paul Delvaux continues to paint bewitching nocturnes, in which nude women wander, like sleepwalkers, amidst strange structures that are difficult to localize in time or space. The atmosphere of the waking dream still pervades his works, such as his large decorations executed for Gilbert Périer in Brussels; they are not, strictly speaking, Surrealist, but these scenes combining modern figures and ancient buildings, and breathing a serene and peaceful order, give off an impression of intense and enigmatic magic. We may also note the constant presence, in Delvaux's paintings, of the skeleton, which relates him to James Ensor, and further back in time to Bruegel, creator of *Triumph of Death*. This petrified world surrendered to phantoms, in which moonlit shadows move about gracefully, serves as an appropriate setting for such dramatic scenes as his *Crucifixion* (executed in 1954) or the striking *Entombment* showing skeletons burying a skeleton, and providing a lugubrious illustration of the saying "Let the dead bury their dead (plate 37)."

While Paul Delvaux's paintings contain a symbolism that is difficult to discover and define, no symbolism intended in the works of René Margritte (plate 35). The unusual as such, surprise mingled with amusement, alarm, and fear, are the sole content of his compositions which induced Salvador Dali to refer to their creator as "one of the most ambiguous painters of our time." As Magritte puts it, what comes between "the absolute mystery of a presence" and the image that reveals it, is not a poetic interpretation but the poetic state of mind. According to Magritte, the object is both real (i. e., valid as such) and ambiguous; and, illustrating this idea, he often treated the theme of a painting representing a landscape, which is superimposed on a window opening on the same landscape: the image and the object become interchangeable, yet each retains its identity. *Le Balcon de Manet* (Manet's Balcony), in which the figures of the famous painting have been replaced by coffins, and a painting showing a coffin instead of Madame Récamier on a sofa borrowed from David's portrait, take us back into the macabre world of the Belgian pre-Surrealists, Antoine Wiertz, James Ensor, Félicien Rops, Jules de Bruycker, Fernand Khnopff.

Nonfigurative tendencies have asserted themselves since 1947, in the group Jeune Peinture Belge, among artists who were no longer satisfied with the realistic aesthetics of the Expressionists or the fantasies of the Surrealists. A contributory cause was probably the exhibition *Jeune Peinture Française* (Brussels, 1946), which acquainted many Belgian artists, cut off from France during the war, with the abstract works of the School of Paris. The foundation of the Salon des Réalités Nouvelles in Paris also furthered the evolution of the Jeune Peinture Belge toward abstract art. But the present flowering of nonfigurative art in Belgium had been prepared previously; aside from the great precursor, Servranckx, and the sympathies aroused in Belgium by De Stijl and Neo-Plasticism, there had also been the example of Georges Vantongerloo who joined the Abstraction-Creation group as early as 1931 and was an active contributor to De Stijl. Finally, Dutch abstract painters, Van der Leck, Mondrian, Domela, Van Doesburg, helped the development of nonfigurative painting, particularly in Flanders. The new movement spread rapidly and has become one of the most productive and significant aspects of Belgian art today. The representatives of geometric or "cold" abstraction are under the influence of Neo-Plasticism; others, closer in spirit, if not in form, to Expressionism, are characterized by a strong sense for the dramatic. The abstract constructions of Antoine Mortier (b. 1910) reflect an almost religious aspiration to master metaphysical anguish, the theme of the Cross serving as the plastic foundation of his paintings and their spiritual focal point. His changeless structures negate movement and transience, while giving free room to the lines of force in which the tide of life flows, restrained and dramatically condensed. Roger Dudant (b. 1929), on the other hand, seeks support in the visual world of scaffoldings, airports, shipyards; in his works, objective truth is summed up in schematic designs of perfect precision, which reflect both sensibility and intelligence. Lismonde (b. 1908, plate 36) could scarcely be classed as abstract if he did not tend to an abridgement of organic form; in painting the human body, or landscapes of ports or ruins, he always seeks to discover the essential outline. All these painters, in one way or another, are inspired by a striving for a rational order, of the kind which has led Delahaut (b. 1911) to a geometric aesthetics related to that of Dewasne and Pillet in France. Whereas Max Mendelson (b. 1915), overcoming a tendency that accounted for the arbitrary schematizations of his *Swimmers* (1950), now expresses the same striving for order in a graphic and hieroglyphic art, which occasionally reaches the dimensions of a decorative monumentalism.

One of the representative artists of this evolution which in less than ten years has brought so many young Belgian painters from figurative to abstract art is Gaston Bertrand (b. 1910, color plate 14). At the beginning he was influenced by Ensor, but he soon liberated himself from the latter's style, embarking on curious explorations of the human figure, which continued in his portraits as late as 1954, when he joined the ranks of the nonfigurative artists. Antoine Marstboom (b. 1905), who produced figurative paintings until 1952, progressively stylized his objective forms, finally transforming his initial subject matter—ships, gulls, ports—into an arrangement of motives without anecdotal suggestions, and expressing the purely dynamic energy inherent in things. Such a reference to objects, which in Marstboom's paintings recalls a certain form of Impressionism, is also present, or sometimes present, in the paintings of Anne Bonnet (b. 1908), but in her case, too, the blurring of the materiality of things, of their substantial aspects, reflects a striving for inner peace and balance, and for external security in an appeased world (plate 38).

The paintings by Luc Peire (b. 1915), Jean Milo (b. 1905), and Jan Vaerten (b. 1909) will not fail to confront us with the familiar problem of "subject matter." Are Peire's forms outlines of bottles or stylized human bodies, similar to Massimo Campigli's woman vases? We should rather say that Peire's statue-like figures and women stems reflect a certain conception of form which is not yet completely developed, but which is incontestably fruitful and promising. Jan Milo spent a long time in the Congo; its tropical atmosphere permeates his very personal art releasing purely instinctual forces from the control of those of reason, a control characteristic of his *Homage to Vermeer* (1951) in the Museum of Fine Arts at Liége. As for Jan Vaerten, his technique combining figuration and abstraction does not reflect the artist's choice but the intrinsic requirements of the painting itself. The plastic figure striving for being manifests its will to be figurative or nonfigurative: the artist merely obeys.

The works of these painters once more demonstrate the artificiality of all attempts to erect an impassable barrier between figurative art and abstract art. The more resolutely a given painter repudiates preconceived systems and dogmas, the more his works are alive and valid. Speaking of Louis van Lint (b. 1909), the Belgian critic Louis Léon Sosset said that for this painter "reality is the embryo of the idea, which is the beginning of its transformation." This definition is true, and it applies to many painters of our generation belonging to various tendencies. Not the least interesting and fruitful of these tendencies is the one that inspires the elemental dynamism of Maurier de Wyckaert (b. 1923), Jan Burssens (b. 1925), and Serge Vandercam (b. 1924), in whose works the organic seething of germs spreads into a torrential stream. In conclusion, we must mention an artist who responds equally to the demands of freedom and those of discipline, Pierre Alechinsky (b. 1927). His works reflect both a calligraphy which is a pure expression of ideal form, and an irresistible surge of natural forces, whose violence and capacity for creating new images manifest themselves with equal vigor in volcanic explosions and slow vegetal maturation.

Victor Servranckx. Opus 5. Collection M. Bilcke, Brussels

15   Georges Braque. 1956 *(Ecole de Paris)*

16 Léon Gischia. 1956 *(Ecole de Paris)*

17   Camille Singier. 1956 (*Ecole de Paris*)

18   Roger Bissière. 1957 *(Ecole de Paris)*

19   Pierre Tal Coat. 1955 *(Ecole de Paris)*

20   Mario Prassinos. 1957 *(Ecole de Paris)*

21 Jean Deyrolle. 1956 *(Ecole de Paris)*

22   Victor Vasarely. 1955–56 *(Ecole de Paris)*

23   Alberto Magnelli. 1950 (*Ecole de Paris*)

24   Camille Bryen. 1957 *(Ecole de Paris)*

25   Jean Fautrier.   (*Ecole de Paris*)

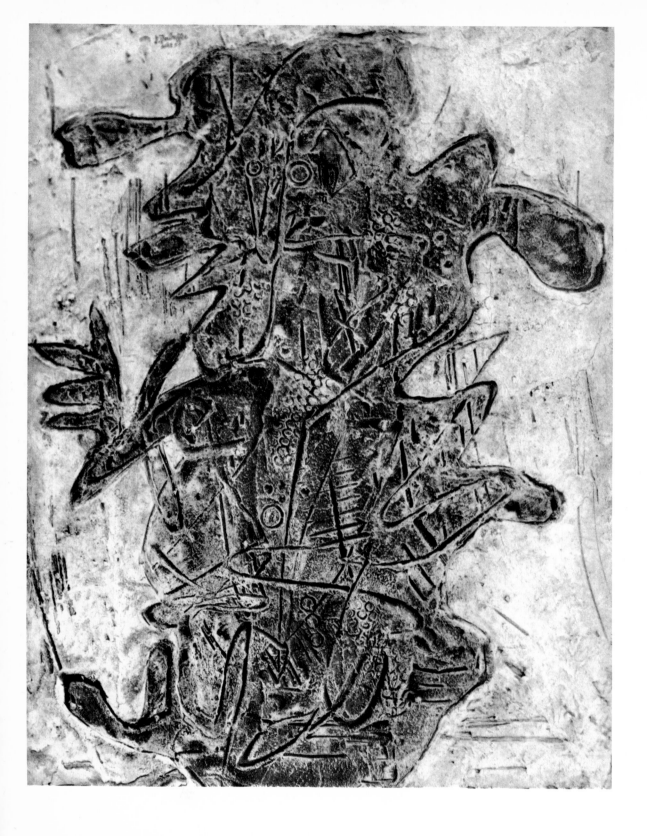

26   Jean Dubuffet. 1951 *(Ecole de Paris)*

27   Zao Wou Ki. 1956 *(Ecole de Paris)*

28   Alberto Giacometti. 1956 *(Ecole de Paris)*

29   Bernard Buffet. 1951   *(Ecole de Paris)*

30 Christian d'Orgeix. 1954 *(Ecole de Paris)*

31   Claude Georges. 1958 *(Ecole de Paris)*

32 a Georges Mathieu. 1957   (*Ecole de Paris*)

32 b Jaroslaw Serpan. 1957   (*Ecole de Paris*)

33   Pierre Alechinsky. 1957 *(Ecole de Paris)*

34   Raoul Ubac. 1956–58 *(Ecole de Paris)*

35   René Margritte. 1955 (*Belgique*)

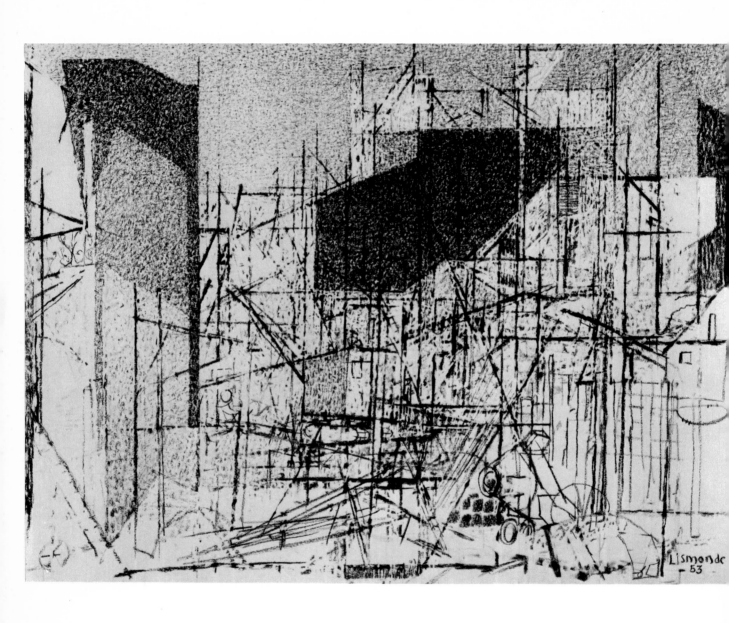

36   Lismonde. 1953 *(Belgique)*

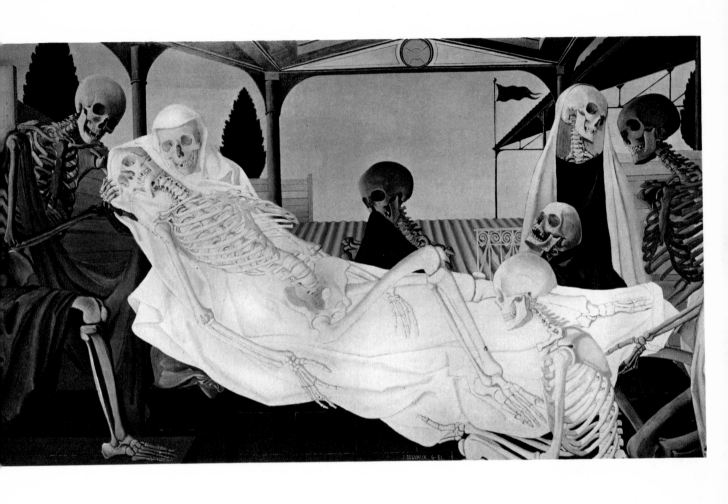

37 Paul Delveaux. 1951 *(Belgique)*

38   Anne Bonnet. 1956 *(Belgique)*

I

The war and the first postwar years marked a decisive turning point in the history of Italian art. Since then Italian artists have become active in the international artistic community and have joined the modern tradition from which they had previously been cut off. It may be in order to explain why Italian artists, having entered this cosmopolitan culture, did not conform to its stylistic fashions but, rather, set about resolving in the only way possible to them a crisis that had been growing in Italian art for years, highlighted now and then by intensely dramatic moments.

The first effort to break the bonds of Italian artistic provincialism was made by the Futurists as far back as 1910. Their program was courageous, but confused and contradictory. They wanted to abolish romanticism and were latter-day romantics. They were directly influenced by the Cubists yet reproved Cubism for its interest in mere formal problems and for its neglect of strongly emotional topics. They preached internationalism, yet desired the triumph and rule of "Italian genius." They cried out for revolution, and were patriots. They proclaimed the end of bourgeois culture, and glorified machine civilization. They were both demagogues and aristocrats. Their confusion was so evident that the best artists quickly abandoned a movement that was more anarchic than revolutionary. Umberto Boccioni died in war in 1916, but his last canvases already showed that he had broken completely with the Futurist theory of "plastic dynamics" and was working with formal and colorist ideas inspired by Cézanne though containing Expressionist tendencies. The first attempt toward a rebirth of Italian art through European experience was a failure. However, it had broached an important problem, revealed a critical condition in Italian life, and raised significant moral questions.

After the First World War, there was also a *rappel à l'ordre* in Italy. "Metaphysical" painting and the movement labeled "plastic values" quickened interest in and serious study of the Italian Renaissance tradition. These movements were in striking antithesis to Futurism. It is clear to everyone today that De Chirico is and, indeed, has always been, a reactionary painter. His metaphysical paintings interpreted widely held feelings, but his more recent paintings are the passé academicism of a hack. Although metaphysical painting and the plastic-values movement opposed all avant-garde tendencies and proposed a return to tradition, they were still part of a European art movement, albeit a European movement that, in Italy as elsewhere, meant the continuation of certain values rather than the free criticism of all value systems.

The situation in the following years became so bitter that it resolved itself into open conflict between "European" and "anti-European." This was partly due to the political situation. Nevertheless one should not exaggerate the direct responsibility of the Fascist regime; nor should it be forgotten that Fascism, though it called itself revolutionary, was only the violent summation of the conservatism, the provincialism, and the cultural mediocrity of the Italian middle class. During Fascism, the Italian artist's condition was difficult, but it was neither so grim nor so desperate as his German colleague's condition under Nazism. Fascism opposed modern art because the regime was conservative and reactionary but it did not have an aesthetic credo, did not impose prohibitions, nor did it promulgate repressive measures. It did not favor the teaching of modern art but did not prohibit it. It denied modern artists official positions and academic honors but did prevent them from working, teaching, showing their works, or receiving prizes in national shows. Objectively speaking, the discomfort of the modern Italian artist was more spiritual than material. There were many controversies, and some of them, in the later years, became rather dangerous. Political bigwigs, third-rate artists, and servile journalists tried in every way possible to outlaw modern art as anti-national, subversive, and decadent; however, there was no persecution in the real sense of the word. It may be that the artists' rebellion was slow and difficult for that very reason: the battle was not so much an outer struggle against an external force as an inner struggle over the sense of moral inferiority arising from denial of liberty, offense to human dignity, and exclusion from the cultural developments of the civilized world.

Just as it had no aesthetic credo, Fascism had no official style (except in architecture alone). An effort was made to manufacture and impose a "Fascist" art, but the results were so meager that laughter was aroused rather than argument. Modern Italian art, therefore, was not born in reaction to the false monumentality of Piacentini's architecture or to the commissioned paintings and sculpture that adorned it. It was a rebellion, a reaction against the Novecento (ninteenth century) style. The vast, confused current called Novecento was widely supported by the regime but it was not programmatically or partisanly Fascist. Indeed, it had no program. It gathered together artists of different tastes and merit. It was, in short, the party of the indifferent and the timid, of those who did not want to face problems or take on obligations and moral responsibility. Seen as a whole, the movement was vaguely nationalistic and traditional, but more from inertia than from purpose, more from indifference than from program. Thus, the art currents that reacted against the moral torpor and aesthetic agnosticism of the Novecento all sought, more or less explicitly, to make contact with the large European artistic current. But this impulse was essentially spiritual: Europe, for these artists, was a mythical entity, a vague ideal of liberty rather than a concrete historical reality. Scipione and Mafai in Rome, the first Milanese abstractionists, the "Six Painters" of Turin, and later, with more clarity, the young artists of the Corrente group, all felt that the most serious aspect of the Italian situation was neither arbitrary political dictatorship nor the ideological fiction on which it was based, but the inertia and callousness it produced in the Italian people. Therefore,

Morandi 1942

39 Giorgio Morandi. 1944 (*Italia*)

they fought the widespread conformism with an acute, throbbing moral sensitivity, with delight in intellectual adventure and strong feelings of dedication.

Of the spiritual tensions that characterize the formation of the various modern Italian currents, the battle of words over architecture is typical. The penetration into Italy of the ideas of Gropius and Le Corbusier took place no later than elsewhere. In 1930 a group of "rationalist" architects had already joined together in Milan. The magazine *Casabella* (House Beautiful) dates from that same period. For more than ten years it discussed the problems of modern architecture with a grasp of ideas and seriousness of critical method not inferior to the most serious architectural publication then published in Europe or America. But modern architects met many serious difficulties on the practical level. The State monopolized building and urban planning enterprises. The "official" architects wrought barbarous destruction upon the center of ancient Italian cities in order to stamp them with the seal of imperial Rome. Behind the false taste for the monumental lay speculative greed and the coldest indifference to the real problems of Italian society. Modern architects knew perfectly well that the new European architecture was born of the need for radical reform in the social structure, and labeled itself "international" and "democratic." However, this social terrain was precisely where the traditionalists lay in wait for the moderns, in order to accuse them, no less, of aiming at the overthrow of constituted government and the establishment of socialism. That is why the modern architects limited their verbal assaults to the problem of form and style; and even when they had united in a group and had drawn up urban reform plans for a working-class section of Milan, they were forced to keep on theoretical grounds of formal design. Abstaining from discussion of social and economic questions, they talked about organization versus disorganization, rigorous method versus superficiality, and modernity versus academicism.

The example of G. Terragni is a dramatic case in point. The works of this architect, who died in the war while still very young, suffice to classify him among the most sensitive and refined European architects of the time. He had an anxiety bordering on obsession for formal purity. Little psychological acumen is needed to understand that what he was seeking to satisfy by that formal purity was a deeper, anxious need for moral purity. However, the historical situation closed all avenues to progress and forced him to express his profound morality in an ideal of rigor rather than in a concrete will to action.

Again, the situation imposed upon G. Pagano, the leader of the modern movement, the task of conducting a bitter, exhausting struggle. Later, this battlefield shifted from art to politics—Pagano died in 1945 in a Nazi concentration camp—and the lengthy struggle unquestionably limited his creative potential.

In 1935, the critic E. Persico (d. 1936), who played a decisive part in the spiritual orientation of the younger group in Italian art, sought to enlarge the horizons of disciplined rationalism to include new experimentation by bringing up for discussion the architecture of Wright and Aalto. However, it was not until the postwar period that Italian architecture's European ideal could develop on a wide front. The discussion was reopened by Bruno Zevi and at first took the form of formalistic opposition to "rational" and "organic," quickly developed to include the entire problem of modern urban development.

The modern architects, it is true, did not succeed in taking leadership of the movement for the reconstruction and reorganization of Italian city planning. And building speculation, even after the war and the downfall of Fascism, advanced implacably, crushing urban development beneath an absurd, chaotic mass of buildings without any aesthetic quality whatsoever. But now the basis of the old argument has been substantially changed and simplified: there are cheap speculation and a mass of confused, anti-social interest on the one hand, and a cultivated outlook, a clear awareness, and explicit affirmation of social needs on the other. Thus, modern Italian architecture, no longer suffocated by a rigorous but arid formalism, has entered into direct contact not only with formal values but with all the living problems of modern architecture. The individual personalities of the artists have an opportunity for expression in this wider context.

P. L. Nervi has perhaps understood better than anyone else the artistic possibilities of the new structural technique. F. Albini has been able to transform his original rigidity of style into a limpid design coherence that is manifest in the forms of city planning as well as in his smaller architectural forms. I. Gardella's chief concern has been the close study of the relation between form and the natural and social environment. P. Scarpa is perhaps the most intransigent spokesman for a movement that is not merely thesis or program but rather a directive to charge form with creativity and poetry. Astengo, Quaroni, Ridolfi, and Rogers and his group have all been active both in the field of architectural forms themselves and in the larger field of urban planning. These men have been the determining influence in a driving movement and have shaped a program whose interest, on the level of international architecture, is beyond question.

Sculptors, too, have had to break out of an encirclement and face a primarily spiritual problem. Their field also knew the cruel drama of limitations in creative possibilities. A. Martini was a leading sculptor in the years between 1925 and 1945. He was an eccentric, extraordinarily gifted with imagination and sculptural talent but erratic and sporadic. He often evaded the demands of earnest, conscientious search. Each of his works springs from a genuine sculptural impulse, contains a spark of creative beauty. Yet many of his works (as the artist himself recognized with infinite bitterness shortly before his death) are the result of improvisation rather than study, of inventiveness that is quickly exhausted in itself and does not give rise to inspired and profound elaboration. His error perhaps lay in thinking that freedom was an arbitrary, natural fact, whereas freedom is a moral conquest and always comes through rigorous discipline. Too confident in the infallibility of his artistic instinct, he played a dangerous game, pretending that he could go in any direction that pleased him and then break away with a flash of genius, or perhaps a gesture, a paradoxical phrase. Many of his works are merely attempts at escape into fantasy, dreams, or myth. His last creations, born of more painstaking sculptural handling, of lately won mastery of the formal language of modern art, and of rejection of all invitations to glorification, must be numbered among the finest works in modern European sculpture. They constitute the point of departure for the younger generation of Italian sculptors.

Marino Marini's work, an example of formal purity and the serious search for an absolute plasticity, is in a sense a critique of Marini's unchecked and sometimes arbitrary genius. Of course, Marini's work, too, tries to give form to myth; and his activity for a long time remained within the framework of a noble, meditative classicism. His myth, however, is no longer escape, just as his classicism is no longer an authoritarian principle. Quite the contrary, the myth in Marini (with particular reference to his main, recurrent them: "the man on horseback") is the result of a profound study of man's spirit and a sounding of the unconscious motives of man's behavior. Marini's classicism is not dogma but history that he has lived and suffered. Accordingly, his sculptural development, which tends more and more toward pure formal abstraction, coincides with an inner psychic development that tends more and more to abandon both naturalistic motivation and emotional escape, seeking its outlet in the strength and immediacy of sculptural handling of material.

G. Manzù took a more radical stand against Martini's mythology. In his thoughtful review of the entire history of sculpture, Manzù plunged deeply into historical studies and courageously substituted the moral values of religious faith for the moral escapism of myth. After the war, his artistic output ceased, and his energies were dissipated in research that was more subtle than constructive, as if the artist were satisfied by experiment as an end in itself. Between 1930 and 1945, however, Manzù's work was of the greatest importance because, like Scipione's painting, it bore witness to the indissoluble connection between aesthetic and moral problems. In his sculpture of that period there was a passionate reference to the romantic experience that the Italians had lived only superficially (was this, perhaps, the reason for their insufficient love of liberty?). A firm refusal to indulge in rhetorical lies, an invitation to find one's self through inner contemplation, and a religious and profoundly humane outlook on history were also there. His Christian fervor was not a vain stand during those troubled years, for he appealed to the fundamentally Christian concept of European culture and civilization. It is because of this, we believe, that Manzù, together with the young painters of the Corrente group, went over to the opposition unhesitatingly and took a stand against the conformism and morality of the Novecento.

40 Renato Guttuso. 1956 *(Italia)*

On another, thoroughly nonreligious ideological level, Mirko's tormented bronzes stated the same things. One can still mention classicism in discussing Mirko's initial output, but one must quickly add that the classic theme was chosen only to be destroyed—consumed, as it were, bit by bit, in the subtle labors of sculpturing. Step by step, what was or had been thought to be the constant and unchanging content of sculpture vanished, to give way to a new content which demanded new formal solutions. In the immediate postwar period, the great bronze gate executed by Mirko for the Ardeatine Memorial Tomb[1] was one of the strongest as well as one of the most human abstract sculptures produced during those years.

This slow, gradual disappearance of the classicism universally regarded as the age-old inheritance of Italy, is perhaps the outstanding feature of postwar art. We find this new anticlassicism in the sculpture of A. Viani. Viani's work is often considered dependent upon Arp, although, in reality, he reverses Arp's process, taking a classic or neoclassic historical theme as his point of departure and then, in his elaboration of it, ridding it of all specific historical reference. In this way the resultant form can communicate directly via the space, light, and reality of the moment.

Of course, other sculptors have also been influenced by contemporary art movements. Leoncillo, for example, has direct sources in the fragmentary composition and color range of Cubism; Consagra was directly influenced by the so-called "Neo-Cubism" of the period following the First World War; and Franchina has been influenced by experiments in the abstract field. Traces of conscious transformation of the mythological and archaic in sculpture can also be found in these artists' works. In addition, their work evidences the acquisition not so much of new expressive means as of more direct and open capacity for emotion. The process of inner freedom and the achievement of a broadened living horizon is also more easily perceptible in painting. One must not confuse the work of that group which the younger Italian artists themselves have labeled the generation of masters with the mediocrity and conformism of the Novecento. Some of these masters (Severini, Campigli, Magnelli, and De Pisis) worked in Paris, in direct contact with the international artistic milieu; and others (Tosi, Rosai, Carra, Casorati), though they worked in Italy in the midst of an increasingly bitter and relentless anti-modern polemic, managed to retain their highly civilized ideal in the dignity and high purpose of their art.

Above them all looms the noble figure of Morandi (color plate 39). The very quality of his work demonstrated how a spiritual ideal could be acquired only by severe application and a continually more profound and jealously guarded intimacy. There is discernible in Morandi's painting a constant awareness, a continually sharper interest in the successive developments in European art, as well as the almost painful consciousness of the need to stand apart, to maintain a defensive position, so to speak. When the defense of an incorruptible moral ideal is entrusted to the purity, the intangibility of poetry, one cannot risk intellectual adventures or participate in idealistic battles that necessarily take place on a wider front than that of art. It now becomes clear, with a more objective and comprehensive view of European history during the last decades, that these artists, and Morandi above all, have had an important place in that history. It is also clear by now that their defense of poetic values had a reason for being that was not limited to the Italian situation alone.

During the difficult years, in a climate of growing tension, Morandi's silent protest and reserve were appreciated in all their nobility by the younger artists. The harsh times, however, demanded much more than a serene, composed *consolatio philosophiae*. The new generation of painters was born in a climate of anxiety and of rebellion that went from secrecy to boldness. Scipione died very young in 1933, but his work represented one of the first acts of rebellion against the Novecento, one of the premises for the young Italian painters. Scipione's Catholic and Baroque Rome, his fundamental theme, is the opposite of the Imperial Rome of Fascist rhetoric. Later, Mafai's Demolitions series is a protest against the inhuman stupidity that prompted the destructive "city planning" of Piacentini. Scipione's feelings of anxiety and guilt are the reverse of the official optimism of the times; his tormented canvases are a prime indication of the will to spiritual opposition. Other artistic currents opposed the Novecento with a program that was less profound, perhaps, but more culturally motivated. The group of Six Painters from Turin (which includes L. Chessa, C. Levi, E. Paulucci, and F. Mazio) explicitly recognized that the main highway of European art, from Impressionism onward, passes through French painting. The first group of Italian abstractionists rallied around A. Soldati, in Milan, in direct rapport with the rationalist architects. The word "Europe" was by then a password, a standard; the problem was to give the word a precise historical meaning and to translate the symbol into concrete terms. This was the task of the Milanese group Corrente (1938). Most of the artists we will later find at work in the intellectual and moral reconstruction of the postwar period were trained in that movement.

Some critics have pointed to the Corrente group as the starting point for socialist Neo-Realism. This latter group, which programmatically opposed the Novecento, included artists with greatly different backgrounds, such as Birolli (color plate 42), Guttuso (color plate 40), Treccani, Migneco, Badosi, and many others. The group's function, more than in formulating a precise program, consisted in expressing a general protest against the Italian situation, which, following the Spanish and Ethiopian wars and the alliance with Germany, became increasingly corrupt and increasingly hostile to all forms of modern art. Finally, the movement had a decidedly neo-romantic character and proposed a critical approach to the main problems of European art and culture.

It is important to emphasize this predominantly critical interest: all the artists who made up the Corrente group took part in the political struggle. Their position was clearly leftist, and they were bent on creating a movement of intellectuals that would hasten the imminent fall of Fascism and lay the groundwork for the total, active integration of Italy into the democratic and progressive community of nations. "Europe" was no longer a dream but a historical reality. Consideration of the ideological and class conflicts of Europe yielded signs of a coming crisis. Making up for lost time was not enough to bring understanding of that historical condition; a profound critical study of all the problems connected with European art of the last fifty or sixty years was necessary. Renato Guttuso revealed the best qualities of his generous nature during those years. His work repeats all the stages of European art, from Cézanne and Van Gogh to the Expressionists, with the evident purpose of separating and emphasizing human and social militant ideas, as well as the revolutionary ferment they contain. Never as in that moment of intense fervor had Guttuso fulfilled the guiding function that Gramsci had assigned the progressive intellectuals.

Naturally, that labor of revision led directly to the bellwether of art, to the man who for many years had been in the forefront of every avant-garde movement and only recently had reaffirmed the need for revolutionary dedication. The road, in other words, led to Picasso, more precisely to the Picasso of *Guernica*. This great painting, perhaps the only great historical painting of the century, became the reference point for the younger generation of Italian and non-Italian artists. The fate of the small city destroyed by Fascist planes became the symbol and, more than the symbol, the portent of Europe's fate. Death and destruction did not delay in coming; Picasso's name was the rallying cry of Italian artists during the terrible war years, the German occupation, and the Resistance movement. Italian artists had considered themselves the outcasts of a free world; now they felt that the world was neither free nor happy, that the crisis in Italian culture and conscience was only an episode in the greater European crisis. The feeling that imminent tragedy threatened humanity in general transcended differences of traditions and national cultures. The problem was the same all over the world: a stalemate had to be overcome by a desperate act of will, by a determined moral effort.

Postwar art reflects this tragic yet fundamentally realistic historical concept. As artists seek in the art of the recent past for those premonitory signs of the tragedy now unfolding, that is, as they look upon the history of modern art with an interest that is essentially moral, so they formulate the moral program of their artistic action in a necessary realism. In general terms, this realism is not and does not pretend to be anything but the abandonment of myth, imaginative escape, and poetry. It is the precise meaning and specific context of this realism on which discussion centers and the contrasting lines and positions of contemporary Italian art are drawn. A final point must be made before going on to a

41   Atanasio Soldati. 1952 *(Italia)*

description of Italian art currents during the last ten years: realism not only is not the same but the exact opposite of naturalism. Realism means not a way of representing but a way of being and acting, not faithful representation of objects but the active presence of the artist in the historical life of society. The attempt to reconcile realism with naturalism can only lead, as in fact it has led the representatives of Socialist Realism, to exhume supposed national traditions, to retrace the steps of the old academicism, to combat all forms of avant-garde, in short, to make the artist a witness of the life of society rather than a factor in it.

When Arturo Martini, undoubtedly the greatest Italian sculptor during the period between the two world wars, died in 1947, Italian sculpture was seeking a way out of a crisis that he had foreseen and lived through. This crisis had led him to pronounce upon sculpture the verdict of a "dead language." At Martini's death, however, a new art of young men was beginning to take shape, based on the traditions that were being established by slightly older masters, such as Marino Marini and Giacomo Manzù.

Marini declared as early as 1935 that he considered the sculptor's creation to be "a true work of art only if it abstracted from and transcended nature while drawing inspiration from it." He had just published an aesthetic credo opposed to Martini's; as the years passed, Marini was to embody this credo in sculptures that were progressively freer and more articulated, concerned with coherent structure rather than with realistic appearance. In this work there was a lesson for the younger artists, even though most of these, as we have seen with the *Fronte Nuovo delle Arti*, were peering outside Italy's borders for meaning and validity in a larger European tradition. Marini's sculpture, too, had European significance, even though it did not go to the extreme of negating the representational image. A Tuscan steeped in the classicism of his region, Marini had been enabled by Cubism to synthesize his sculptural grasp of volumes and to make Cubism act as a corrective on the Expressionism to which it was related. Marini was born in Pistoia in 1901, and now lives in Milan, where he teaches at the Brera Academy.

Giacomo Manzù, born in Bergamo in 1908, was younger than Marini, and was different in cultural outlook. Manzù's origins go back to Donatello, but he stems more directly from Medardo Rosso in his technique, drawn from Impressionism, of dissolving solid form in light. In Manzù's work the theme receives great importance through the created effect, making it impossible to isolate the sculpture in its essence. On the contrary, the effect is of luminous atmosphere seeking to dissolve the artist's material and accentuating content in a dramatic or a sincerely religious aspect. Unlike Marini, Manzù abandoned honesty in his sculpture precisely when he sought to express his subject more solidly. Thus, he arrived at statuary that is sometimes imposing, as in his recent portrait of *Cardinal Lercaro*, but

96

undoubtedly quite removed from the poetic quality of his other portraits or of some of his earlier *Cardinalini* (Little Cardinals).

Another sculptor whose style was formed before 1945 is Pericle Fazzini, born in Grottamare in 1913. Fazzini has written: "Sculpture for me is the union of matter with the spirit that I see and feel with my mind and heart. When I am at my sculpture I feel that there is nothing there except my faith in the work held in my hands." The portrait of *Giuseppe Ungaretti*, 1936 (Rome, National Gallery of Modern Art) was a successful work without any decorative or descriptive intention. With Corpora (color plate 43) and others, Fazzini joined the group that called itself, somewhat inaccurately, "The Neo-Cubists." He later became a member of the *Fronte Nuovo*. Since then, Fazzini has fallen back on a style of sculpture that, judging by his most recent works, fails to show his best creative capacities.

Emilio Greco, born in Catania in 1913, should be mentioned along with Fazzini. In the postwar period Greco succeeded in freeing his forms from certain archaic effects and has arrived at an elegant stylization of his subjects in which the principal objective seems to be the achievement of a harmonious, undulating, and caressing rhythm. Other sculptors, such as Mazzacurati, Mafai, the now elderly Gerardi, and Mascherini have continued to work within the representational tradition and, in their best works, have produced some good results.

Though Martini's work has not been forgotten and Marini still produces works of high quality, there is also a new sculpture that one of its closest students, Marchiori, has defined as the sculpture of the "second act." It was natural, of course, for sculptors to contribute their techniques and ideas toward that renewal of artistic expression proposed by the painter. As well as Fazzini, three of them, Viani, Franchina, and Leoncillo, participated in the discussions and shows of the *Fronte Nuovo*. Consagra had been a member of *Forma* in Rome; and one of his first abstract works, an arabesque in metal, was significantly entitled *A Manifesto for the Future*.

Mirko Basaldella, brother of the painter Afro and a member of the group of Eight Italian Painters, abandoned his efforts at a Cellini-like elegance together with his morbid reminiscences of Renaissance sculpture. He dedicated himself to modifying forms into a kind of abstract and Surrealist heraldry, as though he were creating an animal mythology, real or imaginary, with fawns and chimeras, all valid in their imaginative consistency. Mirko showed all his artistic maturity in a masterpiece created in 1949: the bronze gate for the Ardeatine Memorial Tomb.[1] Here the twisting of the bronze captures the essence of this material, and a rhythm of light accentuates and conceals its volumes so that the gate reveals the authentic imaginative power of one of Italy's most talented sculptors rather than the work of an artisan craftsman. Mirko was born in Udine, 1910, but, artistically, is more Roman than anything else. His first show was at the Galleria della Cometa (The Comet Gallery) in 1935, where the liveliest talents then working in the capitol exhibited. Mirko's sculpture has now achieved international recognition. He has followed his aesthetic bent to its extreme. His subjects are still cast in a Surrealist style and have a totemic, a symbolically hieratic quality. In the relief characteristic of his most recent work, the artistic concern is solely with relationships of space, of unity in temporal dimension, highlighted by the varied color of his materials, now green copper, now shining brass. Mirko's monumental sculpture has nothing whatever to do with statuary: his sketch for the *Monument to the Unknown Political Prisoner*, which won second prize at the London Exhibition in 1935, shows a man staring upward at the top of a high, symbolic wire fence. The figure of the man is solid and substantial within its limited volume, as if to indicate a compactness more spiritual than material. Mirko is now in America, and teaches at Harvard's School of Design.

Viani, Franchina and Leoncillo, who had exhibited together at the *Fronte Nuovo's* show at the Venice Biennale in 1948, had thoroughly dissimilar temperaments. Of the three, Leoncillo, born in Spoleto in 1910, tended toward realism after the dissolution of the *Fronte Nuovo*. However, as with Guttuso, his realism was a return to a special kind of Expressionism based upon a thorough knowledge of post-Cubism. *Bombardamento Notturno* (Night Bombing), a work done in 1954, is also suggestively entitled *Guernichetta* (Little Guernica). This work has marked a critical point in Leoncillo's art. He has learned through it an intuitive need for a less programmatic use of volume; and in his most recent work he tends to avoid the "populist" type of representation. Leoncillo cannot do without a dialectic exchange with nature. His is a seething temperament, and his sculptural materials, in his case, ceramics, intensify his expression in a singularly naturalistic, though not objective, manner. In this regard, Leoncillo has drawn close to the recent work of painters like Morlotti, without a doubt the best among the movement that has been called "Neo-Naturalist" (color plate 44).

Viani's sculpture is quite different. He was born in Quistello (Mantua) in 1906, and was Martini's assistant at the Academy of Fine Arts in Venice after 1946. The master's teaching was undeniably important and is recognizable above all in the sense of monumentality that characterizes his work, though this is more evident in dimension than in spirit. However, his work shows that he has gone beyond the sense of pessimism that inspired Martini to say that sculpture was a dead language. Sculpture may have been a dead language so far as statuary was concerned, but Viani was not so much concerned with this as with the problem of modern classicism. His sculpture shows influences by Brancusi and Arp but is profoundly unlike theirs. For one thing, Viani's way of conceiving volume and

42   Renato Birolli. 1951 *(Italia)*

space is radically different, concentrating them so that the emotional content will not slip away. He also rejects *a priori* any sign of Romantic overabundance, since he conceives of sculpture as a tangible witness of man's condition and thus as part of human history.

Nino Franchina was born at Palmanova di Udine in 1912. He, too, had his beginnings in an Expressionism that tended to make volume concrete through the practice of Cubist ideas. His *Sammarcota* of 1946–1947 made a vivid popular impression. However, this did not meet the needs of his innately elegant artistic temperament. Franchina was to express this quality better later, above all with new materials such as sheet metals, iron and even traditional bronze, but with an emphasis more on linear qualities than on plastic volume. His monument to Giovanni Paisiello is planned as a tall, slender, fused form for completion in stainless steel. The model of the work (for the monument has not been completed yet) shows his concern with placing a modern form in a precisely planned environment. So true is this that the architect Sissa has collaborated with him on the project. However, the elegance of Franchina's sculpture does not mean an escape into decoration. In his most recent works, the various metals accentuate the dynamic rhythm of the composition but do not escape the laws of a thoughtful architecture of abstract form.

Consagra has certainly kept some of the plastic interests that he showed when a member of the *Forma* group. Born in Sicily at Mazzara del Vallo in 1920, Consagra mastered some of the features of European abstract painting while with *Forma*. He did not follow the lead of the *Peintres de la Tradition française*, preferring instead the *Cercle et Carré* and *Abstraction-Création*. All of this was modified by his contact with Magnelli. His deepest convictions and personal outlook led to a conflict between pure abstraction and representational sculpture. Thus, while Consagra's style has continued to be abstract, his forms always act on a human plane; indeed they are sometimes vaguely anthropomorphic. This is certainly far from geometric abstraction and is closer to Cubism. Consagra's sculpture in metal and wood is two-dimensional, but the contrast of planes avoids the effect of low relief. His sculpture is always deeply rooted in a profound human awareness and reflects his outlook as a man. It is not accident that Consagra, as if opposing Martini's pessimism, has written a booklet entitled *The Need for Sculpture*.

The panorama of Italian sculpture in the postwar period does not end here. Fontana is also a ceramic artist of refined taste and a developed technique. In his most recent works, Fontana has fully preserved the free quality of his imagination and the elegance of his concrete forms.

Edgardo Mannucci, born in Fabriano in 1914, began his artistic career before the war. In the postwar period he has developed an original, coherent style by using metallic materials whose surfaces are bare and corroded, with islands of color formed by molten metal.

Lorenzo Guerrini, born in Milan in 1914, studied in Italy and Germany with Erich Adolf and Arno Breker, and lived for a while in Austria. There is still a reminiscence of Wotruba in his work. He is also a goldsmith and metal designer. He has reached his most expressive period in recent years with sculpture on bare stone whose surface is kept almost in its natural state, in order to emphasize a barbaric violence in his concentrated volumes and his deliberately charged emotions.

Luciano Minguzzi, born in Bologna in 1911, tends in his more recent work to restrain his aggressive violence, the contortion of his forms, within a geometric cage. The cage enters into the organic structure of the composition, defining and resolving it into highly organic motion. Volume is not done away with, and the full significance of modeling is retained. Umberto Mastroianni, born in Fontana Liri in 1910, has developed his original Cubist compositions to a highly accented dynamism featuring large masses moving in various directions.

On the other hand, Salvatore (Salvatore Messina), born in Palermo in 1916, seeks an elegant, almost linear rhythm in all his forms despite the importance of volume. Franco Garelli, born in Diano d'Alba (Cuneo) in 1909, was first a painter, then turned to ceramics and finally went into metal sculpture composed of soldered elements left in a crude state as if to induce an emotional shock in the onlooker. A similar direction, though perhaps more dramatic, marks the work of Barisani, born in Naples in 1918. Aldo Calò, born in San Cesario di Lecce in 1910, was schooled in Florence. Later he traveled in France and England, where he came into direct contact with the work of Henry Moore. The English sculptor's influence is noticeable, though the manner is less Surrealist in Calò. There is a kind of baroque nostalgia buried in Calò. He has resolved this problem by creating forms determined by the nature of the material itself, wood, stone, metal. The qualities of these materials influence the volumes and rhythms of his sculpture. Carmelo Cappello, born in Ragusa in 1912, began in a representational style which he has left behind today, though reminiscences of this style are still discernible in the elegant allusiveness of his compositions. Agenore Fabbri, born in Barba (Pistoia) in 1911, has been one of the most faithful sculptors, perhaps more faithful than Leoncillo himself, of the realistic school formed shortly after 1948. However, in his work in ceramics or his sculpture in stone and metal, despite the populist emphasis, he has created a style stemming from an Expressionist culture whose impact symbolized the social conflicts and the political ideas felt by the artist.

Among the Italian sculptors residing abroad we must include Berto Lardera, born in La Spezia in 1911, and Carlo Signori, born in Milan in 1906. Both artists live in Paris. Signori was even a pupil of Maillol, but the artists who have most influenced him are undoubtedly Brancusi and Arp. Signori won the competition for the monument to the

Rosselli brothers[2] at Bagnoles sur l'Orne in 1947. His forms are simple and tend to an absolute geometrical purity even though there is always a hint of anthropomorphic representation behind them. Signori is little known in Italy but he represents one of the best aspects of Italian sculpture, principally because he has created an individual language. Though this language has been clearly influenced by other European movements, there are no apparent regrets or hesitations in his work. Berto Lardera moved to Paris in 1947 and he, too, seems alien to the process of rebirth that took place in Italian sculpture during those years. His unwavering experimentation in abstraction has seemingly had no need of a representational period of meditation. Lardera went from almost two-dimensional low-relief sculpture to an architecture of metallic planes and surfaces that crisscross in their own organic asymmetry, with a rhythm in which the voids have the same value as the full, though thin, surface of the sheet metal.

Other Italian sculptors of good quality may also be mentioned. Like painting, sculpture has overcome the crisis that so depressed Martini. It has done so by turning its back on traditional representation or, in any case, on the badly understood tradition of Renaissance sculpture. Crippa, among the younger artists worthy of attention at the present time, has been mentioned already as a painter. His sculpture follows the Surrealist style of his painting; he plays with the pictorial effects of oxidized metal or with the graceful horror of his "monsters." Francesco Somaini, born in Lomazzo (Como) in 1926, is a young man who has not yet hit his full stride. Salvatore Meli, born in Comiso, Sicily in 1929, is an accomplished ceramic artist who exploits a notable popular vein with sophistication.

It is probable that Italian sculpture, at the beginning of the century, was somewhat more backward in taste than other modes of art, even though these did not really belong to their own time. From Medardo Rosso to Boccioni and Roberto Melli an attempt was made to reform sculpture. The teachings of this movement indirectly influenced first Martini and later Marini and Manzù, chiefly by example. But in Italy academic vulgarity is always lying in wait and real values are displaced by the false values of such as Baroni, Mariani, and other celebrated rhetoricians; to them sculpture meant statuary. Martini's loss of faith in sculpture derived from this. However, the crisis did not last long. The real values of sculpture, beyond the statuary and monumental, were sought in a climate of liberty. In fact, Martini's own last works, his *Woman Swimming Under Water* of 1941, and such reliefs in simplified form as the terra-cotta *Horse* of 1945, proclaimed a new spirit. Martini made every effort to arrive at a meaningful tradition that would be different from the rhetoric of Renaissance imitation or false primitivism. Marini backed his horses, driving them outside everyday logic to achieve a new stylistic logic intimately connected with the sculptural act. Sculpture, no longer concerned with the monument, again became objective form; that is, it reacquired the meaning it had lost by turning to the cultural tradition

43 Antonio Corpora. 1958 (*Italia*)

of contemporary Europe. The capacity for poetic intensity was recognized to belong to the resources of sculpture. Rejection of the cloying, academically modeled followed, as well as of false skill in craftsmanship. Craft and technique were to be inherent in style and not superimposed on it. The sculpture-object was not an entity of academic abstraction separate from the reality of stone or marble; sculpture, chiseling, clay modeling regained their meaning as "work" in their own right. Through them the artist's creative imagination would be realized in a particular way.

The whole "second act" of Italian sculpture seems to be characterized by this common search of all artists, regardless of their individual preferences, education and whatever else tends to keep them separate. The result, so far as the artists we have mentioned are concerned, has been that Italian sculpture has rejoined the European sculptural tradition.

II

After the liberation of Italy at the end of the war, the younger generation of Italian artists was faced with the problem of rediscovering a language for art. Consequently, they turned to an examination of Italian artistic experience in the period between the two world wars in order to find out what was still valid. Analysis of Italian art from the end of Futurism to the retreat into a consciously Italian tradition led to a negative judgment of the artists belonging to this period, especially since the new artistic generation had had no contact with Fascism's cultural policies. On certain occasions, moreover, the younger artists of the prewar period, such as Guttuso, Vedova, and others, had been the first to protest clearly and openly against those policies, both in word and deed. For example, during the Premio Bergamo (the Bergamo Exhibition) of 1942, Vedova notes in his diary (*Letteratura* No. 29, Rome 1957), that there were signs of "disturbing incidents: precise symptoms of a more or less conscious upheaval." Furthermore, the very artistic groups that tended to break with the "official" character of the art practiced during the previous twenty years often had had a clear anti-Fascist basis for their cultural ferment. Indeed, there had been rebellion against the deliberately heroic attitude cultivated in the climate of those times as far back as 1930. An effort was made in painting, sculpture, and architecture to seek a more "European" quality, to create a culture that would consciously tend away from nationalism and nationalist themes and find a grounding in the European avant-garde movement. These new cultural indications showed themselves in a number of cities and took various directions. In Turin, as far back as 1930, the University had anti-Fascist teachers such as Luigi Einaudi, and, in the arts, Lionello Venturi. Here the reaction took an Expressionist bent in what was called "The Group of Six," made up of Galente, Menzio, Paulucci, Jessie Bowel and Carlo Levi. In Rome, the reaction also took an Expressionist turn with Scipione (1904–33) and Mafai. Scipione's style was Surrealist and mystical;

44   Ennio Morlotti. 1956 *(Italia)*

Mafai's adhered more closely to realism. The reaction was Expressionist in Milan as well, in the Corrente group. Numerous artists who had participated in this movement later reappeared on the scene in the postwar period, seeking a new form of artistic expression (Cassinari, Birolli, and Vedova himself, then very young). Another Milanese group favored abstract art, with a taste for pure abstraction recalling the Dutch exponents of Neo-Plasticism as well as the important examples of Klee and Kandinsky. These artists gathered at the Milione Gallery after 1932; and, though the group was not truly homogeneous, it did contain artists who were pursuing similar studies: Soldati and Reggiani, Licini, Bogliardi, Ghiringhelli, Radice, and Rho. Even later, all these artists remained faithful to their grounding.

It should not be forgotten that some of the second generation of Futurists continued to work and experiment. For example, in Rome, Prampolini intensified his experiments with various materials, and he was to produce his best results in the postwar period. Nor should we overlook Magnelli's experience outside of Italy, where he had been in contact with the European avant-garde since the first decades of the century. Within the borders of Italy, however, it was Morandi (color plate 39) who, representational if you like, still kept intact his poetic driving force and through it influenced many other artists, including abstractionists. Morandi was born in Bologna in 1890, and has always lived there. Between 1918 and 1920 he underwent an intense metaphysical experience, after which, in a summary style, he went on to do paintings that were usually very much alike in subject: some landscapes, but particularly still lifes of bottles and jars. These varied in color from painting to painting, creating an art that was ever new, unpredictable, but authentic, the coherent expression of highly reserved but determined personality. Paralleling Morandi's painting activity was his work as a graphic artist, for Morandi is a superbly skilled etcher with boundless imagination.

The younger Italian painters could not overlook Morandi among the older masters of Italian painting, despite possible differences in their approach. For example, some of Morandi's Surrealist suspensions in space, certain tonal values used not for self-sufficient descriptive ends but for arriving at a kind of "semantics of color" were precious even to artists like Atanasio Soldati (not to be considered among the younger artists, since he was born in Parma in 1896 and died in 1953), whose intentions, as we have mentioned before, were thoroughly dissimilar.

Morandi is still active today. The prize given him at the Sao Paulo Biennial Show in Brazil in 1957 conferred upon him the international recognition that he undoubtedly deserved. In spite of those who have repudiated him, Morandi's work has influenced the development of Italian artistic expression in the postwar period.

The rebirth of Italian art in the postwar period can be said to date from the establishment

45   Bruno Cassinari. 1957 *(Italia)*

of the Fronte Nuovo delle Arti (The New Front of the Arts) which held its first show at the Galleria della Spiga in Milan in June 1947. Naturally, it had been preceded by preparatory activity in various Italian cities and art groups, however ephemeral. All the most important art groups finally joined together in the Fronte Nuovo delle Arti.

The end of the war brought new ferment to Italy. Artists no longer wished merely to react against that involution which had been the Novecento movement in Italy. The problem faced by the younger generations of artists and sculptors was to handle the new content of art coherently. The problem of artistic language or expression was foremost, so much so that the movement of protest centering around the Corrente group, for example, which was actually more moral than artistic, was no longer sufficient. In the last analysis, the Expressionism of the Corrente group ceased to be important to all those artists who, between 1945 and 1947, went to Paris both to bring their knowledge up to date and to participate wholeheartedly in the European tradition that had been denied them by the rigid barriers of Fascism and by the once revolutionary Italian avant-garde movements which had ended by being installed in the Academy.

In Rome, among the first artists to face the problem of assimilating the new Late Cubist style of painting, that is, establishing a direct relation to contemporary French experience, were Corpora (born in Tunis in 1909, color plate 43), a member of the Fronte Nuovo, as well as Turcato (plate 51), Monachesi, and the sculptor Fazzini. Turcato later joined the young abstractionist group called Forma, together with the sculptor Consagra and other very young painters of the time, like Perilli (born in Rome in 1927, plate 52) and Dorazio (also Rome, 1927; plate 53).

The two groups quickly clashed with the movement of Roman Expressionist painters founded in 1946 (Stradone, Scialoja, Sadun, Ciarocchi), all of whom had taken Mafai and Scipione to heart. Scipione had died when very young in 1933. Mafai had continued enriching his painting with tonal color and, between 1933 and 1942, had arrived at an extreme expressive accentuation of form in his *Fantasie*, where spiritual possibly outweighed artistic considerations. Roman Expressionists of the postwar period wanted to keep his teaching in mind, at the same time studying Morandi's color tonality.

Meanwhile, some young artists, Turcato among them, had joined in what came to be known, after the name of their art magazine, as the Forma group. Their program was signified by this name: there needed to be new discussion of the very concept of artistic language or expression. The value of formal concept was to be indicated but without complete abstraction; and they declared that the content of art born in the new cultural climate should be realized within a framework unconcerned with naturalistic representation. All this was due not only to a new cultural sensibility, which led these young painters to look outside their country's borders for artistic values, but also to a spiritual need. They

46   Giuseppe Santomaso. 1957 *(Italia)*

sought a philosophy alien to all forms of romanticism and religious influence. They hoped, through purely plastic and figurative elements, to express the new social and historical condition of man that had taken shape during the war, above all through the Resistance movement.

"We proclaim ourselves Formalists and Marxists, in the belief that the terms Marxism and Formalism are not irreconcilable, especially today when the progressive elements of our society must maintain positions that are *revolutionary and avant-garde*, and not slip into the equivocation of a conformist and played-out realism. Its most recent manifestations in painting and sculpture have shown what a narrow and limited road it is." This was how the manifesto of March 15, 1947 read, as published by *Forma* and signed by Carla Accardi, Ugo Attardi, Pietro Consagra, Piero Dorazio, Mino Guerrini, Achille Perilli, Antonio Sanfilippo, and Giulio Turcato. The Forma group was a training ground more than anything else, although, at the time that the manifesto appeared, the artists had already defined their interests clearly and steered confidently through the troubled waters of Italian art. Moreover, they showed solid grounding when judged by certain indications from other European art movements. Besides, the entire Italian art world was in ferment and concerned with new problems. In Milan, the early group of abstractionists who had gathered at the Milione Gallery around 1930 was highly active again. There appeared a review of art, entitled "45," in which the Expressionist members of the Corrente group aired their problems. In Rome, meanwhile, Prampolini (plate 57) reinvigorated his old experiments of the avant-garde Futurist movement, arriving at a new treatment of the many different materials that went into the surface of his paintings.

Most of the younger Italian artists of the period first discovered Cubism between 1945 and 1948. Of course, they were anxious to make up for lost time. *Guernica* was seen as the critical point of Picasso's transformation from Expressionism. Their stated aim was to go beyond *Guernica*; but not everyone agreed on the proper direction to pursue. These differences all found their way into the Fronte Nuovo delle Arti which, in the long run, tended to exacerbate rather than reconcile them.

The ferment of renewal throughout Italy needed to find some unifying center. However, as we have mentioned, controversy raged for many months before the formation of the Fronte Nuovo, although the artists recognized a common ground that mostly came out of the Resistance and anti-Fascist movements. Finally, a group of these artists, together with the critics Marchiori and Apollonio and several others, drew up a program in Venice, October 1946, which they called the Nuova Secessione Artistica (The New Artistic Secession). The declaration was signed by Renato Birolli (color plate 42, plate 54), Bruno Cassinari (color plate 45), Renato Guttuso (color plate 40), Ennio Morlotti (color plate 44), Giuseppe Pizzinato, Giuseppe Santomaso (color plate 46), Emilio Vedova (color plate 47),

47　Emilio Vedova. 1957　(*Italia*)

and the sculptors Leoncillo and Alberto Viani. The painter Carlo Levi, who had joined the movement, later resigned. The new declaration stated: "Nine Italian artists, who are replacing an aesthetic of form by a dialectic of form, intend to have their tendencies, which conflict outwardly only, converge toward a synthesis that will be recognizable only as it develops in their work. This is a sharp break with all preceding syntheses, which came about through theoretical decision made a priori. Each of the artists intends to keep his observations and his individual statements in the world of art close to a primary basis of ethical and moral imperatives, and sum up these activities as living acts. As a result, painting and sculpture will become declarative instruments and methods of free exploration of the world, thus increasing contact with reality constantly. Art is not the conventional face of history but history itself, which cannot exist without man."

The Secession movement later changed its name to the Fronte Nuovo delle Arti in order to emphasize further the collective will of its artists. The first show was held in Milan, at the Galleria della Spiga, in 1947. The membership of the Fronte Nuovo had changed in less than a year: Cassinari had resigned but the painters Corpora and Turcato and the sculptors Fazzini and Franchina had joined. Though they did not resign, Birolli and Morlotti did not exhibit with the others. The most reputable critics supported the movement, but the first show was not a success because of a great confusion of ideas and the lack of genuine understanding of the artistic problems. However, as Marchiori stated in the preface to the catalogue, the Fronte Nuovo declared itself "a group of free men rightfully proud in the belief that they represent the most disparate directions of contemporary Italian art." The writer, who had played a large part in the creation of the movement, emphasized the points of disagreement and continued: "Is it possible, within a general definition, to reconcile the differences of means and ends proclaimed by the artist of Fronte Nuovo? It seems better, through their successes and failures, to document the reality of a vital impulse guiding all of them toward a common destiny . . . This is a time of unresolved conflicts, of unconfessed sacrifices, and bitter rebellion; in short, a time of crisis for men bent on freeing themselves of the past and being reborn."

The principal fault of the Fronte Nuovo consisted in its grouping together of artists of different schools developing in different directions. Some of these artists were exponents of recent thinking in art, and had turned away from representation. However, there were others ready and willing to cultivate a tendency that was well on its way to becoming rhetorical. Guttuso had already proclaimed the need to go beyond *Guernica*; everyone agreed on this point, but Vedova, Corpora, Turcato, and Birolli intended to follow an abstract direction. These artists wished to establish a new dialectic relation with nature; they sought a reality that was not based on appearances but rather on concern with man's destiny. They had rediscovered a tradition of the most genuine

48   Osvaldo Licini. 1951   *(Italia)*

European kind, with ties to the *Peintres de la Tradition Française*—Birolli to Pignon and Gischia, Corpora to Bazaine. On the other hand, the social concerns of a Pizzinato or Guttuso threatened to overshadow artistic problems, which, indeed, developed later.

While the Fronte Nuovo was readying its show for Venice in 1948, some strange articles began appearing in newspapers that had been continuously sympathetic to the movement. An attempt was made to reinstate the art tradition which the Front itself, in its first manifesto—largely the work of Birolli—had tried to combat. Guttuso, for example, attempted to reassert the value of some Italian masters after the Front had declared it did not wish to recognize any masters. It is also worthy of note that artists such as Afro (plate 55) and Mirko never joined the Fronte Nuovo, despite the decidedly abstract turn their artistic vision had taken and the equally decisive shift in their tastes.

However, the formation of the group was an important historical event. It brought artists together, prepared them for later developments, and presented them to the sarcastic attention of the Italian public, which could no longer ignore the group. There could be no misunderstanding this time. Above all else, the purpose of the Front was to place each man on his own, to clear away misunderstandings, and to point out the real significance of artistic integrity. In a world that had been bogged down for years in rhetoric, it finally spoke about painting and sculpture in new terms.

Success was achieved at the Biennale of 1948. The first Biennale of the postwar period was not only an immense contribution to Italian culture but also the springboard from which Italian art, largely because of the efforts of the Fronte Nuovo, was launched toward recovery of its international position. And even today, despite the various directions taken by the artists and the originality achieved within the framework of European art itself, it must be pointed out that the Fronte Nuovo served a necessary initial purpose.

It was a compact group that presented itself at the Venice Biennale of 1948 with Marchiori as spokesman. The group was more completely represented than it had been at the Galleria della Spiga because it knew that more was at stake. The concluding section of Marchiori's introduction read: "On the occasion of the Fronte Nuovo's first show at the Galleria della Spiga in Milan (June 12 to July 12, 1947) . . . Italian critics, with few exceptions, were hostile to the Fronte Nuovo without understanding the theoretical reasoning which was, and still is, valid and continually in keeping with the times. Today, in fact, the critic's moral need to understand is made more critical by the growing solidarity of the most authentic artists who, through the valid medium of their works, seek that understanding and trust which, although manfully requested, has been denied them because of one excuse after another. The Fronte Nuovo delle Arti has come to the Biennale for the purpose of justifying itself historically, faithful to the trust it has come to assume as shown by the reality of these works."

49 Giuseppe Capogrossi. 1957 *(Italia)*

The artists represented in the show were: Turcato, Santomaso, Corpora, Pizzinato, Guttuso, Vedova, Birolli, Morlotti, Leoncillo and Franchina. The show was a success. Above all, foreign critics noted that Italian art was on the move once more.

The artists had come to the Venice Biennale show of 1948 after a year of intense and feverish work during which each artist had sought for clarity above all else. The great presence of Picasso was still in the atmosphere, especially the Picasso of *Fishing at Antibes*, but there was already a search for and a realization of a different dimension, a different space, new contact with material reality. Guttuso's own themes, like Pizzinato's, foreshadowed the realism that was to follow. They were treated with greater liberty, roughed out in a formal violence, composed entirely of abstract energy insofar as it was purely pictorial, and concrete insofar as it dealt with a life of insistent reality—the moment of history in which these artists felt they were living. At the same time, Vedova was announcing his dramatic subjects, which were followed immediately by his *Protests*; Birolli was shattering the human form in order to accent emotion but never relying on the forced design of Expressionism; and Morlotti, in his still lifes, was experimenting more intently with Picasso's forms.

The dispute in Italy between realists and abstractionists began after 1948. The Fronte Nuovo had by now given all that it could, and the member artists went their separate ways. On the one hand, Guttuso and Pizzinato, involved in their political stand, continually rejected any transformation of seen reality. However, Guttuso understood realism not as a pure and simple reference to objective representation but as a return, with a certain amount of freedom, to realism's Expressionist origins. Guttuso always tried to maintain pictorial quality. Others, lacking his artistic capacities and temperament, could not escape a crudely naturalistic style.

Six other members of the Fronte Nuovo, i.e., Birolli, Corpora, Morlotti, Santomaso, Turcato, and Vedova, joined with Afro (plate 55) and Moreni (plate 61) and appeared at the Venice Biennale of 1952 as what has been called Il Gruppo degli Otto Pittori Italiani (The Group of Eight Italian Painters). It should be borne in mind that this group's intellectual origin was in the theorizing of the Fronte Nuovo, although the Eight had more homogeneity than the earlier group. Lionello Venturi, who in a sense was the group's co-ordinator, wrote that these artists "are not and do not care to be abstractionists; they are not and do not care to be realists; their purpose is to abandon this antinomy which on the one hand threatens to transform abstract art into a new mannerism, and on the other obeys political orders destructive to liberty and to creative spontaneity . . . The eight painters use the pictorial language of the tradition begun around 1910 which includes the experience of the Cubists, the Expressionists and abstract painters."

116

50   Fausto Pirandello. 1957 *(Italia)*

Each of the Eight represented in the group show at the Biennale of 1952 has a pre-eminent position in Italian art today. There are others on the same level whom we cannot ignore. Nevertheless, the greatest interest has centered on the cultural position of the Eight; and even today, when every artist has developed his own independent style, major credit must be given the Eight for having discovered the expressive potentialities of a new artistic language.

Other artists were following separate but simultaneous paths. Painters like Reggiani, Soldati, Licini, and Prampolini remained faithful to their search for a pure abstraction. It had a geometric and spare quality in Reggiani (plate 56); an attenuated metaphysical character in Soldati (color plate 41); a Surrealist spirit in Licini (color plate 48); and a concern for the poetic significance of materials in Prampolini (plate 57). Magnelli, too, had kept faith with his vision, nonetheless enriched in his last canvases by a more subtle use of color. Other painters, however, abandoned their earlier experimentation. Foremost among them was Capogrossi (color plate 49), who had been a member of the Roman 'tonalist' group. After 1949, Capogrossi did a painting that, although flat in treatment, gave a feeling of space between the brushstrokes. An extra dimension was created that the ancestral character of the brushstroke itself placed outside time and history. Alberto Burri (plate 58) also, at first, cultivated a type of Expressionist painting. Later, he went on to bold experimentation in materials of the most nonpictorial kind: burlap sacks, burnt wood, and plastics. A rigorous Neo-Plastic type of imagination is ever present with him, but the visual result is quite different, in view of his denial of all consideration of form. Form, indeed, tends to disappear in order to emphasize more strongly the brutality of his materials. Luigi Spazzapan (plate 59), who is closer to the younger Futurists, is also concerned with plastic materials, but with intense colors and without straying too far from the traditional techniques of painting.

Corrado Cagli, together with Capogrossi, was another representative of the Roman group. He went to live first in France and then in the United States, returning to Italy after the war. He is vastly cultured and sensitive, and has sometimes alternated between abstract and representational experimentation, but always with a refined Surrealist style that is recognizable above all in his particular vocabulary of forms symbolizing mental states between consciousness and the unconscious.

Bruno Cassinari (color plate 45) is closer to the Eight in culture. He was a member of the Fronte Nuovo at first but later resigned when, after a trip to Antibes, he put together an idiom learned from Picasso with the form simplifications derived from the Expressionists (he had also been a member of the Corrente group), without, however, destroying that emotional intensity which the Expressionists had brought to the structural organization of composition. Nature is present in Cassinari, but his painting, as Umbro Apollonio

118

has noted, "transports us into a region which is no longer that of naturalistic enthusiasm . . but rather of absolute lyricism."

It is worth while mentioning here that Mafai himself, who began around 1930 in an Expressionistic style and later took up his own brand of realism, has felt the need in his most recent works, the *Paesaggi* (Landscapes) and *Mercati* (Markets) of 1957, to go beyond objective representation. He has blurred naturalistic appearances in fiery colors. These are often arbitrary and, consequently, have an abstractionist dimension. Franco Gentilini (plate 66) too, though he is undoubtedly connected with a representational model, brings his image to a point of geometric stylization and restates it on the surface where the use of sand mixed with color enlarges it beyond natural dimensions. Among the representational painters Fausto Pirandello (color plate 50), with his Cubist composition, has, more than anyone else, perhaps, achieved an equilibrium between abstraction and representation, woven together by a precious, solid light that gives solid form to his volumes.

Lucio Fontana (plate 62), sculptor, painter, and ceramic artist, was one of first Italian abstract sculptors. In 1934 he had joined the Abstraction-Creation group of Paris. After the war, together with some younger artists, among them Dova (plate 63) and Crippa (plate 64), he became the leading member of the "Spatial" movement, which originated at the Galleria del Naviglio. All of Fontana's work is characterized by great imaginative freedom. Fontana already foresaw his later Spatialism when in 1946 he published his Manifesto Blanco in Buenos Aires. In this manifesto he declared that the prime aim of Spatialism was "to achieve works of art with the new materials science offers the artist." Dova and Crippa are the two young artists of the movement who have shown the greatest spontaneity and ability. Indeed, Dova (b. 1925) today ranks among the best painters of the last generation. His technique is precise and painstaking, and he adds to this a taste for Surrealism which, though it may recall Max Ernst, is highly original. His fantastic animal and bird shapes, losing their characteristic forms, are suitable to the pictorial effects of his brilliant, enameled surfaces, so that Dova's Surrealism escapes all literary association and has its own autonomous form.

Other painters have been more closely influenced by the activity of the Eight. Scialoja and Sadun, who had already been opponents of Roman Neo-Cubism, later went beyond Expressionism. Sadun never lost sight of the example set by Morandi; Scialoja went to greater extremes, abolishing all representation and seeking a textural quality of painting in the large, scattered forms he prefers. This work has a dramatic emphasis that is still not completely alien to Romantic heritage. Even Antonio Scordia, a painter whose early training was in the Roman "tonalist" tradition, later took the Cubist examples to heart and through them arrived at a structural freedom that allowed a greater emotional freedom. Felicity of color and rigorous use of brushwork also characterize the works of Alfredo Chighine.

Meanwhile, the young artists are developing styles of painting along the various directions taken by their elders. Brunori (plate 60), born in Perugia in 1924, and now working in Rome, has been one of the most significant artists of recent years. His painting is based on a dialectic exchange with nature in which reality is recreated with rhythmic intensity and the fragmented composition of Cubist derivation subordinated to light. Ajmone and Carmassi in Milan, Romiti, Vacchi, and Bendini in Bologna, Raspi, Marignoli and De Gregorio in Spoleto, all transform their responses to nature and matter into abstract forms. The young painters who had created the Forma movement continue to be active in Rome, but they have come a long way from their initial positions. Perilli, Dorazio, Sanfilippo, and Carla Accardi have distinguished themselves as the best of the group. In Florence, Gualtiero Nativi has remained faithful to his geometric forms. In Naples, Barisani, who is also a sculptor, finds all his expressive values in allusive design. Other young painters in Milan, among them Baj, Bertini (now living in Paris), and Dangelo have founded a movement of "nuclear art."

Tendencies multiply and the results are often uncertain. However, a constant level of quality is now present, even in the very young, like Ruggeri and Saroni of Turin, who are still under twenty-five. Many other names could be mentioned, for the younger artists have received from their elders a lesson of freedom and an open door to artistic integrity. For the most part, the younger painters have put these gifts to good use.

During the first decades of the twentieth century painting in Spain remained at the level of mediocre academicism, and the great Spanish painters belonging to the modern schools —Picasso, Gris, Miró, and Dali—had no influence in their own country. Only sporadic interest was shown in the experiments being carried out outside Spain: Francisco Iturrino (1864–1924) was influenced by Fauvism, and Juan de Echevarria (1872–1932) by Cézanne and Gauguin. However, the more recent developments did not originate in the work of these painters, but rather in the work of Daniel Vazquez Diaz (b. 1882) and Francisco Cossio (b. 1898).

Vazquez Diaz introduced into Spain the Cubists' discoveries, notably in his frescoes in Santa Maria de la Ravida at Vuelva, where he abandoned illusionist perspective in favor of a geometric treatment of space. Francisco Cossio, too, had spent some time in Paris, and returned with some valuable lessons. His painting, which contains Cubist elements, is noteworthy for its subtlety and a certain attenuated splendor, which is wholly free from rhetoric. Cossio enjoyed a period of favor after the First World War precisely because he combined a baroque spirit with modern formal solutions, avoiding the ponderous naturalism in which Spanish painting had been lingering until then. However, these two painters, for all their accomplishments, have not been engaged in original stylistic research. On the other hand, no attention was paid to the authentic and charming primitivism of Vicente Perez Bueno, now in his seventies, whose paintings are still capable of arousing great interest.

Spanish painting has shown more signs of life since 1945, when it joined the stream of contemporary art. This is seen most clearly in the work of a group of artists who were less than thirty at the end of the Second World War. Taking Surrealism as their point of departure, they gave rise to an anti-academic movement, at the basis of which is a quest for a new art, capable of refashioning the legacy of traditional ideas and values, and of expressing spontaneous lyrical impulses.

This development was preceded by a number of memorable episodes, among them, the Second International Exhibition of Surrealism held in Tenerife; the organizer of this exhibition was Eduardo Westerdahl, founder and editor of the *Gaceta de Arte*, the importance of which is now universally acknowledged. In 1948, Westerdahl founded the *Grupo de Canarias* (Canary Islands Group), and the same year the first group of abstract artists was formed at Saragossa. It was, however, at Barcelona, again in 1948, that there was formed the most important group of all, the one which more than any other has enabled Spain to become a part of the new creative movement. Its inspirer was the poet Juan Brossa, founder of the review *Dau al Set*, and it included the art historian Juan Eduardo Cirlot, the writer Arnald Puig, and the painters Antonio Tapies, Modest Cuixart, Juan-José Tharrats, and Joan Pons who later moved to Brazil. In 1949 and 1950 two congresses devoted to the new currents were held at Santander, under the auspices of the *Escuela de Altamira*, a school founded in 1948 by the critic Riccardo Gullon, the historian Pablo Beltran de Heredia, the sculptor Angel Ferrant, and the German painter Mathias Göritz. In 1951 the first Spanish-American Biennale marked a further stage in the artistic development of Spain: for the first time modern art was accepted in an officially sponsored exhibition which included works by Millares and Plansdure. In 1953, the first international exhibition of abstract art was held at Santander, and the exhibition of fantastic art at Madrid. Also in 1953, the Hispanic Institute established the Westerdahl Museum of Abstract Art in Tenerife, containing works by Miró, Prampolini, Millares, Ferrant, Platschek, and others. Equally valuable were the activities of the *Associación de Artistas Actuales*, founded at Barcelona in 1953 by the critic Cirici Pellicer. To this Association we owe the *Salon de Mayo*, and the *Grupo Taull* (founded 1955), which includes Tapies, Tharrats, Cuixart, and Guinovart. All these factors contribute to the exceptional vigor of the artistic life of Spain, with centers in Madrid, Barcelona, Santander, Valencia and the Canary Islands. Up to 1954 Eugenio d'Ors' *Academia Breve de Critica y Arte* participated in this activity, although D'Ors had never displayed great enthusiasm for the new experiments, preferring the neo-Picassian style of Rafel Zabaleta (b. 1907). Nevertheless, he has encouraged the younger artists, accepting some of them—Tapies is one—in his *Salon de los Once*. Architects also played an important part—the *Grupo R* in Barcelona is among the foremost contributors to the modern movement in Spanish architecture—as did sculptors such as Angel Ferrant, Eduardo Chillida, Jorge de Oteiza, and Martin Chirrino.

Other notable developments included the shortlived emergence at Valencia of the painter Manuel Gil Perez, who died in 1957 at the age of thirty-two, and whose Constructivism largely influenced the theories of Oteiya, the sculptor. Perez was a member of the *Grupo Parpallo*, which brought together writers, painters, sculptors, and architects bent on promoting the integration of the arts. This group put out a review, *Arte Vivo*, which was edited by Vicente Aguilera Cerni, one of the best informed art critics in present-day Spain. Finally, in 1957, a number of leading Spanish artists, including the painters Millares, Feito, Canogar (plate 70), and Saura, and the writers Manolo Conde and Josè Ayllon gathered together in the El Paso group in Madrid, which champions the cause of *art informel*. According to the critic J.E. Cirlot, *art informel* is characterized by "a realism of limited scope," by images comparable to those obtained with an electron microscope (e.g., in metallographic sections) and evocative of worlds far beyond our own, by the use of techniques such as decalcomania, blots, *frottage*, *fumage*, etc., and by the emphasis on the creative act, determined by no formal or figurative considerations.

In a survey of contemporary Spanish painting we cannot fail to pay homage first and foremost to Antonio Tapies (b. 1923, plate 67), an artist of great richness and complexity. He came to the end of his Surrealist period c. 1952, turning to essential forms and excluding references to natural objects or recognizable symbols. He soon arrived at a point where the medium itself determines the form after its poetic implications have been revealed. Tapies has in fact grasped the vital origin of the medium and brought it into an expressive order without having recourse to cultural quotation. His work is characterized by a graceful poetry, suggesting an ecstatic silence, almost entirely detached from any earthly harmony.

Juan-José Tharrats (b. 1918, plate 69) is moving in a similar direction; his vision is, however, less austere and more romantic, while Manolo Millares (b. 1926), after a period of Surrealist experiments and magical abstraction, in 1952 turned to *art informel*. Tharrats reveals in his dazzling and vivid colors a taste for the sumptuous. Millares is less reserved; he attacks his medium directly, almost allowing himself to be carried away by his spontaneous impulse. "I act in utter freedom and in a world that is delectably strange and disconcerting. I maltreat different fabrics. I pierce infinite space and I torture it with the dynamic entanglement of a few pieces of cord. Sometimes non-form – out of stubbornness – remains contained, entire. Sometimes it floods out in a torrent towards the cosmos. Great mouths may yawn into being; like explosions these spew out white or intense black towards infinity, forming telluric wounds, fissures, hypergenetic strength, organic dynamism, etc."

Antonio Suarez (b. 1923) is more delicate in his subdued tones, and extremely sensitive in his compositions; like Vicente Vela (b. 1931, plate 71b), he seems precious with his uneven grounds, sweetly tinted and lightly silvered over. Rafael Canogar (b. 1934), on the other hand, emphasizes compositional structure; he often aims at effects of relief, as though attempting to wrench ever new values from his fantasies. "We must not strive to discover the law of the chaotic moment, but reality itself in an essential contradiction between the explicable and the inexplicable . . . The sign as expression of vital energy in action . . . The creative method must be dynamic, which implies a perception in time . . . Realization of structures which complete each other, in search of a rhythm . . . A tension created by signs which contain the world and the same time infinitely extend its limits" (plate 70).

Antonio Saura (b. 1930, plate 68) follows a different tack. He also came under the powerful influence of Surrealism, breaking free after five years, in 1953. The reaction was so violent that from then on Saura has used black and white only, impetuously tracing upon a wide canvas large signs from behind which there emerges an intense light. "A painting is first and foremost a blank surface," he once stated, "that has to be covered with something. The canvas is a battlefield that has no boundaries. The painter faces it in a tragic hand-to-hand encounter, transforming a passive and inert material by means of his own gestures into a

cyclone of passion, into a cosmic and eternally radiant energy . . . Beyond all vain discussions of abstract or representational art, beyond all preoccupations of purism, fanaticism, of
aestheticism, there is the peremptory need to cry out, te express oneself in one way or
another, making ours all the possible energies of the universe, whether this is through the
love of a woman's body, of a natural thing, of a *nada* or of an All, through an unlimited need
for love, knowledge and energy, through despair, through a cosmic hunger, through total
expansion or dynamic concentration''.

In the work of Luis Feïto (b. 1929, plate 71a) imagination is almost contemplative. His
exquisitely austere colors include extremes, subtle grays and browns, refined with intensely
modulated dark passages. "A surface I like, I make, I plow over. I dig down among its
roots. I open it up until I find my channel. The surface grows and I encounter it. I strike it,
I break it, I destroy it. I am bruised. Sometimes I caress it. Sometimes the light—hope—
suddenly appears, sometimes nothing. And I go on wandering about. Traveling about over
it—dry, scorched. Sometimes I come across water. It opens up. I fall into its dark depths.
Bottomless. I knock against a virgin rock. Pure. Space is created. I jump in. I wrest its
silence from it. I twist out its mystery. And it is born''.

Other talented Spanish painters include Enrique Plansdure (b. 1921) who is a colorist by
temperament; Manuel Mampaso (b. 1924) who is frequently over-decorative, but nevertheless displays unmistakable vigor; Modesto Cuixart (b. 1925) who achieves magical effects
by means of reliefs and skillful fusing of black and gold; Francisco Farreras (b. 1927) who
still leans towards geometrical formalism which he loosens up by means of chromatic
modulations, and Antonio Provedano (b. 1921), who relies upon geometrical elements
of naturalistic rather than fantastic provenance.

While official art in the countries of eastern Europe is marked by a narrow-minded natural-ism and a primitive materialism, painters in Yugoslavia, followed a few years later by those in Poland, have found their way back to the problems and techniques of modern art. In both countries the bonds with the West, though outwardly allowed to lapse, had been kept intact, and recent works by young Yugoslav and Polish artists affirm once again the universal character of the modern movement. They also contribute certain original elements to it, elements which are social rather than national in origin. These young artists began their careers at a time when the new ideas in art, for which their elders had been able to win recognition only after a long struggle, had come to be taken for granted.

The teachers of this young generation had participated in the great adventure of the School of Paris. Before the First World War talented artists of all countries had made pilgrimages to the French capital, where they joined the new movements, often contribut-ing to their development. Some chose to remain there; others returned, transplanting the foreign seeds to their native soil and achieving new syntheses. In Yugoslavia the latter group includes Milo Milunovic, Marko Celebonovic, Petar Lubarda, and others born around 1900. Milunovic's works express the Cartesian ideal of a balance between feeling and reason; along with the influence of Cézanne and of Braque we find in them elements derived from the late-Hellenistic style of Pompeii. Celebonovic's canvases, in which color and light are redefined in terms of simple, vital truths, have the unmistakable flavor of medieval Slavic frescoes. The wild rocky landscapes of his native Montenegro are indelibly present in Petar Lubarda's paintings, although his rocks, skies, and human and animal figures have lost their familiar contours, and been transformed into fantastic abstract constructions, the visual experience having been reduced to its essentials.

These artists of the older generation who went through Fauvism and Cubism still play a leading part in the creative experiments of the present generation, and have their influence upon it. But the younger artists also draw upon other, more complex, sources. They have assimilated the idiom of nonobjective art, and in their works, the techniques of Abstraction, and Surrealism or Magic Realism, are put to the task of reinterpreting visible and invisible reality.

Gabrijel Stupica's autistic allegories of the human condition are projected beyond the domain of the rational. In his paintings, the boundary dividing reality from the semblance of reality is blurred. The silvery cast of his colors has hardened progressively, becoming the somber coating of a ghostlike, tormented humanity.

Miljenko Stancic shares with the older Stupica a predilection for somber tones. His figures emerge as though hesitantly from a dreamy background into the flickering light of day. Intellectually, he seems to be indebted to Cubism; his imaginative visions derive less from the literary repertoire of Surrealism than from a personal experience of the submerged areas of the psyche.

Marij Pregelj, too, draws upon the treasury of images within the unconscious. His grotesque visions depict the concentration camps of life, the prisons of convention, an overcrowded civilization in which men are reduced to abstract entities reminiscent of the figures on the reliefs of the Kings of Lagash.

The terrors of the soul which find expression in the work of many of the younger artists are a reflection of actual experiences of death and destruction. Their art conveys a sense of being on the brink of an abyss. Their symbols point to a realm beyond the scope of representation, evoking the chaos that prevailed before the Creation or anticipating the landscapes of some post-human era.

Lazar Vozarevic's rigorously drawn archaic figures seem to inhabit some mythical domain. Ljubo Ivancic, Mire Cetin, and a number of other, younger artists depict the existential themes of anguish and isolation. Miodrag Protic breaks up familiar forms, and with their elements constructs well-proportioned new objects in which we find echoes of Chardin, Braque, and Milunovic, Protic's teacher. Mladen Srbinovic's subtle creations are spiritually related to the works of his teacher Marko Celebonovic.

Some of the Yugoslav abstract painters were influenced by the Fauvists, and preserve the latter's sensual forms and evocative colors. Others, such as Stane Kregar and Edo Murtic, whose art combines logic with passion, and is characterized by formal inventiveness and playful rhythms, owe more to the influence of Kandinsky. Kregar, the older of the two, began to paint in the abstract style before the Second World War. Murtic at first used representational elements, arranging them in expressive and colorful groups; then he turned to abstraction, and his earlier primitive animals and plants have yielded to luminous arabesques which only vaguely resemble their prototypes in nature (plate 72).

Stojan Celic, too, has gradually shifted from his earlier spontaneous renderings of visual experience to abstract combinations of colors and forms, in which organic and inorganic elements are interwoven. Sime Peric, relying on his spontaneity and the artistic values inherent in color and its vibrations and the structural effects it conveys, expresses himself in the Tachiste idiom.

The Exat 51 group is faithful to the spirit of Mondrian's puritanical rationalism. Ivan Picelj, Bozidar Rasica, Aleksandar Srnec, and the other young painters and architects belonging to this group aim at reducing the pictorial elements to forms expressing purely spatial relationships.

Reacting against the modern alienation from the object, some Yugoslav artists are seeking to restore contact with the representational world by means of a Synthetic Realism, which reinterprets archaic symbols and folk traditions in the light of modern techniques and

126

insights. This trend found its expression before the Second World War in the founding of the *Zemlja* ("Earth") group; and a sense of reality combined with a magic view of human relationships characterizes the works of Krsto Hegedusic, an artist of the older generation. Under his inspiration and guidance a number of peasant painters banded together in the village of Hlebine. Their leading representative, Ivan Generalic, paints objects both observed and invented, fantastic plants and human and animal figures, with a charming naïveté.

Lazar Vujaklija (plate 73) is also essentially a modern Primitive. Drawing his motifs from the medieval Bogumil Stones and from colorful peasant embroideries, he creates — by no means unconsciously—a naive, expressive paradise of children and animals, in a style reminiscent of early religious tapestries. In his and other artists' works we may discern a quest for a new definition of reality, one which would combine a strictly personal inner vision with a naive experience of the outside world.

Modern painting is not a recent phenomenon in Poland. Here, too, the debate with visible reality has led to Fauvism and Cubism, and then to Abstraction and Magic Realism. Wladyslaw Strzeminski (plate 74b) taught at the Academy of Vitebsk with Malevitch, and from there he returned to Poland bringing with him Suprematist and Constructivist conceptions. In 1924 he and Henryk Staszewski were the leading members of the group of abstract painters associated with the magazine *Blok*. The same year Henryk Berlewi published in Warsaw his manifesto for a new school of painting, whose program was to combine his own conceptions with those of the Dutch Neo-Plasticists and the Russian Constructivists. In 1930 Staszewski took part in the programmatic exhibition of the *Cercle et carré* group in Paris, where his works were exhibited next to those of Mondrian, Kandinsky, Arp, Pevsner, Schwitters, and Vantongerloo. His austere and crystalline constructions are inspired by mathematics and technology.

Artistic developments in Poland were interrupted by the Second World War. Those artists who survived its technologically organized holocaust returned to their ruined studios with memories of their underground experiences, but also new visions of human and cosmic realities. Their revolutionary attempts to penetrate the conventional façade of existence, to explore new dimensions, and to overcome the divorce between art and inner reality were once again interrupted, this time by the new regime, which advocated so-called Social Realism to the exclusion of all other styles. However, since 1956, following "the thaw," Poland has seen a reawakening of the creative impulse, and Polish artists have made up for some of the lost time, tackling contemporary artistic problems with courage and energy.

127

Tadeusz Kantor's passionate will to expression had won him recognition during the period between 1945 and 1955. Then, in the heyday of Social Realism, his name vanished from the catalogues of the exhibitions, reappearing only in 1956, with a number of works which the years of isolation had stamped with symbols of terror and gloom. His color has become autonomous, detached from all subject matter, and obeying only the demands of instinct. In his paintings (plate 74a) he displays a sensitive Tachiste pattern of hovering spots of color and fluid rhythms governed by musical laws.

Maria Jarema, Jonasz Stern, and Marek Wlodarski, who belong to the older generation, have also abandoned representational art to devote themselves to the task of reinterpreting the world in terms of their inner visions. Maria Teresa Tyszkiewicz, starting from a geometric Constructivism with an admixture of Surrealism, has evolved toward pure abstraction, conceived of as a universal idiom. Her swift hallucinatory "script" and spontaneous inspiration contradict only superficially the perfection of her geometric forms. Stefan Gierowski began with an Expressionistic distortion of objects and human figures; now his deliberately crude compositions, suggesting the violence of primitive instincts, are organized along Cubist lines. Jerzy Nowosielski ran through all the stages from figurative art to Tachisme, retaining throughout the characteristic features of his style, which is based on an emphasis of the plastic elements.

The evolution toward abstraction could be exemplified by the mention of other distinguished names. But only a few Polish painters have completely abandoned all reference to visual reality. This is not because they think that pure form needs the support of symbols, but because they find purely abstract art an inadequate medium for forcefully rendering an underlying mood of grayness and spiritual conflict. Thus, Tadeusz Brzozowski expressively distorts visual reality, yet at the same time fights his way toward it, seeking a new means of access to it. In his analytical dreams, man and objects lead an underground existence, from which they are elevated to become the vehicles and signs of a magical vision. The unreality of his colors lends his works an aura of the superreal. The world depicted in the canvases of the younger Jan Lebenstein is very much like that of Kafka's novels, filled with the consciousness of vague presences, powers which are feared but to which there is no direct approach. Extremely sensitive, Lebenstein is deliberately simple, consciously naive, seeking to recover a directness which our civilization has lost, and a primitive sense of the mythical world.

The efforts of the young Polish painters to extend the range of their art, the political pressures of the past several years having been lifted, are characterized by a chiliastic conception which tends to transcend the boundaries of abstraction. Common to all these artists, beneath their individual differences, is a new conception of reality, broader and deeper than that of all the schools that have been called "realist" in the past.

BIOGRAPHICAL DATA

A. *Polish painters*

Tadeusz Kantor, b. 1915. Studied at the Academy of Fine Arts, Cracow, from 1934 to 1939. Exhibited in Warsaw 1956–57, and with the Red Rider group. Founder of the experimental theater Cricot 2 in Cracow.

Maria Teresa Tyszkiewicz, b. in Cracow. Studied at the F. Kowarski atelier, Warsaw, from 1929 to 1939. Belongs to Modern Plastic Artists group. Exhibition in Warsaw, 1956.

Stefan Gierowski, b. in Czestochowa, 1925. Studied at the Academy of Fine Arts, Cracow. First exhibition, Cracow 1955. Represented at Polish exhibition in Brussels, 1956–57.

Jerzy Nowosielski, b. in Cracow, 1923. Studied in Cracow, under Prof. Kamocki and Eibisch. Devotes himself, in addition to painting, to designing stage sets and costumes. Member of Modern Plastic Artists group. Exhibited in New York, Chicago, Prague, and 18th Venice Biennale. Exhibition in Cracow in 1956.

Tadeusz Brzozowski, b. in Lwow, 1918. Studied at the Academy of Fine Arts, Cracow. Represented at Polish Art Exhibition, Chicago 1946; Modern Exhibition, Cracow 1955, and Polish exhibition, Brussels.

Jan Lebenstein, b. at Brzesc, 1930. Studied at the Academy of Art, Warsaw; graduated in 1954. First one-man show, Warsaw 1956.

B. *Yugoslav painters*

Miljenko Stancic, b. at Varazdin, Croatica, 1926. Studied at the Academy of Art, Zagreb. Exhibited in Prague, Tokyo, 18th Venice Biennale, Amsterdam, Brussels.

Miodrag Protic, b. at Vrnjacka Banja, Serbia, 1922. Private studies. Essayist, art critic. Exhibited at home and abroad, including 18th Venice Biennale, Amsterdam, Brussels, and Prague.

Mladen Srbinovic, b. at Susice, Macedonia, 1925. Studied at the Academy of Art, Belgrade, where he is an assistant instructor. Exhibited at home and abroad.

Stojan Celic, b. at Bosanski Novi, Bosnia, 1925. Studied at the Academy of Art, Belgrade. where he is an assistant instructor. Exhibited at home and abroad.

Sime Peric, b. at Antofagasta, Chile, 1920. Studied at the Academy of Applied Art, and worked under Prof. Hrsto Hegedusic. Exhibited at home and abroad.

Lazar Vozarevic, b. at Sremska Mitrovica, Serbia, 1925. Studied at the Academy of Art, Belgrade. Exhibited at home and abroad.

Lazar Vujaklija, b. in Vienna, 1914. Former typographer, began to paint during leisure hours. First exhibited in 1952. Represented at many exhibitions, including 18th Venice Biennale, Amsterdam, and Brussels. Designs rugs.

51　Giulio Turcato. 1958　*(Italia)*

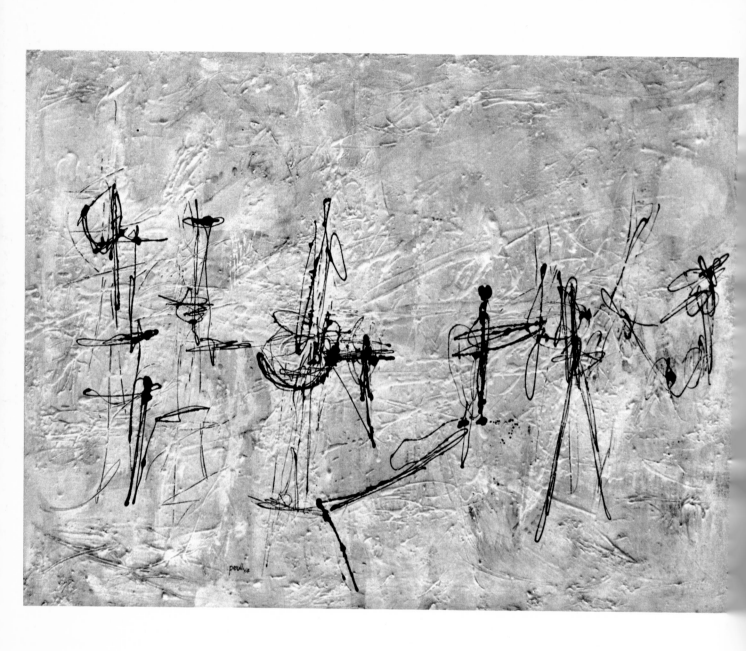

52   Achille Perilli. 1957 *(Italia)*

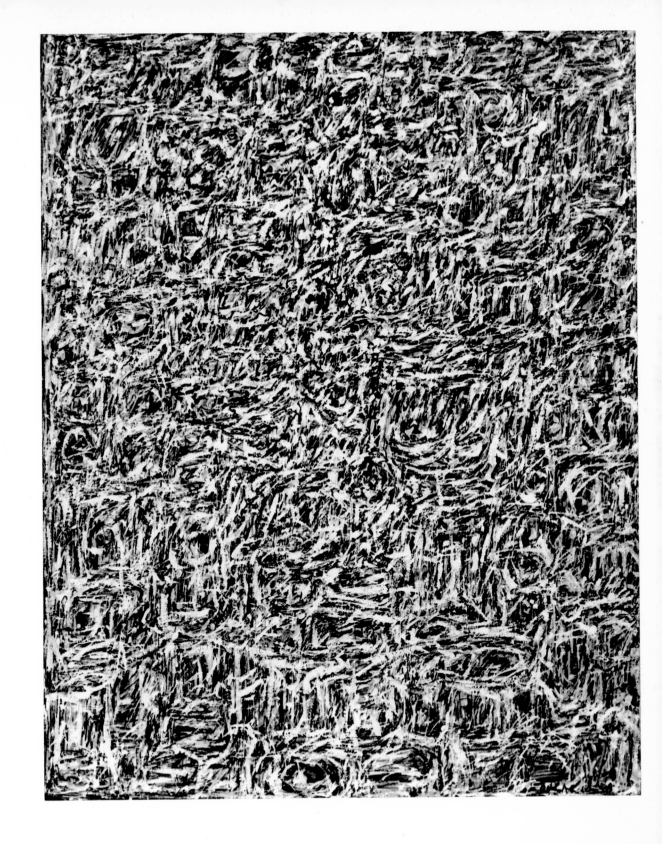

53   Piero Dorazio. 1958 *(Italia)*

54   Renato Birolli. 1957 *(Italia)*

55　Afro. 1956　*(Italia)*

56   Mauro Reggiani. 1955   *(Italia)*

57   Enrico Prampolini. 1950 *(Italia)*

58   Alberto Burri. 1958 *(Italia)*

59   Luigi Spazzapan. 1957 (*Italia*)

60   Alberto Brunori. 1957   *(Italia)*

61   Mattia Moreni. 1957 *(Italia)*

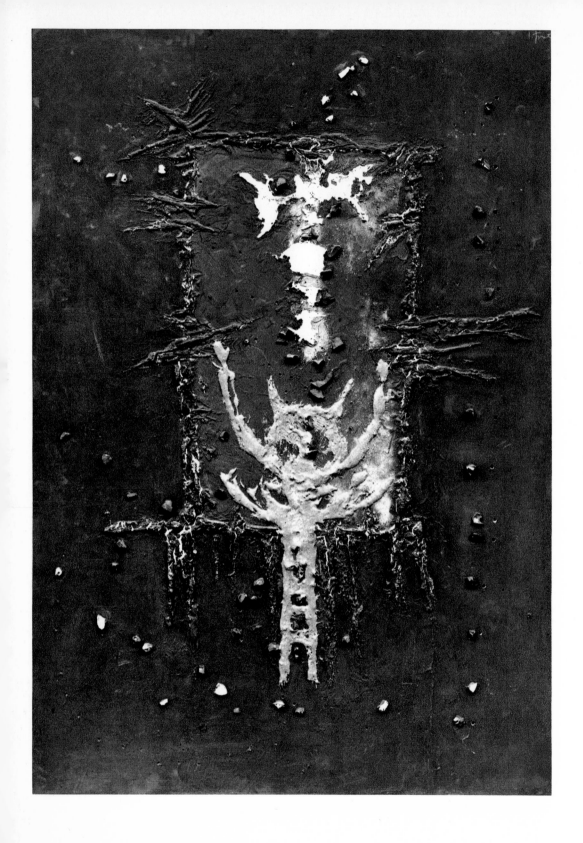

62   Lucio Fontana. 1958 *(Italia)*

63   Gianni Dova. 1957 *(Italia)*

64   Roberto Crippa. 1958 *(Italia)*

65   Zoran Music. 1954 *(Italia)*

66   Franco Gentilini. 1957 *(Italia)*

67   Antonio Tapies. 1958   *(España)*

68 Antonio Saura. 1958 *(España)*

69   Juan-Josè Tharrats. *(España)*

70 Rafael Canogar. 1957 *(España)*

a Luis Feito. 1958 *(España)*

b Vicente Vela. 1958 *(España)*

72   Edo Murtic. 1958 *(Jugoslavija)*

73   Lazar Vujaklija. 1954 (*Jugoslavija*)

74a Tadeusz Kantor. 1958 *(Polska)*   74b Wladyslaw Strzeminski. 1948 *(Polsk*

In 1945, when the Second World War ended, it was not even known whether such a thing as German art still existed, let alone when conditions might be such as to permit the resumption of artistic activities. The twelve years of the Hitler regime kept two generations of painters from becoming known to the public at large. The dictatorship suppressed real talents forbidding them to work and to exhibit. All literature on modern art was banned from libraries and schools, and all the major modern works were removed from the galleries and sold. The situation appeared hopeless: the younger artists had only a vague idea of what German art had been like before 1933, and the older artists were grief-stricken over their own personal tragedies and over the fate of the nation. If anyone had said then that in ten years Germany would again have an active and vigorous artistic life, he would have been looked upon as an irresponsible dreamer.

Today we realize that the damage caused by those twelve years of dictatorship, though vast, was superficial: it did not destroy the will to create. Older painters such as Schmidt-Rottluff, Erich Heckel, and Emil Nolde had quietly gone on working, and friends and collectors continued to buy their paintings, so that they were able to survive, though on a reduced living standard. The generation after them, which included painters such as Willi Baumeister and Theodor Werner, and the even younger E. W. Nay and Fritz Winter, who exhibited for the first time about 1930, had survived the war and resumed their work – Fritz Winter after ten years of military service and Russian captivity. The younger artists, whose training, after 1933, had been rather inadequate, took this latter generation as their models, and Baumeister in particular exerted a great influence upon them. In all the German states, after the war the younger artists formed small groups or congregated around art schools, for instance, those at Berlin and Stuttgart. Only in the Russian zone was there no resumption of artistic activity: the regulations regarding art that were laid down by the Russian authorities were like those of the Third Reich. Almost every East-German artist of note has moved to the West in the course of the postwar years.

It must be admitted, however, that German art did suffer grievous losses between 1933 and 1945. Some of the finest artists died before the new era began (Christian Rohlfs in 1938, E. L. Kirchner in 1938, and Oskar Schlemmer in 1943), and a large number of architects, writers, composers, and painters emigrated, among them Wassily Kandinsky, Paul Klee, Lyonel Feininger, Max Beckmann, Josef Albers, Kurt Schwitters, Ladislaus Moholy-Nagy, Hans Richter, Johannes Molzahn, Hans Hartung, Wols, and Rolf Nesch. The German artistic and intellectual climate grew less propitious from year to year, for each of the exiles left a gap. The dissolution of the Bauhaus deprived German artists of an outstanding school, and of the fecund intellectual influence that had been built up, over twelve years of effort, by the group that included Kandinsky, Klee, Feininger, Schlemmer,

Albers, and Moholy-Nagy. This influence has not been replaced to this day, and other art schools have not yet attained the stature of the Bauhaus. Its disappearance was a loss equaled only by the plundering of the sections devoted to modern art in the museums, which deprived the public of any contact with contemporary movements. Fortunately many artists found shelter abroad. A new Bauhaus was opened in Chicago, and Klee was influential in Bern as Kandinsky was in Paris. Most of the valuable modern works in the German museums were transferred to galleries abroad (Basel, New York), or went into private collections in Switzerland, Holland, and America. Germany itself was the greatest sufferer from the evil days it had fallen upon. But the spirit that the Nazi government set out to destroy refused to die.

The artistic situation in Germany in 1945 was completely different from that in France or America. In the latter countries, too, the war marked the end of a period, and for most artists had meant an interruption of work; on the other hand, the war had brought about greater contact among the various nations. A number of French artists spent the war years in the United States (Fernand Léger, Marc Chagall, Max Ernst, André Masson); emigrating there after the Bauhaus masters, they represented a second influx of European artists into America. They returned to Europe, however, as the Germans did not. All the Bauhaus men have become used to their adopted homeland, and have gained in strength there. They have been unwilling to return to Germany also because the artistic climate there has never been altogether favorable, except perhaps during the 1920s. The revival of art immediately after the First World War aroused great interest, and a number of good galleries and art periodicals furthered contacts between painters and the public at large.

In Germany today, as in the past, the government plays a larger part in artistic life than in France or America. The art schools, like the universities, are run by the government, and an artist can often gain recognition and material security by winning a government prize. This state of affairs has many advantages, but its drawbacks are even greater. In France recognition comes with achievement. In America, the museums and art institutes, which are almost without exception privately financed, provide leadership, usually steering the public in the right direction, thanks to their superior organization. In Germany, the artist's lot is unquestionably less enviable. His only real advantage lies in the fact that Germany has a large number of cultural centers—Berlin, Hamburg, Cologne, Düsseldorf, Essen, Hannover, Frankfurt, Mannheim, Stuttgart, Munich. Since 1945 the decentralization of cultural life has even been pushed further, and even small towns such as Recklinghausen, Siegen, Constance, or Reutlingen try hard to help young artists by means of acquisitions and commissions. New galleries, such as Der Spiegel in Cologne and the Zimmergalerie in Frankfurt, have become meeting places for painters and collectors, and regional groups of artists, such as those of the Junge Westen contribute to the spread of new ideas. The period of stagnation has been left well behind.

When artistic life was resumed in 1945 a few German Expressionists still survived. They were treated with the greatest respect, but they had no influence whatsoever, although several of them—Schmidt-Rottluff, Heckel, and Pechstein—were given posts as teachers. Sometimes their students, after following their guidance for a few semesters, chose to emulate utterly different models, for instance, Mondrian. Oskar Kokoschka, who had remained in London, had as little prestige with the young painters as Karl Hofer; the Expressionist who came closest to achieving some influence was Max Beckmann (d. 1950). His late paintings and triptychs, painted in Holland and America, attracted attention though they were known only through mediocre reproductions. His works dealing with contemporary reality, such as *Temptation* and *Hide-and-Seek*, were as effective as his *Night*, done immediately after the First World War. His "transcendental Realism" might have been the inspiration for some authentic new work, but none of the younger artists was capable of achieving the proper balance between the real world and the transcendent world—possibly because they lacked experience of the kind that had enabled Beckmann to represent the great drama of the world on the brink of total destruction as a kind of *divina commedia*.

Most of the work by disciples of the German Expressionists remained far behind the goal pursued by their masters. There were, however, exceptions, such as Alexander Camaro, who had been Otto Müller's pupil in Breslau, and Rolf Nesch, who for some time worked under E. L. Kirchner; others, such as Werner Gilles, built on entirely different foundations. In all of them, Expressionistic features gradually yielded to Symbolism.

The part played by Cubism in France and other countries, was played, in Germany, by the Blaue Reiter group, which included Kandinsky, Klee, Jawlensky, Marc, and Macke. Only Kandinsky and Klee exerted a direct influence on later painting; Marc an indirect and delayed one. Kandinsky and Klee had a number of pupils at the Bauhaus, among them Fritz Winter (b. 1905) and Max Bill (b. 1908) who produced original work. The majority contented themselves with applying their teacher's theory, but since it contained both formal and spiritual elements, even lesser talents achieved a fairly high level (Fritz Levedag, Wilhelm Imkamp, Hubert Berke, Gerhard Kadow, Jean Leppien). Polls among young painters repeatedly show that Kandinsky is held to be the most influential painter of the early twentieth century, and it is a fact that for the generation that determined the direction of art after 1945 he has meant more than Picasso. This is true of Kandinsky in all the phases of his development, the Blaue Reiter, the Bauhaus, and the Paris periods. Even the Tachistes pay homage to him. Some aspects of Klee's art were fertile sources for post-1945 painting (his "schemata," "magic squares," and the "black bar" pictures of his last years), but his poetic and musical conceptions were too closely bound up with his personal intuitions to influence the younger painters.

The widespread Neue Sachlichkeit movement (Otto Dix, Georg Grosz, Georg Schrimpf) bogged down in the official naturalism of the Nazi period, and had no issue. And although the Dada and Surrealist movements had outstanding representatives in Germany (Max Ernst worked in Cologne until 1922; Hans Arp paid frequent visits to Germany, where Kurt Schwitters was active in Hannover, and Richard Hülsenbeck and Raoul Hausmann in Berlin), they had no lasting influence; the principles of a "relativistic existential realism," with its mixture of the playful and the serious, of psychoanalysis and Constructivism, found little response. Only Richard Oelze (b. 1900) and Hans Bellmer (b. 1902) have continued in the Surrealist vein down to the present, and after 1945, Heinz Trökes (b. 1913) produced authentic works in this style.

Lisitsky's and Moholy-Nagy's Constructivism has dropped out of the picture as completely as has the Stijl movement, although Theo van Doesburg influenced the Bauhaus group in Weimar for some time. Only Vordemberge-Gildewart (b. 1899), who emigrated to Holland and is presently teaching at Ulm, and the Swiss artists Max Bill and Fritz Glarner (now in America) have continued the Constructivist inspiration. This is all the more surprising because the Bauhaus encouraged Constructivist tendencies; Naum Gabo and Antoine Pevsner both lived in Germany for several years, and Casimir Malevitch came to Germany in order to supervise the publication of his *Nonobjective World*.

To summarize, the heritage of the pre-1933 period does not amount to much. In 1933 all artistic development was interrupted, and it was not until 1945 that German painters were able to collect themselves and to strike out in new directions.

The dominant trend during the last ten years has been toward the nonobjective. Every group exhibition (the Extreme Malerei exhibition in Stuttgart in 1947 was one of the first) has disclosed a preponderance of abstract painters, and in the course of the years several figurative painters have, not always to their own advantage, adopted the abstract style. The catalogues of the reconstituted Deutsche Künstlerbund (1951–1958) clearly reveal this trend, and even Gilles and Camaro are increasingly moving away from visual reality. Willi Baumeister, in a statement printed in the first of these catalogues, says correctly that "even representational paintings have come to be interpreted in terms of nonobjective art."

This may suggest that our age can largely dispense with the object, but it does not imply that a painting done in 1950 by Max Beckmann is inferior to the works of a Baumeister. It is still possible to endow the object with symbolic force. The forms of our vision wear out just as do the forms of our thinking, but genius is occasionally able to overcome such limitations.

75 Willi Baumeister. 1955 *(Deutschland)*

It would be erroneous to conclude that contemporary art, because it is predominantly abstract, is homogeneous; it is no more so than realism was in the nineteenth century. What similarities, for instance, are there to be discovered between Theodor Werner and Fritz Winter? Only the untrained viewer fails to see the differences; he lumps all non-objective painters together, and while he may comprehend a work such as Werner Gilles' *Legend of Orpheus*, he does not grasp the meaning of the forms. Indeed, judging from the statements abstract painters make about themselves, it would seem that differences among individual artists have never been greater than they are today. This is true even within a single school. Willi Baumeister and E. W. Nay regarded themselves as diametrically opposed to each other, and today a painter like Bernard Schultze would be extremely surprised to be compared with Winfried Gaul or Emil Schumacher. Broad classifications are always resisted the more violently, the closer the basic conceptions originally were to each other. Nor is this new: we know how the Brücke painters resisted such classifications.

The meaning of abstract (or "concrete" or "absolute") art must be determined by studying each case separately; we may then be able to decide, at the end, whether we are being confronted with an experience of reality, a means of direct communication, or an attempt to restore painting for its own sake. The modern artist is no longer confronted with nature: he has become a factor in the interaction of man and nature. "For the first time in history man is thrown back on his own resources, he can no longer find any other partner or opponent" (Heisenberg). As a result new patterns are being developed which the painter is compelled to take into account; he must adjust his art to the new situation. As the purely visual elements tend increasingly to be arbitrary, the painting comes closer to resembling a musical score. The former concept of matter in space is a thing of the past, and non-perspective vision, whose chief component is time, has eliminated traditional ideas of space. Painting is indeed becoming as abstract as music, a development that was anticipated by Van Gogh and Gauguin. This musical quality is asserted most strongly in the work of painters such as Nay, but its presence is discernible, in various degrees, everywhere.

After 1945, Willi Baumeister (1889–1955, color plate 75) was the most respected German artist, the only one to enjoy any popular success. His sixty-fifth birthday was celebrated in his native Stuttgart as though he were an important public figure. Baumeister had something of Picasso's adventurous spirit, always making bold experiments and striking out in new directions. (His friend Oskar Schlemmer, who died of a malignant disease two years before the end of the war, was unlike him in this. When memorial exhibitions of Schlemmer's works were held, the modernists discovered to their disappointment that the old Bauhaus master had not been abstract at all; and they declared that it was not the task of the present to portray "figures in space." How silly. For Schlemmer's compositions, seemingly representational and done in perspective, were actually based on mathematical constructs and on space-time conceived as a unit, and transcended the antithesis between abstract and realistic art, confounding their critics.) Like others of his generation, Baumeister was influenced by Cézanne and by Cubism. He felt that analysis was indispensable. Cubism and the Blaue Reiter group had in general a greater influence than Fauvism and Expressionism in Germany, because the dissolution of forms preceded their construction. With his *Mauerbilder*—"mural paintings" (1920–22)—Baumeister made his first successful advance into new territory; he was aiming at a synthesis of painting and architecture, as well as an enlargement of pictorial space. By means of raised objects attached to the surface, emphasizing the contrast between appearance and reality, he endowed the wall with an active quality, and through the addition of figurative elements related it to the theme of man in space—a theme that also interested Schlemmer. The *Mauerbilder* found a favorable reception in France; an essay devoted to them was published in *Esprit Nouveau* in 1922. Le Corbusier and Fernand Léger were enthusiastic about these works; their friendship with Baumeister survived the war.

The *Mauerbilder* were followed by works on the themes of sport and the machine. Baumeister destroyed many of these, finding them unsatisfactory. In 1930 he began a series of works that included paintings done on sand with hollowed out colored planes. This was followed by the *Flämmchen* paintings (1931), the Ideograms (1937), the Eidos pictures (1938), the Rock Gardens (1938), the African and Sumerian histories (from 1942 on), the Metaphysical Landscapes (1947), the Epochs (1947), and the so-called Montaru, Monturi, and Aru Series (1953). Each of these consists of from six to twenty works, variations on a single theme, which may derive from formal invention or an expression of the unconscious. The successive groups often overlap, and within a given group we sometimes discover what seems to be a sudden recollection of a painting from another, previous sequence. Like Matisse, Baumeister must be judged on the basis of his entire series; only then do we become aware of the potentialities of the individual paintings.

His titles are not always a reliable guide to subject matter or treatment: his *Chess Player* of 1927 is merely a constellation of dots, while another version of the same subject evokes a player and a chessboard; a scene entitled *Gilgamesh* may be figurative or architectural, or merely a web of forms suggesting the bark of a tree; paintings such as *Blocksberg* (1952), *Faust* (1952), or *Phantom* (1953) are no more literary in content than the painting entitled *Dur* (1951). The subject matter can scarcely be separated from the manner in which it is treated, but even the most abstract compositions contain references to visual reality. This distinguishes Baumeister from his German contemporaries, and relates him to Picasso and Léger, and more generally to the French school, which has always mistrusted pure abstraction. And Baumeister, though referring to himself as an abstract artist, often half-seriously interpreted his paintings to his friends, saying that two pointed black forms represented the cathedral at Cologne, that in his *Epochs* he was showing giants, and in the Montaru series continents in the process of formation; he called one of his black and green compositions, *Cézanne and his Motif*. Needless to say, such associations occurred to him after the fact. He painted without having the slightest idea of what his works were going to resemble; like Kandinsky he spoke of this as a quest for the unknown, and in 1947 he published an interesting book on this subject, *Das Unbekannte in der Kunst* ("The Unknown in Art"), which he had written during the war.

Baumeister's preoccupation with the archaic, the fact that so many of his paintings and titles refer to African rock paintings, Sumerian legends, the history of Babylon and Israel, Mexico, and occasionally the Far East, indicates a presdisposition, a natural affinity with things primeval. His works are permeated by forgotten and repressed elements, psychological archaisms and atavisms, "remnants of the memory of mankind." In the 1940s these elements became dominant, and in his last works they are expressed as symbols. In his Aru paintings the forms resemble Chinese ideograms, and yet they are the logical outcome of his previous inventions. Baumeister was a man governed by his instincts: the phenomenon of regression was something he took for granted, and long-buried layers of his mind responded to new sensations. It was in this way, and not through research in museums and libraries, that he came close to reproducing the primordial language. His visit to Altamira on the occasion of some international congress was a great experience for him, and a confirmation of his art, although the paleolithic cave paintings are "naturalistic" hunting scenes, executed for purposes of magic. He dreamed of visiting Africa to see the later rock paintings, of which he had read descriptions in the works of Frobenius and Obermeier. Baumeister absorbed, with a remarkably sure instinct, everything he thought could be useful to him. He was amazingly well informed about both ancient and modern art.

The critics and his colleagues often regarded his versatility and inventiveness with suspicion. They were mistaken. While it is true that Baumeister could have devoted himself profitably to any one of his conceptions, he wanted more than that, he wanted to test his strength and to explore the world. And the world, for him, was not only nature, but also history, the fate of mankind, from the earliest beginnings to Einstein.

He relied always on instinct, on the cunning of his own hand. He never made a false stroke, he always found the right place for the right touch of color. It was a pleasure to watch him at work, as he sketched with his brush, chose the proper color for the ground in order to build on it, and, after the main lines were laid down, tackled the details, strengthening or weakening them, occasionally also "embellishing" them.

162

76   Theodor Werner. 1957 *(Deutschland)*

His fondness for "paintings in relief" began in 1920 with the *Mauerbilder* and persisted until the beginning of the Montaru series. He was fascinated by the contrast between the graspable, tangible elements and the ungraspable, the purely painterly nonmaterial elements. But over the decades he also produced works confined to a flat surface, for example, his metaphysical landscapes, and the Montaru and Aru compositions. Even in these, however, he occasionally used mixtures of plaster and sand, or built up a relief effect by laying on the paint thickly.

His works are as varied in content as were his expressive means. He produced mythical paintings (the series of the African and Sumerian Histories, the Epochs, the Aztecs, etc.) and symbolic ones (the Eidos and the Aru compositions). But all of them are characterized by a kind of realistic unreality. The tremendous black forms of the Montaru series, with the variegated ornaments at the edges, actually do suggest continents in the process of formation or disintegration, the white discs of the Monturi series suggest stars, and the Aru pictures hieratic figures. Baumeister stood halfway between Picasso and his own contemporaries, he was a link between yesterday and today, and for this reason the younger painters saw him as "the grand old man," both as artist and as human being, for he always courageously championed their cause, frequently intervening in public debates.

Just as unique as the case of Baumeister is that of Theodor Werner (b. 1886; color plate 76). He came into prominence only in 1947 when many Germans saw his works for the first time, at the exhibition held at the Galerie Rosen, in Berlin. The works of his that had been shown at German exhibitions in the 1920s—Post-Impressionistic still lifes and landscapes—had not revealed his true originality. In 1930 he had gone from Germany to Spain, and thence to Páris where he lived between 1930 and 1935. He had achieved some recognition there, and Christian Zervos had seen his talent. Carl Einstein had introduced him to Braque and Miró, but as a result of the political situation, he had no exhibitions either in France or, after that, in Germany. It was only after his return to Germany in 1935 that he discovered his personal style, a very un-French rhythmic figuration, based on linear and musical elements, in which he expressed himself for many years. This style has nothing in common with Cubism, although he was fond of Juan Gris.

Few of Werner's early works have survived: almost all the paintings he produced prior to 1935 and many works of the later 1930s were destroyed during the war. On a visit to Paris in 1938 he did a number of paintings, among them *Aeginete* and *Pan and Nymph*, in which figures emerge out of linear forms and transparent colors. These are reminiscent of the early geometric designs, the Celtic "mirrors" of the Latene period, the Irish miniatures, and occasionally the Scythian animal art, as well as early bronzes of China and Luristan. Such sources inspired him, just as Baumeister was inspired by the prehistoric rock paintings, and Picasso by early Mediterranean art. Only in Klee do we find a similar regression, in his case to an Islamic strain. There is nothing surprising in this, since the human soul is, as we know, "a creation of prehistory."

In Werner's paintings of the early 1940s, such as *Loge* (1941) and *Pierrot Lunaire* (1942), rhythm rather than color is the primary means of expression, and often the works look like wash drawings. The titles are arbitrary, referring only to associations after the fact, for this artist, too, merely follows his inner impulse in drawing his forms. The rhythmic pattern grows increasingly intricate, the colors more intense, and in the end the form stands out clearly from the network of lines, as though it had been planned in advance. *Creatio ex nihilo* (1943) and *Scythian Finds* (1947) are composed with precision and have great suggestive power. The rhythm of each seems to be embodied in the theme that reveals itself spontaneously. Something intangible is given visual expression, as in the early geometric designs; as in the early *Book of Kells*, art is the process of creation itself. The image arises freely, seemingly out of nothing, and has no precise reference; it is indeed a *creatio ex nihilo*, as is the painting called that, which shows two transparent figures that have detached themselves, as though accidentally, from the course of events.

Although this conception proved fruitful, in 1949 Werner adopted a different manner. In his variations on the theme of flight, i. e., the overcoming of gravity, time, and space, the forms are no longer seen against a network of lines. The effect, however, is not one of immobility; on the contrary, the forms seem to move about, and the background advances and recedes. It is no longer rhythm that serves to link the two, but color. Werner now thinks in terms of color, and uses his color musically. A new chapter has begun in his work, which is now entirely given over to "the reverse side of the world." All references to objects are eliminated; the fragmentary forms are signs whose meanings must be deciphered. These paintings are *imagines* in the original sense of the term, and they embody Werner's interpretation of the real world, which, after all other attempts to represent it have failed, is seen as a complex of symbols.

Werner still invented titles after 1949, but they were now metaphors of metaphors, referring to isolated features of a given work or to effects that the painter ascribed to it. Thus a color harmony struck him as *Autumnal*, an emphatic form as a *Star Flower*, a dynamic accent as a *Vortex*, a series of signs as a Chinese *Inscription* (1951). But after 1954 even these almost meaningless titles were eliminated, since they tended to limit the viewer's experience of the work. Without them the way is opened to multiple interpretations. The composition causes the beholder to react in certain ways, but it is not easy for him to partake of the very delicate tensions expressed. The transitory quality of the means of expression also determines the medium: Werner favors tempera on heavy paper, he only rarely uses oil on canvas.

165 One of Werner's recent works is called *Anywhere*; others might be called *Any time*, since this painter makes no distinction between time and space, his mind "moves along time, as it were." The events are there before him, the artist merely encounters them (Eddington, quoted by Gebser in *Abendländische Wandlung*). All of life is conceived as unity within space and time, time being all time, including past and future. Possibly Werner is not aware of what he is expressing, he is merely obeying an inner compulsion, and calls something *Origin* or *Emergence* that in reality is both beginning an end.

Since 1952, Werner's paintings have been characterized by a dictatorial formal idiom: the means of expression assume the initiative and create forms that do not exist anywhere except in these paintings. The invisible is made visible, and the painting becomes "the key to the great code of the world" (Novalis).

Apparently Werner feels most secure when his work is thus removed from the world of appearances: his colors become intensive and glowing, their harmonies are often surprising and always highly intricate, the fragmentary forms increase in size and become emphatic. When lines accompany them, they are like luminous traces (the title of a painting done in 1952) left behind by the movement of the forms. Regular figures—circles, triangles—are superimposed, like signposts on several of these later compositions.

In 1954 Werner painted a mural of about 55 feet long and 10 feet high for the auditorium of the Hochschule für Musik (designed by the architect P. Baumgarten). In executing this difficult commission he drew on the whole of his experience as a painter since 1945. His mural is a rhythmically organized metamorphic painting, which is divided into three parts and yet constitutes a whole, for the movements of forms within it have no beginning or end, and the colors serve to articulate the transformations. After finishing this mural, to which he devoted all his energies for a whole year, Werner returned to small scale painting, and since then has produced a number of works of extraordinary richness of invention, often very concisely formulated.

It is typical of Germany that the contrast between Baumeister and Werner is seen again between the painters Fritz Winter and Ernst Wilhelm Nay. In the work of Winter, a native of Westphalia (b. 1905, color plate 78), as in Baumeister's, we find echoes of nature and history, while Nay often achieves figurations that refer in various ways to the "Absolute," and that, to use Paul Valéry's expression, are "intellectual feasts." Kandinsky's antithesis between "great reality" and "great abstraction" seems to be repeated here on another level.

Winter studied at the Bauhaus and had the good fortune of being a pupil of Kandinsky and Klee and attending their courses in art. Since their teaching dealt with the elements and the basic laws of artistic creation, with the origin and function of form and color, Winter was under no compulsion to paint in the style of his teachers, though he did paint

77   Fritz Winter. 1956 *(Deutschland)*

in their spirit. They had always urged their "apprentices" not to take as a point of departure the *natura naturata* but rather the potentialities of *natura naturans*, and encouraged them to discover their own methods of visual communication.

At first Winter painted in a naturalistic style. During a visit to Switzerland he discussed the subject with E. L. Kirchner. Kirchner showed an understanding of Winter's desire for independence, and Winter showed a similar tolerance for Kirchner's rejection of all formalism. Kirchner had tried to discover the "hieroglyphs" of nature. Winter was seeking a language of signs which would not contradict the spirit of nature. Like Klee, he aimed at "the rebirth of nature."

From naturalistic representation Winter progressed to using ideograms in the manner of Hans Arp, and later to even freer conceptions. The colorful works shown at his first exhibition (Galerie F. Möller, Berlin, 1931) were distinguished for their simplicity and sureness of feeling. At a showing a few years ago of about a hundred of his earlier works that had been taken out of Germany during the Nazi period, critics were amazed at the maturity of his *Variations on a Spatial Theme*. We can understand Feininger's having been enthusiastic about them. Winter freed himself from the object only gradually: as late as 1939 he could still entitle one of his paintings *Farbenreichtum von Sirmione*—his work, with its mosaic-like planes, is an actual evocation of southern light. (Klee knew the extent to which the colors of a locality are important to a painter: Elba, for instance, disappointed him in this respect, while Corsica fully satisfied him.) In the 1930s Winter also did black paintings and grisailles (*Black Picture*, 1936): he was the son of a miner, and had worked for some time in a coal shaft, and black plays in his works a part similar to that which caves play in the sculptures of Henry Moore, whose background is similar to Winter's. In later paintings Winter expressed a preoccupation with subterranean rocks, their formation and color. He is the only painter of his generation to display such a predilection for blacks and grays, although he is personally a cheerful man. "I am glad for red and yellow, but I long for gray, the infinite" *(Diary)*—gray is for him an indefinite color, related to white. After 1933 Winter worked near Munich, and after 1935 at Diessen on the Ammersee. Like many of his fellow painters, he was regarded, under the Nazis, as a "degenerate," and lived for the end of the Third Reich. In 1939 he was called up; in 1945 he was taken prisoner by the Russians, and was not released until the end of 1949. During those ten years he did not produce much; he managed nevertheless to execute a series of about a hundred very beautiful drawings while in the field, and during a stay in the hospital at Diessen (1944) did a series of oils, entitled *The Driving Forces of Nature*. There are about forty of the latter, each a valid work. They are pantheistic poems, related to Franz Marc's last paintings, the *Animal Destinies* and the abstractions, but also to Marc's sketches from nature, to whose titles *(Arsenal for a Creation)* Winter's show some similarity. Na-

168

ture is introduced into the composition for pictorial reasons, and is the product of meditation and creation. During the war years Winter often had occasion to observe nature at close quarters. A leaf, a crystal, a forest, a cobweb, but also the dampness rising from the earth, the light that distorts objects and transforms them, the flow of hours at twilight and at night, all this was nature for Winter, and merged with his inner visions. A forest grows out of accented verticals, out of angular and round forms, and out of colors that give the painting its quality.

In 1949 Winter resumed work, executing a number of paintings somber in expression (*Dark Signs*, 1950, and a black *Lunar Landscape*, 1951). His visit to Paris in 1951 gave a new impetus to his work; there he was once again in contact with talents of other countries, as he had been at the Bauhaus, and he was particularly fascinated by the paintings of Hans Hartung. Along with small gouaches he painted large canvases, in which curved black lines cover the surface as with a net, as though to protect the secret of the sensitive world of color. The structure of his composition has gradually become more elaborate with small islands of color superimposed on the ground, and dynamic linear elements dividing or connecting them. Perforations and emblematic figurations have made their appearance, loud color accents have begun to glow in the foreground: it is as though Winter were writing for a full orchestra after having long composed for a chamber ensemble. But he has adhered to his original conception, and while his work no longer directly reminds the viewer of reality, it sets chains of associations in motion. His paintings of recent years have titles such as *Spring* (1954), *Spring Tree* (1955), or *Solstice* (1957): they evoke nature in the same way a spiral line evokes the flight of a bird.

Ernst Wilhelm Nay (b. 1912, color plate 78), a native of Berlin who lives now in Cologne, is, as I have said, as different from Winter as Werner is from Baumeister. A freethinker, he does not philosophize, except as a painter, and he has said of himself: I paint, therefore I am. This is the more surprising because, like Werner, he has intellectual interests, and is fond of modern music and poetry. He is the musician among contemporary German painters, not because of his love for music, but because he works in the manner of a composer, setting note next to note, not positing the end result, but letting it gradually develop.

Nay was not trained by teachers of modern art, but by Karl Hofer: his first paintings were realistic. His *Portrait of a Boy* (1925) hangs in the Hamburg Kunsthalle, and is still a good portrait. From E. L. Kirchner's paintings he learned how to read meaning into nature; he also learned how to schematize figurative elements and to endow them with rhythm. In 1937–1938 Munch invited him to Norway, where he painted his Lofoten Island landscapes. These paintings are decorative in the French sense, but very German in their apodictic transformation of natural forms. A second successful stage of his development was marked by his metamorphic paintings, which were executed in France (before 1945) and later in Hofheim (Taunus). These are, as to subject matter, Ovidian metamorphoses, with titles such as *Thetis Fleeing* (1941), *Queen on Her Throne*, or *Orphic Picture* (1948). Figures are treated in a purely formal way, having no relation to objects (triangle-breast), as constructions rather than representations. The arabesque-like contours are freed of any descriptive function, the colors obey laws of their own. Nay modulates from green to blue, from orange to vermilion. His delight in decorative effects occasionally reminds one of the Nomadic style.

In 1950 he entered upon an entirely abstract phase of development, a phase which has lasted to this day. Nay's new manner is deliberately austere, as though he wished to emphasize the change by using cold colors and precise forms. Up to 1952 details were discernible—"butterfly" paintings, and metamorphoses in which pearl necklaces, almond eyes, and interlacings appeared—but these gradually yielded to his new formal canon, to series of dots, pointed ovals, feathers, and fans. Figurative inventions have been replaced with general dynamic forms, reminiscent of leaves, flying birds, flashes of lightning, and, less frequently, of geometric figures—triangles, lozenges, half-circles. Nay weaves these into the surface and arranges them in sequences of rhythm and color. He orchestrates his colors, which have gradually gained precedence over other elements, and gives his paintings titles such as *Instrumentation, Rhythms in Purple and Gray*, or *Triumph of Yellow* (1952). Linear elements contribute to the general effect, but the lines are surrounded by color, or else form a third pattern overlaid above the patterns of the dynamic ground and that of the color planes and spots.

In 1953, the pictorial space in Nay's paintings became clearly spherical; the arrangement was most often horizontal, but in some works was vehemently diagonal. In 1954 the circles and ovals yielded to discs, and the polygons to aggressive pointed forms hard as glass; the compositions became more dramatic, projecting the mythical elements of his work of the 1940s onto the plane of pure relationships. The checkerboard pattern made its appearance, and "the motion picture reel" was used to order the chaos, or to form an antithesis to the scattered-dots pattern. In 1955 Nay began to use his discs in a way which, quite unlike Delaunay's use of them, exploits the weightlessness and infinite mobility of the circle. But comparisons are misleading here: we are dealing with pictorial inventions, based on complete mastery of crucial elements such as surface, form, color, rhythm, dynamics, and agogics, which have more than the usual significance for Nay. His paintings ara characterized by a weightless quality, and even his blacks have a luminous effect. At a certain point the artist himself seems to have been seized with vertigo, and he began to interlock and overlap his discs, to differentiate them by means of his brushwork, and to anchor them

78 Ernst Wilhelm Nay. 1958 *(Deutschland)*

more firmly with the help of irregular figures (*Alpha*, 1957). Something like expression suddenly made its appearance, though certainly not with the artist's intention, for he is obsessed with formal, not with expressive values.

Nay's own statements suggest that he looks upon each painting as "a problem in computation," like Edgar Degas. He speaks of "arithmetical" pictorial form, based upon surface, number, and rhythm, and on color. These elements give rise to form and space, the latter as a metaphor of the inconceivable. Communication is not the object, "the human is not the artist's concern," but it can be a consequence of his work if everything goes well, if his creation is congruent with the universe. Then "contact" comes about of itself, and the painting "adds a grain of love to the whole." Klee said that paintings should, among other things, contribute to human happiness.

The contrast between Baumeister and Werner, or between Winter and Nay does not reflect a purely German trait—we find similar contrasts everywhere. It would be erroneous to interpret it in terms of classicism versus romanticism, Constructivism versus Expressionism. It should be viewed rather as two different aspects of the same attitude toward the world and the self, aspects which reflect differences in temperaments rather than in methods.

Hans Hartung (b. 1904) who has become a French citizen and is one of the leading painters in Paris (cf. p. 40) clearly illustrates this relationship between object and method. The vitality of his line, which was a characteristic even of his Tachiste works in the 1920s, points to Expressionism, the poetically differentiated colors to romanticism. The unconditional character of the form, however, suggests a search for ultimate boundaries. The language of painting achieves autonomy and carries a significance that cannot be revealed through any other medium, as is the case with René Char's or Saint-John Perse's poems.

Nationality has nothing to do with all this, but it is perhaps no accident that the German artist Wols (Wolfgang Schulze, 1913–1951, color plate 79), who emigrated to Paris in 1931 and died there, falls within the same category as Hartung—of those who derive their forms through a direct transcription of existential realities. Wols's paintings never emerge from the *status nascendi*, they reveal their creator. His drypoints were published as illustrations for books by Kafka and Sartre, and they are characterized by the same absence of preconceptions about life and art as one finds in those writers. He had the Zen adept's indifference toward his works and their success. He never spoke of them, and made no effort to sell them, as though it were the most natural thing in the world to put all one's energy into such expressions. He experienced greater difficulty in the mastering of the medium of oil than in drawing and watercolor, but he succeeded in the end in producing

79 Wols. 1950 *(Deutschland)*

paintings in a distinctive style. Nevertheless his graphic works are the more effective ones. His oeuvre is fragmentary, for he died early. His posthumous influence on the younger generation has been very great, although not as great as that exerted by Hartung, who also influenced painters of his own generation by his openmindedness and incisive forms— qualities he shares with the writer Samuel Beckett.

Wols of course belongs to a generation younger than Hartung's—to that of Hann Trier and Karl Otto Götz as well as of the Tachistes. The age groups overlap somewhat: for instance, Fassbender is counted among the younger generation although he was born about the same time as Nay. The same is true of a number of Bauhaus students who were born between 1900 and 1910. But after all we consider Baumeister, Werner, Max Ackermann, Julius Bissier, and Ernst Geitlinger as being in the same group as the fifty-year-old artists, though they are older than that, because they kept pace with the younger men, or because they achieved personal expression only late in their lives. The year of birth is not always of crucial importance.

Ackermann was born in 1887, Bissier in 1893, Geitlinger in 1895. We know them as abstract painters, for their later works are the more important ones. Geitlinger painted romantic works, such as his *Mississippi Steamer*, even after the Second World War, and did not abandon representation until 1951. Ackermann, a pupil of Adolf Hölzel, switched to nonobjective art earlier, but for a long time he continued to include references to reality in his paintings, and only recently has he applied in them principles derived from music (plate 99a). Bissier, a friend of Baumeister's, went over to abstraction in the early 1930s, and his latest India ink sketches and colored monotypes are reminiscent of Chinese painting. They also resemble Hartung's early Tachiste experiments, but Bissier's style tends toward a pictorial script: to him his productions are as legible as a poem. They too contain reflections of nature, and represent the extreme case of a transcription of insights from reality through intellectual concentration (plate 99b).

It is more difficult to classify a painter like Carl Buchheister (b. 1890), a friend of Kurt Schwitters of Hannover, who combines the methods of Dada and of "action painting." Despite his advanced age he exhibits with the youngest artists, and is judged by the same standards as they. Rolf Cavael was born in 1898, Marie-Luise Rogister and Eduard Bergheer in 1901, and Boris Kleint in 1903, the same year as Josef Fassbender, and with these painters we come back to the generation of E. W. Nay, who is in his fifties. Titles such as *Blissful Dog* (Fassbender, plate 95), *Città Meridionale* (Bargheer, 1956, plate 96a) or *Green Massif* (Rogister, 1957) suggest references to reality, however remote, though they are metaphorical as well. When Cavael entitles his India ink sketches *Ye-Pi-Tu*, he intends a reference to the Orient, though his treatment is very different from that of Bissier in his Eastern meditations. The tension between

80 Werner Gilles. 1954 *(Deutschland)*

the art of yesterday and today is more clearly discernible in the works of the older than of the younger artists: for the latter reality is questionable to begin with, though it is present in many of their works. This tension accounts for the rapid changes of style among this group. When we are confronted with a new work by one of them, we are often reminded of Hartung, de Staël, or Poliakoff. The clinging to earlier influences is true of painters in all countries, who, faced with "existential relativism," naturally seek support and confirmation. In the work of Fassbender, for example, the difference between 1951 and 1957 is considerable, and suggests that a new consciousness of time has made itself felt in his pictorial world.

A special case is that of Woty Werner (b. 1903, color plate 84) who began as a painter, but who achieved a personal style only after she took up embroidering and weaving. Her designs evidence the same feeling as characterizes modern painting; the fact that her medium is a different one is even less important today, when so many painters are resorting to alien materials in order to enhance the plastic effects of their work. Woty Werner's earliest designs (1940) were naturalistic, and related to the figurative works of Munch and the Brücke group. By 1946 her forms had begun to show greater freedom, and her *Homage to Rousseau* (1947) is reminiscent of the Blaue Reiter style. Her *Three Rings* of 1948 inaugurated a series of autonomous creations, amazingly inventive and free of any kind of schematism. The technical requirements of the weaver's art often result in a sterile ornamentalism, but this is not so in the case of Woty Werner, to whom the limitations of her craft are a stimulus to creative independence. For a time, her work, particularly such humorous designs as *Circus, Rooster* (1947), *Carnival* (1948), *Lantern Feast* (1951), contained references to zoomorphic forms and arabesques, but these were gradually eliminated, and her later designs permit only occasional realistic associations, as in Klee or Miró. As her forms became freer and her works increased in size, she used titles more sparingly. Her large tapestry for the Forschungsinstitut in Godesberg (1956), with its rays, swelling curves, and glowing colors—various greens and pinks on a gray-green band—could be called a "Hymn to Springtime." Her sense of color is as infallible as is her faculty for inventing ever new forms and combinations of forms. To some extent she remains bound to nature—this may be due to the fact that she is a woman—but her inventions are essentially intuitive.

Before dealing with the youngest generation of painters, we shall discuss a group of representational artists. Most of these were born in 1900 or earlier, and their number is as small as it is in other countries. They are Symbolists rather than realists, for they use objects merely as a pretext. Kandinsky's "great reality" is increasingly being supplanted by "great abstraction," and one of the chief characteristics of the present situation is the

81   Heinz Trökes. 1952 (*Deutschland*)

predilection displayed by these painters for the ambiguous and the hidden. The old modes of vision have become almost completely obsolete, and neither science nor society have so far provided us with new principles for the formulation of visual reality. That is why many painters who were still painting objectively as late as 1945 have since gone over to other camps, some of them achieving interesting results (Georg Meistermann, Gerhard Fietz, Ernst Geitlinger). The few who have persisted in their adherence to nature—Alexander Camaro, Rolf Nesch, Werner Heldt, Werner Gilles, H.A.P. Grieshaber—have considerably altered their styles, each in a different way, but each turning away from the object, which is transformed into a hieroglyph. It would be possible to classify these artists according to their backgrounds and teachers: Camaro was a pupil of Otto Müller, Nesch worked under E.L. Kirchner, Scholz was influenced by Nolde, Heldt studied at the Berlin Academy, and Gilles at the Bauhaus under Feininger. But whatever these artists learned from their teachers was evident only in their early works, and was gradually discarded as they found their own paths.

Alexander Camaro (b. 1901, plate 87), a native of Silesia like his teacher Otto Müller, made his debut almost simultaneously as a painter and a dancer, appearing with Mary Wigman in the performance of *Funeral Repast* given in Munich in 1939. The illusionary quality of the theater to some extent characterizes Camaro's postwar paintings, among them his *Wooden Theater* (1946), eighteen oil canvases that were greatly admired. He shows us not excited actors and spectators, but emptiness, the loges and the lobby after the performance is over. One lone figure is enough, almost too much. Camaro tries always to conjure up the disquieting feeling of that which has gone by or has not yet emerged, the sense of what cannot be grasped; like the nonobjective painters he suggests rather than represents. His forms are not discovered but invented, and they are largely independent of visual reality. His landscapes have a primeval quality: his *Lake Dwellings* (1950) and *Gulls on the Beach* (1951) are not unlike works by Fritz Winter, and in his variations on the theme *East* (1955) he makes use of grid forms and faded colors as well as choreographic symbols. A poetic quality remains discernible in the late works, but what was originally descriptive of a situation, has taken the form of color and harmony.

Werner Heldt (1904–1951, plate 88), a native of Berlin, was a more rigorous painter than Camaro, and rather unlike him, though his bare streets and squares and views from windows also express emptiness, solitude, and anguish. His *Still Life with Houses* and *Sunday Afternoon* (1954) have a definite elegiac quality. His outlines and colors are intense, precise, and effective. Like the planes in Juan Gris's late works, his objects are shifted off their axis. He also uses marbled planes, black and white next to pink and light green ones. In his works the objects are always clear, the poetic element being inherent in the construction—a rare thing in representational paintings. But what are the objects in these

82   Bernhard Schultze. 1958 (*Deutschland*)

works? One of Heldt's paintings is entitled *Berlin on the Sea* (1948), and the unreal forms correspond to this unreal reality. The objects are mere expedients.

The work of Werner Gilles (b. 1894; color plate 80) differs from that of both Camaro and Heldt. Instead of Camaro's empty places expressing existential anguish, we find in Gilles the myth of Orpheus (*Orpheus I*, ten drawings, 1947; *Orpheus II*, eleven drawings, 1949); and whereas in Heldt the structure of planes serves as the principle of organization, in Gilles this function is performed by "mystic construction." He uses the object as a theme on which he composes variations, as Picasso, whom Gilles admires, occasionally does. His inspiration is poetic, he is at home with Rimbaud and Mallarmé, as well as with Greek myths and the Italian landscape. The island of Ischia has been the setting for much of the dialogue Gilles has conducted with the past. His poetic compositions *Ophelia* and *Oedipus*, or his *Pagan Tombs by the Sea* (1955), painted as a tribute to his friend Werner Heldt, are not fantasies but versions of reality, just as his unreal figures are not distortions of reality but pictorial signs, words. They recur and must recur since they are part of his mythological vocabulary. He is like Rimbaud in his predilection for the unreal, and like Mallarmé in his tendency to let the medium take over. But being a German, he does not carry these tendencies to extremes, and it is precisely his lyricism that makes him a favorite with the German public. This public still is infatuated with ancient Greece, though today it is also acquainted with the mysteries and the chthonic powers. Gilles conjures these up in unreal colors that scarcely permit a distinction between Hades and the Elysian fields.

Rolf Nesch (b. 1893, plate 89), too, is a special case among the representational artists. Since 1940 his works have shown no trace of being influenced by Kirchner, whom he met in 1924 or by Munch, whom he met in 1933 (when he settled in Norway). The expressive quality of his metal reliefs is so suffused with Surrealist and abstract elements that these works take on an entirely different significance. The invention of "printing on metal," a process whereby a plate of copper and zinc is transformed into a kind of relief with the help of pieces of wire and metal, completely changed the character of his etchings, and also affected his style, in that the new process introduces archaic features into the work. Since 1935 Nesch has constructed reliefs with metal, wood, semi-precious stones, and pieces of ceramic, some of which are barbaric in appearance: he himself compared his high relief *St. John* to a Melanesian idol. His color prints, which he always does by hand, and which for the most part exist only in single copies, remind us of his reliefs; great demands are made upon the paper, which must take on quite unusual protuberances and hollows, and the figures have a rough quality. As in Irish miniatures, these figures often seem to be composed of various materials. When metal buttons are used to indicate eyes, and copper wire to indicate hair, and when a wire netting becomes a crown and perforations in the metal become white pearls, the figurative elements acquire a nonfigurative quality. Nesch's

Juggler (1952) and *Caterpillar* (1954) thus owe more to their purely pictorial elements than to the models they depict. In reliefs composed of more than one unit, as the triptych of 1956, the diverging and overlapping rhythms further emphasize the purely constructed quality of the work.

H. A. P. Grieshaber (b. 1909, plate 90) studied at the Stuttgart academy, and visited Paris, Africa, and the Near East; between 1933 and 1940 he did odd jobs at Reutlingen; from 1940 to 1945 he served in the army, and in 1945–1946 he worked as a miner in Belgium; since 1947 ha has been giving private lessons in art. His career is as remarkable as his artistic personality. Where are his origins? His early works were inspired by the Brücke group, as were those of Camaro and Nesch; but his recent works show little of that influence. Like Nesch, Griesbacher works almost exclusively in the graphic medium. He produces large prints (often on several blocks, each measuring as much as 7×3 feet). Some of his latest color woodcuts are close to the post-Cubist French manner; though he introduces references to reality into his forms, his work derives its force from an inner impetus, not from nature.

The group of artists just mentioned, who are tackling the problems of symbolic realism, have played a more productive part in Germany of the postwar years than many of the "turncoats" who eagerly jumped on the bandwagon of abstraction. The object may have lost its symbolic force, but it is not dead, and may one day be restored to an important function. The symbolic realists interpret the tradition in terms of a rebirth of art under the spiritual sign of a changed era. But after the war another group of artists, those to whom the tradition means the carrying forward of the revolution that began at the turn of the century, have shifted the emphasis from the object to the autonomy of the composition. Thus, Max Kaus (b. 1891), a pupil of Heckel, has turned his attention from the constructing of individual forms to their combination: his *Ruins of a Temple* (1956) is a system of planes. In the works of Xaver Fuhr (b. 1898) small surfaces have been replaced with large, all-inclusive ones, and Walter Becker (b. 1893) has introduced Surrealist elements into his paintings. The Brücke tradition persists most markedly in the works of Thomas Niederreuther (b. 1909) and Karl Kluht (b. 1898).

Werner Scholz (b. 1898, plate 91) met Emil Nolde at a crucial period of his development, and he has aimed at a more solid construction of the surface. His paintings are not superficial, but they are not emotional either (*Steel Triptych*, 1950). In many of his works the objects become unrecognizable as a result of the emphasis on structure, and an arrangement of colors becomes the actual theme.

Much the same thing might be said of Friedrich-Karl Gotsch (b. 1900, plate 92) who, like his classmate Hans Meyboden (b. 1901), was a pupil of Kokoschka. Both are natives of northern Germany, talented, and as students impressed their teacher; they were not, however, susceptible to his influence, althoug Gotsch's early works disclose his admiration for Edvard Munch, and Meyboden's for Paula Modersohn-Becker. When they recently re-emerged, after a long period of not showing, they were regarded as out-of-date, like all representational artists without the prestige of a Gilles. Their works still showed no trace of Kokoschka, either of his psychological interests or of the intoxication with color that marked his Dresden period; at bottom both remained true to themselves, and Meyboden is even today closer in feeling to Paula Modersohn-Becker than to Kokoschka (psychologically his paintings are reminiscent of the Rilke of *Malte Laurids Brigge*, and formally of the early Bonnard). The dreamy arabesques of his interiors emanate an old-fashioned meditativeness. Gotsch has preserved the tragic attitude toward life that led him originally to Munch, but his forms no longer have anything to do with the Norwegian's work: they aim at the psychological shock. His *Girl with an Orange* (1956) reminds us of a Picasso of the 1930s, and his *Woman Artists* of the early Beckmann. At present his chances for public recognition are unfavorable: there is a tendency to regard as authentic only the unique. (Is there such a thing?) The use of pointed, piercing, unrestful forms even in the treatment of restful themes, of repellent colors even in family pictures, and the detachment of North-German Gothic art are essential features of Gotsch's recent work. He is closer to the northern German painters than to the Viennese Kokoschka, although his world is so much his own that no one could think of him as a successor to Beckmann.

Astonishingly little has survived of Surrealism in Germany, althoug Max Ernst (plate 93), who in 1922 moved from Cologne to Paris, has never been forgotten. For a time Heinz Trökes followed in his footsteps, and among the youngest painters, Manfred Bluth (b. 1926) may be regarded as his disciple. Mac Zimmermann (b. 1912) and Heinz Battke (b. 1900) are painters of the grotesque rather than Surrealists, and the term "grotesque," used in the sense of E. T. A. Hoffmann, may also be applied to the animal and human figures of Hans Jaenisch (b. 1907), which often possess a mysterious quality of humor. Whether Bruno Goller (b. 1901) belongs in this category is difficult to decide; the term "magic realism" may perhaps be applied with greater justice to his descriptive variations on Surrealist themes, as the head, the umbrella, the coffee mill, etc. His case is rather unusual, all the more so because his paintings often come close to those of the *peintres naifs*, or modern primitives, a group that has virtually no representatives in Germany. The only authentic Surrealists are the etcher Otto Coester of Düsseldorf (b. 1902), whose prints (portfolio *Zweierlei*, 1947) are witty and technically perfect, and Hans Bellmer (b. 1902), now living in Paris, whose variations on the theme of the Doll were begun in 1934 and resumed in 1949. Bellmer frequents the French Surrealist poets, and in 1947 his works were noted favorably at the great Surrealist Exhibition (Galerie Maeght). To these names one should add Richard

83   Georg Meistermann. 1958 (*Deutschland*)

Oelze (b. 1900; plate 94) who was active in America until 1939, was caught by the war in Germany, and at present works at Worpswede. He is a very able artist, represented in the Modern Museum of Art in New York, but practically unknown in his native land.

The younger generation today is in the camp of the so-called Tachistes, but before discussing the Tachistes, we shall mention a few younger artists who do not belong to any group. Meistermann (b. 1913), Heinz Trökes (b. 1915), and Hann Trier (b. 1915) are all talented painters who follow their own paths. All three come from Westphalia, a province which played a leading role in postwar German art. Meistermann (color plate 83) became known in 1950 when he was awarded the Blevin-Davies prize, in Munich, for his *New Adam*, a painting in the style of Picasso in his late period. Meistermann had achieved some recognition previously for his paintings on glass, and after the war he was commissioned to decorate some religious and secular buildings, among them the St. Kilian church in Schweinfurt and the Radio Building in Cologne. His large stained-glass windows are works of art just as are Woty Werner's woven designs; formally they are halfway between representation and imagination, and the composition is given a certain, not always predictable, logic by the leaded bars. Much the same may also be said of several of Meistermann's paintings before 1954, which treat, in part, the same theme as the windows (for instance, the fish-bird motif) and achieve their ambivalent effects by interweaving observed and invented elements. Painting on glass also taught him how to define space by means of juxtaposed planes, and in his *Groundplans* and *Spatial Plans* (1957–1958) he painted a fugue of juxta-position and succession, which embodies the theme of time. Recently a critic called his *Four Variations in Red* (1958) icons, for the well-calculated simplicity of surfaces and colors suggested to him something transcendent.

Since 1945 Heinz Trökes (color plate 81) has gone through many phases; he is a Ulysses rich in cunning, whose innate imagination, lightness, and freedom are qualities rarely encountered among German artists. He began as a Surrealist, as a close follower of his fellow countryman Max Ernst, and his paintings such as *Barbaropa* (1947) are legitimate contributions to Surrealism, born out of the chaos of the early postwar years in Berlin. Abstraction was for him only a short interlude; the Surrealist element will presumably always remain a crucial component of his work. Through his teachers Itten and Muche he is indirectly a pupil of Klee, and as one of the few who really understood Klee, he does not imitate him. But he shares Klee's delight in ways of painting that call forth associations, as well as the pleasure Klee took in experimenting in various directions simultaneously, and profiting from technical discoveries. At Ibiza (1952–1956) Trökes learned the essential qualities of color, and while his *Castle in the Air* (1953) and *Tropical Flora* (1955) still reveal the trained hand of the draftsman, they also reflect his insights into the relationship between color tones and color rhythms, which he captures precisely each time in accordance with what he has in mind. He does not execute ideas formed in advance, nor does he let himself be led away by his impulses and then surprised by the result. He is always inspired and controlled by the poetic element.

Meistermann obliterates the traces of the creative process from his finished painting; Trökes associates this process with poetry; Trier (plate 98) glorifies it. He paints his pictures in such a way that the viewer sees the process of painting itself. He began this in 1950, and has done it with increasing vehemence. One of his paintings of 1952 is called *Express Train*, others are *Bird in Flight* and *Vibration* (nine versions). In the latter the movement manifests itself first in only one or two directions, but gradually becomes a vibration that spreads out on all sides or gravitates around a center. In other paintings the vibration has no direction, and spreads over the color spots like a net or a black veil. The spots represent nothing, they are as though "written on the wind," as nature itself writes in tree tops, on rocks, on the sand of beaches. The technique conjures up the absolute, of which time is a function. *Zapateado* (1957), the name of a dance in three-quarter time, is a metaphorical title, given to a composition in which the representational elements are transformed into arithmetical but not geometrical figures: Time-Being, Art-Another World.

In such works Trier approaches certain experiences that Karl Otto Götz (b. 1914, plate 97) and K. R. H. Sonderborg (b. 1923, plate 100) have shown in a different way. These two artists were for some time regarded as related, until a joint exhibition in the Kestnergesellschaft (Hannover, 1956) clearly disclosed their differences. These are partly accounted for by their background. Götz made his debut 1933, Sonderborg in 1950; Götz went through Surrealism, while Sonderborg began with avant-garde experiments about 1950, studied with William Hayter in Paris in 1953, and found his own style at once; Götz has been interested in high frequency techniques, Sonderborg in nuclear research. But their differences also reflect different artistic predispositions: Götz is primarily a painter, while Sonderborg is equally interested in graphic elements. Beginning in 1950 the two painters catalogued their works merely by the date, for instance, "9.9.54;" Sonderborg even adds the time shown on the clock when the picture was completed. Opposites have always some point of similarity, if only—as in this case—a fondness for the monochrome.

Götz has built up his own idiom consistently and independently; in 1945 he compiled a *Primer* illustrated with many woodcuts, variations on a number of themes—a kind of pictorial grammar, which he used for his compositions, for instance a mural of 1950, reproduced in the magazine 'CoBrA' (the name stands for Copenhagen-Brussels-Amsterdam). Issue No. 5 of this magazine contained essays by him, and by Baumeister, Appel, Buchheister, Alechinsky, and others. Beginning in 1948 he published the magazine *Meta* at his own expense; its first ten issues contained pieces about a number of young artists, including Bryen, Sam Francis, and the Rhenish painter Müller-Kraus (b. 1911), who lives in Stockholm, and whose early works had points of contact with the woodcuts of the *Primer*. Götz has always been alert and well-informed; the poems he has chosen to print in his magazine are remarkable, including, in 1952 and 1953, works by René Char and Hans Arp.

All this has not prevented him from painting, and in 1952 he found his own idiom, with the broad expressive roads he is able to extract from the paint-drenched ground with rubber sponges and rags. Nothing can be revised in such works; he discards many sketches, making four and sometimes five attempts before a painting comes out as he wants it to. What we see in the final product, is the pattern of a hurricane or an eddy, always dynamic in the extreme, and pointing to those unfathomable regions of space in which dwells the ineffable.

Sonderborg paints chiefly on thick sheets of drawing paper, leaving some parts of them blank; he then marks up these areas of the surface with black India ink, and scratches in the internal contours with a razor blade or other suitable instrument. Whatever is still lacking is added with India ink. The results have the subtlety of Chinese drawings done with an India ink brush, and occasionally their character. Sonderborg is preoccupied not only with time and speed, but also with contemplation. It is true that his *Bohemian Rose* is not a rose, but it is just as miraculous and mysterious a thing, made of white traces as subtle as breath. A reproduction of Altdorfer's *Battle of Alexander on the Issus River* inspired a particularly beautiful sketch with spears, intersecting straight lines, and dots, as though he had tried to translate the meaning and essence of the masterpiece into his own language, and succeeded. Speed and repose, action and meditation, technology and "the pulsation of the heart," as he puts it: life as a paradox and art as the guiding thread.

Only a few contemporary German painters have followed other paths. Rupprecht Geiger of Munich (b. 1908, plate 105) has remained uninfluenced by his environment, and his paintings suggest that he is striving to extend Malevich's Suprematism on the basis of the more recent notion of space-time and a conception of color as an immaterial force which can record the slightest tremors. His works—done mostly in two colors, blue and black, for instance, with their crescendos and decrescendos, are as precise as a mathematical equation. Rudolf Mauke (b. 1924, plate 106), an outsider like Geiger, is younger, but already lends a distinct voice to the orchestra. A pupil of Schmidt-Rottluff, afterward a follower of the Mondrian style of 1913, he has produced incisive figurations, in which linear elements indicate the rhythms, and the colors, concentrated in one area, indicate the spatial relationships and their balance. As in the case of Geiger, these works reflect modern scientific preoccupations.

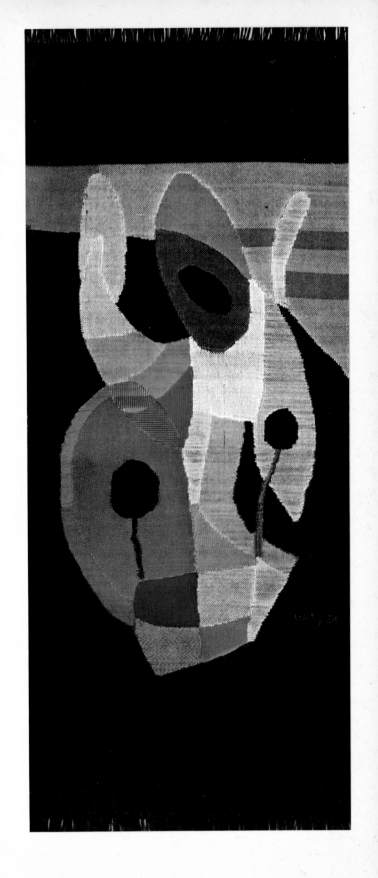

84 Woty Werner. 1956 *(Deutschland)*

In conclusion we shall deal with the Tachistes. Curiously enough, this term is used to designate a large number of painters who use color spots in a way that resembles that of the Impressionists, for example, Monet in his waterlilies or his series of Cathedrals. As usual in the history of art, a part stands for the whole.

The chief representatives of this movement in Germany are Bernard Schultze (b. 1915), Emil Schumacher (b. 1912), Winfried Gaul (b. 1928), Gerhard Hoehme (b. 1920), Fred Thieler (b. 1916), Karl Fred Dahmen (b. 1917), Otto Greis (b. 1913), and Heinz Kreutz (b. 1923); newcomers include Peter Brüning (b. 1929), Hans Platschek (b. 1923), Herbert Zangs (b. 1929), Klaus Fischer (b. 1930), Kurt Bartel (b. 1928), Erwin Bechtold (b. 1925), Albert Fürst (b. 1920), and many others. Westphalia leads the way here, too. Outside Germany the movement began somewhat earlier, during the Second World War, with Tobey, Pollock, Matthieu, Riopelle, Bryen, Wols; in Germany it began in 1952.

What this type of painting means will be clarified by individual examples. The first to apply its principles was Bernhard Schultze (color plate 82). When his paintings were shown for the first time, viewers were independently reminded of other paintings, for instance, Delacroix' *Death of Sardanapalus*. Some element in the rhythm or color or expression aroused such associations. The furrows in the green impasto suggested nature, streams, moss, underbrush; the streaks of yellow, fungus, the sea coast; lines in ocher, trails in the sand; occasionally the associations went back as far as Tiepolo. Photographs of the painting, dated 1955—photographs which exaggerated the relief effects produced by the thick layers of paint—suggested excavation sites or early Babylonian cavalry battles. And yet, in each case, the painter seems to have worked without any definite intention in mind—though not without a general conception. This conception, however, may have come to him while he was painting the picture; there is an element of chance in this, but it has to be controlled. However spontaneously the painter may proceed in such works, he must continually make decisions. What is exactly his purpose? He reduces the process of painting to its most fundamental components, to the raw materials themselves, and imprints upon them his vital experience, his experience of his own self and of his relation to the world. He does this directly, translating his impulses as he goes along, not in the form of linear elements but by laying on paint, continually breaking up the surface, modeling it, and choosing his means in such a way that they suggest the actual progress of his work, creating structures and fields of energy which end by evoking realities of the most various kinds. However much the paint (and occasionally the other substances used by the artist) may retain its quality of being raw material, the controlling activity of the painter produces entirely different effects. A red may suddenly begin to glow amid the chaos like a promise, and a brown rag evoke decay and death. Titles like *Riverbeds* (1927) or *Before Time* must not be taken literally, for the paintings say more than that.

85 Max Bill. 1955 *(Schweiz)*

At first Schultze exhibited with Greis and Kreutz, and in 1953 the three painters were friends; they differ from one another in temperament rather than in their basic approach. Kreutz is more lyrical, more given to revery, more Impressionistic: he occasionally reminds one of Bonnard. Greis's work was allied to Kreutz's, but at some point he took a different direction, and his most recent paintings bring him close to Alechinsky and to Chinese ink drawings. Such Oriental analogies recur time and again. Schultze is relatively more "obsessed" than the other two, more reckless, more dramatic, driven by and submitting to a kind of fate.

Similarly, Gaul (plate 101) and Hoehme (plate 102) had at first much in common, but in the course of the years they have followed diverging paths. Gaul comes closest to so-called abstract Impressionism; his paintings are spread evenly over the surface. They are not without articulation, they clearly show phases and centers of gravity, but they remain well-balanced both pictorially and psychologically. Some of them are symphonies in gray, reminiscent of certain portions of Monet's series of Cathedrals, and revealing an advanced technique. Even when Gaul envisions terror, he gives it a title such as *Splendor of Destruction* (1957). Hoehme is more extraverted, more violent, he digs into his colors, and pushes forward in various directions. In so doing he has become aware of the discrepancy between the vital character of the creative act and the limitations imposed by the traditional rectangular shape of the frame. He has broken out of this by painting on unstretched canvases, which he later hangs on the wall as pictures divided into several sections. He also paints objects with oils and lacquer, which he places next to the wall like totem poles or hangs on the wall like friezes. Whereas Gaul often gives an impression of serenity, we feel in Hoehme the presence of a demonic element.

As late as 1956 the works of K. F. Dahmen contained elements of construction, and even today we can sense in some of them the presence of scaffoldings, but increasingly these have yielded to an organization of the surface based on lights and shadows, and planes and reliefs. His black pictures are his most impressive; Dahmen is able to wrest the most harmonies from blacks.

For a time Emil Schumacher (plate 103) made "tactile objects" out of paper pulp, cardboard, and oils. These were irregular in shape and looked like fragments left behind by some cataclysm. His latest paintings suggest something similar. They make us think of cave paintings, of old walls with cracks and traces of decay, such as Leonardo da Vinci was fond of, and as Wols observed during his walks through Paris at night. Schumacher scratches up the surface and bores into it also producing the effect of various degrees of elevation by means of color, without transforming his paintings into reliefs. When he traces a line on such a "wall," it looks like a riverbed, not like the product of a human hand. He has a special talent for guiding his hand in such a way that it seems to guide itself. His works,

86 Karel Appel. 1953 *(Nederland)*

Hans Fischli (b. 1909) has introduced, through his works, several elements of the Bauhaus theory into Switzerland. Fritz Glarner (b. 1899, plate 110b) brought in Piet Mondrian's theories and those of the Stijl. Now living in New York, Glarner is at present the most successful Swiss sculptor abroad; in his paintings and drawings he has retained the Surrealist quality that characterized his early sculptures, which are among the most vigorous produced by Surrealism and by Switzerland. He is generally regarded as a member of the School of Paris, and only a very few persons know that he was and still is Swiss. The highly talented Walter Kurt Wiemken (1907–1940) might have achieved great distinction as a Surrealist had he not died at the age of thirty-three. In down-to-earth Switzerland Surrealism has gained a firmer foothold than in Germany; the country became something like a second home to Hans Arp, and painters such as Gerard Vulliamy (b. 1909), Hans Erni (b. 1909) Serge Brignoni (b. 1902), and Theo Eble (b. 1899), who has now become an abstract artist, as well as many others, have made important contributions to Surrealist art.

Since 1945 "concrete art" and Tachisme have come to the forefront in Switzerland. Recent exhibitions have revealed that painters of international rank belong to these two movements. Among those practicing "concrete art" are Max Bill (b. 1908), Richard Lohse (b. 1902), Leo Luppi (b. 1893), Walter Bodmer (b. 1903), and the previously mentioned Glarner (Sophie Täuber-Arp died in 1943). Tachisme is represented by René Acht (b. 1920), Charles Rollier (b. 1912), Franz Fédier (b. 1922) and Rolf Iseli (b. 1934). As can be seen, "concrete art" in Switzerland is represented by the fifty-year-olds, and Tachisme by the youngest generation.

According to Bill's definition, "concrete" art is an art "based on its own peculiar resources and laws, without any reference to nature, and does not arise out of a process of abstraction." Its basic premises are color, space, light, and movement. Concrete art strives for law, order, harmony; therefore it is also called "harmonical." It is both realistic and spiritual, non-naturalistic and yet close to nature; it aims at universality and yet cultivates uniqueness. This is more or less how Bill describes it. The term "concrete" goes back to Theo van Doesburg who used it in 1930; Kandinsky, too, used it in the 1930s.

Bodmer (plate 110a) is, next to Lohse and Moilliet, the oldest Swiss painter; in addition to paintings, he produces wire reliefs, and the two media are closely related. In his paintings, linear elements are superimposed like wires in the colors, and the contrast between the two produces vibration and an effect of space. In the reliefs, some of them painted, space is constituted by the configurations of the wires, and by their relationship to a wall or a montage replacing the wall. Bodmer's works are inspired by musical concepts, and partly by mathematical ideas, but even so they are anything but purely abstract.

Max Bill (color plate 85) goes one step further, championing "Mathematical Modes of Thinking in Contemporary Art"—the title of an essay of his in *Werk* of 1949. By this he does not mean an art based on computation, but on feeling and thinking. He regards mathematics as a means for gaining insight into the world, a science dealing with relationships and modes of behavior that cannot easily be communicated and that require a visual embodiment. The art which provides it need not be mathematically precise, but its vision must be true. Art explores realms that have never existed, and that are not formulable in terms of numbers; it fashions new rhythms, relationships, and laws, and creates symbols such as that of the limited infinite—i.e., deals with realities of interest to the present epoch, rather than expressing the artist's personal view of the world.

Bill's own paintings and sculptures confirm the truth of his theses. For instance, in one of his works, he represents visually a space that begins on one side, and ends in altered form on the other side, the second side being the same as the first. He represents limits that have no limit, fields of energy consisting entirely of variables, etc. In short, what he gives us is thought become form, insights perceived by the senses, primordial ideas rather than primordial images or archetypes. Although with Bill we are never in doubt of the successful outcome, each of his works has a stimulating effect. Paintings such as *Vibrating Colors on the Pythagorean Triangle* or *Construction with Two Similar Boundaries* have a mysterious quality for all their deliberateness.

As more and more things are explored, the realms of the unexplored and of the unexplorable grow vaster. Art remains a mystery, and its symbols remain irreducible. Planck once said that the complicated mathematical symbols that explain the world cannot be visualized. Art sometimes succeeds in lifting this veil, and in making visible that which cannot be made visible in any other way.

Boris Kleint. Variation No. 10

87   Alexander Camaro. 1953 *(Deutschland)*

88   Werner Heldt. 1952 *(Deutschland)*

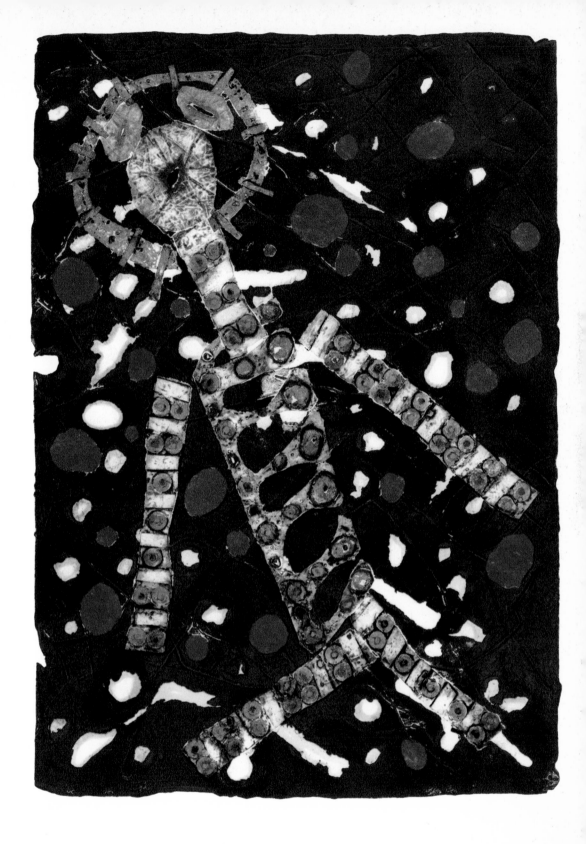

89   Rolf Nesch. 1954 *(Deutschland)*

90 H. A. P. Grieshaber. 1957 *(Deutschland)*

91 Werner Scholz. 1950 (*Deutschland*)

92 Friedrich-Karl Gotsch. 1956 *(Deutschland)*

93   Max Ernst. 1950   *(Deutschland)*

94 Richard Oelze. 1949–54 *(Deutschland)*

95   Joseph Faßbender. 1957   *(Deutschland)*

96a Eduard Bargheer. 1956 *(Deutschland)*

96b Margherita Russo. 1957–58 *(Deutschlan*

97   Karl Otto Götz. 1958 *(Deutschland)*

98   Hann Trier. 1957 *(Deutschland)*

a Max Ackermann.
1957 *(Deutschland)*

b Julius Bissier.
1958 *(Deutschland)*

100   K. R. H. Sonderborg. 1958 *(Deutschland)*

101   Winfred Gaul. 1957   *(Deutschland)*

102   Gerhard Hoehme. 1957 *(Deutschland)*

103 Emil Schumacher. 1957 *(Deutschland)*

104 Fred Thieler. 1958 *(Deutschland)*

105   Rupprecht Geiger. 1957 *(Deutschland)*

106   Rudolf Mauke. 1958 *(Deutschland)*

07 a
osef Mikl.
057 *(Österreich)*

07 b
ritz Hundertwasser.
057 *(Österreich)*

108a Carl Unger.
   1957 (Österreich

108b Karl Anton Wolf.
   1958 (Österreich

109   Varlin. 1955 *(Schweiz)*

110a Walter Bodmer. 1951 *(Schwei...*

110b Fritz Glarner. 1954 *(Schweiz)*

I.

The internationalism of modern art makes it difficult for the critic to claim a distinctive type of art for his own country. There is no British art since 1945 – there is an art, more **vigorous** than any art Britain has known since the death of Turner (1855), which has made a distinctive contribution to the world-wide movement of the arts. It will be my aim in this essay to describe the present situation of art in my country, but in order to bring out the significance of recent developments, I must first, in a very few words, describe the situation as it existed before 1945.

Great Britain did not contribute a single artist of international status to the great movements of the second half of the 19th century: we cannot claim Whistler, who was an American, and our native Impressionists, painters like MacTaggart and Sickert, never gained a reputation abroad that in any way corresponded to their provincial fame. We had our parallels to the Nabis and the Fauves, but when the Post-Impressionist exhibitions of 1910 and 1911 were held in London, the public was taken by surprise, so insular had its taste become. The further shocks of Futurism and Cubism followed soon after, but the only attempt to assimilate this new development, the Vorticist movement associated with the name of Wyndham Lewis (1882–1957), was abortive. Lewis himself, whose precise draughtsmanship did not compensate for a complete lack of essential painterly qualities, turned to portrait painting and literary satire. His inability to inspire a new movement in the arts – an inability due to defects of character rather than of talent – was one of the tragedies of the inter-war years.

The decisive change in the situation that took place between the wars was due to two or three native artists who, partly owing to the war, had no direct contact with the situation on the Continent – that is to say, the situation in Paris. The artist who has contributed most to the change – the sculptor Henry Moore – was born and educated in the provinces, and though he was to gain scholarships which took him to London in 1921 and to Italy in 1924, he had no studio experience in Paris or elsewhere outside England. The same may be said of the best painters of the inter-war years – Paul Nash and Graham Sutherland. They owed more to the English romantic tradition than to any external influence. In spite of superficial elements of modernism, they descended from Turner rather than from Matisse or Picasso. If they were to flirt with the disreputable muse of Surrealism, as Paul Nash did, it was with the conviction that that movement was essentially English – William Blake had been its first prophet.

By 1933 a group of English painters, sculptors and architects with what then seemed to be a common purpose had begun to emerge – it called itself Unit One, and in a publication devoted to its aims and early achievements which I edited in 1934 I could already use the word "international" to characterise its aims. "In architecture, and in sculpture as well as in painting," I observed in my Introduction to this volume, "a new awareness of the real purpose or function of the arts has been slowly evolved during the last fifty years, and this consciousness is international in its extent. Whatever happens in England will be part of what is happening in Europe and America generally, and though there is still room for local differentations (most obviously in architecture owing to different climatic conditions) yet such differentations will take place within a coherent movement of worldwide scope."

That prophecy has been fulfilled in the intervening twenty-five years, and the war which occupied six of those years did a good deal to integrate English art with the international movement. This was not a consequence of war itself, which is always destructive of art, but was due to the creation of certain institutions designed to educate or entertain the armed forces, or to "project" British culture among war-time allies or nations whose friendship seemed desirable to the Government. For these purposes the British Council and the Council for the Encouragement of Music and the Arts[3] were established (in 1934 and 1939 respectively), and their general effect has been to give the British artist a patronage such as he has not enjoyed since the Middle Ages. State patronage can be deadly, but the British constitution has evolved that anomaly among political institutions, the chartered corporation, and both Councils are established on this basis, which means that their financial subvention is controlled in gross and not in detail, and that within the limited duration of the funds thus provided the piper is free to play his own tune. Under enlightened guidance these two institutions have brought the contemporary art of other countries to Britain, where it can be seen and studied by British artists; and they have sent British art to other countries, where it can be measured against the highest prevailing international standards.

By 1945 this system of interchange was firmly established. The British Council was charged with the administration of such international events as the Venice Biennale, and in the first postwar exhibition, in 1948, Henry Moore was the principal exhibitor, and he was awarded the International Prize for sculpture. It was the beginning of a new epoch for British art. British art, after a hundred years, had once again achieved international status.

The immediate postwar situation in England should next be realised. The bombing of London has dispersed the artists, and many of them who found the country to their taste were never to return. Henry Moore settled about fifty kilometres to the North of London; Ben Nicholson and Barbara Hepworth went much further away, to St. Ives in the West of Cornwall. Graham Sutherland went to Kent, and since the war has lived for part of every year in the south of France. These facts, which might seem trivial, account for the

222

111   Ben Nicholson. 1957 *(Great Britain)*

characteristic individualism of British artists. There ist no "school" *of* London, and whatever artistic activity there is in postwar London, centres round the schools *in* London, and in the Institute of Contemporary Arts, which was founded in 1947 with the specific intention of providing a meeting-place for artists and their friends. In general, however, British artists have preferred to develop their talents "in der Stille."

During the war, as a consequence of the official patronage already mentioned, a number of artists were enlisted to make official records, and from this experiment there remained, for postwar reflection, at least three remarkable achievements – the shelter drawings of Henry Moore, the aerial landscapes of Paul Nash, and the sketches of furnaces and mines made by Graham Sutherland. None of these achievements had any direct bearing on the war: in each case the artist expressed an obstinately personal vision. Moore's recumbent figures are images of the archetypal womb, in which life itself seeks shelter from external stress. Nash's wrecked aeroplanes are symbols of a defeated attempt to mechanise life; and Sutherland's fiery furnaces are alchemical in their significance and assert the presence of spirit in matter. All these "engaged" artists took evasive action, and subdued the occasion to their artistic will.

In describing the masterpiece among his war paintings, the large *Battle of Britain* now in the Imperial War Museum, Nash wrote: "To judge the picture by reference to facts alone will be unjust to the experiment. Facts, here, both of science and nature are used "imaginatively" and respected only in so far as they suggest symbols for the picture plan which itself is viewed as from the air. The moment of battle represents the impact of opposing forces . . .". Commenting on this painting and on another of its kind, Sir Kenneth Clark told the artist that "in this and in *Totes Meer* you have discovered a new form of allegorical painting . . . You have discovered a way of making the symbols out of the events themselves, which I think very important!"[4]

A "new form of allegorical painting" would serve as a general description of whatever positive character British painting possessed at the end of the War. It should be remembered that immediately before the War, 1936–9, a belated effort had been made to establish a Surrealist group in England, and both Moore and Nash, though not manifesting any doctrinaire adherence to the movement, were sympathetic participants. But in England, as elsewhere, Surrealism did not survive the war as a coherent movement, and the English artists gladly relapsed into a more original individualism.

This individualism imposes on the art critic a piecemeal treatment of British art. One can trace influences from artist to artist, but they have no coherent character, and our greatest artists, Henry Moore for example, have perhaps had more influence abroad than at home. Let us begin with Henry Moore, for he is not only the most outstanding British artist of our time, but one who is at the same time characteristically British.

112 Graham Sutherland. 1952 *(Great Britain)*

II.

The main outlines of Moore's development are by now well known, and the only purpose in retracing them here is to emphasise the uniqueness of the position he had achieved by 1945. Moore, like every great artist, is a meeting point of diverse influences, influences which are assimilated and transformed. He has never disguised the debt he owed to the early sculpture of Picasso and Archipenko, and, perhaps mediated through Jacob Epstein, to the sculpture of Modigliani, who in his turn had been influenced by African sculpture. More potent influences came from the Mexican and Sumerian sculpture Moore studied in the British Museum, and from the early Italian painters, particularly Masaccio, whom he studied in Italy in 1925. He has even acknowledged a debt to the sculpture of the Saxon churches in the North of England with which he was familiar as a youth. But all these influences, and others I may not have mentioned, would have ended in a superficial eclecticism but for the all-powerful plastic sensibility which assimilated them to the form as such, and rejected all the surface excrescenses due to the mannerisms of period or personality. Moore has described how he has also been influenced by natural forms – bones, shells and pebbles – and he remarks that "out of the millions of pebbles passed in walking along the shore, I choose out to see with excitement only those which fit in with my existing form-interest at the time. A different thing happens if I sit down and examine a handful one by one. I may then extend my form-experience more, by giving my mind time to become conditioned to a new shape." For pebbles we may substitute the various works of art which Moore has studied: some have fitted in with his form-interest at the time; others have enlarged his form-experience. Throughout his development, what has developed is an innate response to three-dimensional form.

During the war Moore's sculptural output had been much restricted, but in 1943–4 he achieved, after many preliminary sketches, a work which marked a climax in his career – the Northampton *Madonna and Child*, a seated figure in Hornton stone 59 in. high. At one and the same time it represents a summary of his development up to the end of the war, and presides over his development since 1944. Its naturalism, relative to the extremes of abstraction that had immediately preceded the war, seemed to indicate a return to figurative humanism – a prediction (for some people a hope) that was not to be fulfilled. To think of Moore's work in ideological terms is to show a complete misunderstanding of its formal constancy. Moore has declared that for him "the humanist organic element will always be . . . of fundamental importance . . . giving sculpture its vitality." On the same occasion ("Notes on Sculpture," 1937) he suggested that his sculpture was becoming less representational, more abstract, because "in this way I can present the human psychological content of my work with the greatest directness and intensity." Naturalism and abstraction, form and vitality, represent for Moore, as for all great artists, the two terms

226

of an endless dialectic, and the one cannot triumph over the other without destroying the harmonious unity that characterises a great work of art. From this point of view one might say that only an artist capable of the abstraction of the stringed figures of 1939 would have been capable of holding in such perfect tension the folds and bosses of the *Madonna and Child* of 1944.

The postwar period begins with a series of *Family Groups*. The first sketches date from 1944, and the conception emerges naturally from the *Madonna and Child*. There were no less than fourteen sketch models in terra cotta made in the latter part of 1944 and the early months of 1945. The earliest of these was developed into the stone *Family Group* of 1954–5 now erected in Harlow New Town. One of the latest became the model for an edition of seven large bronze groups (H. 60 in.), of which one is in the Tate Gallery, another in the Museum of Modern Art, New York. Further versions of this theme, to be cast in bronze, followed in 1946 and 1947. Meanwhile Moore resumed the theme to which he has been most constant, the *Reclining Figure* (plate 121), dormant since 1940. Fourteen terra-cotta sketches and three bronzes were produced in the year 1945. Some of these were sketches for the *Memorial Figure* designed for the garden of Dartington Hall, Devon (1945–6), or for the gigantic *Reclining Figure* in elm wood (L. 75 in.) now at the Cranbrook Academy of Art, Bloomfield Hills, Michigan. In general treatment (massive rhythm and serene humanism) the Dartington figure achieves the same formal synthesis as the Northampton Madonna, but the Cranbrook figure with its attendant sketches marks the beginning of a new plastic theme – the correlation of external and internal forms. This theme was to receive its final expression in the still more gigantic *Internal and External Forms* of 1953–4 (also in elm wood, H. 103 in.) which was acquired by the Albright Art Gallery, Buffalo, U.S.A. As an archetype this theme is an extension of the "great Mother" theme which has been Moore's obsession since his beginning: it is a foetal image, the child enveloped by the mother. It is perfectly combined with the reclining figure motif in the bronze *Working Model* of 1951, which developed into the *Reclining Figure (internal and external forms)* of 1953–4 (plate 122). A minor variation of the theme is represented by the lead *Helmet Heads* of 1950 with variable interiors.

Hardly a year has passed without its series of Reclining Figures, and it is significant that when in 1957 Moore had to decide on a theme for the monumental sculpture commissioned for the new headquarters of UNESCO in Paris, after much deliberation and experiment he again chose this theme.

It is impossible to review all Moore's creations since 1945, but mention must be made of two significant pieces. One is the bronze *Standing Figure* (87 in.) of 1950, conceived for a landscape setting (one of the edition of four has been erected on a rock on the bare open moor at Shawhead, Dumfries, Scotland). This is the first of a series of columnar figures, rather like totem poles. The Shawhead figure is derived from a human model; some recent figures of a columnar form (1956) are more vegetal in their inspiration. Another piece that must be mentioned is the bronze *King and Queen* of 1952–3 (plate 123). of which there are five copies, one on the same moor at Shawhead in Scotland, one in Middleheim Park, Antwerp, the others in private collections. The impressiveness of this group, which in form is a development of the Family Groups of 1945–9, is due to the emission of a chthonic power or mystery, concentrated in heads reminiscent of Mycenaean pottery grave-figures, but a power and a mystery that is diffused in every detail and outline of the group.

Moore's creative energy is undiminished, but in more than thirty years he has accumulated an *Oeuvre* that is unrivalled for its consistency and integrity. The contributing influences have long ago been merged into the flow and force of his original genius, and we can now discern, not one more variation of modernism, only significant as part of a complex movement, but an independent achievement, universal in its appeal. This universality is no doubt due to the artist's immediate contact with archetypal images of whose significance even he is not necessarily aware. The instinct that leads him to the reclining figure and makes this the obsessive image of his career is a sure one: it corresponds to a general desire to identify vague unconscious desires with an "objective correlative," with an external symbol of enduring matter. We, the artist's public, find these vague desires materially satisfied or visibly incorporated in an icon, a object we can touch, or occupy with our plastic sensibility. The form of the object is at the same time aesthetically satisfying, pleasurable to the senses, and we therefore enjoy the moment of identification. It would be superficial to identify this process with a vicarious sexual satisfaction: the underlying desire is more primeval, for the Reclining Figure represents the procreative Mother, life-giving and life-preserving, whose image, always latent in the human psyche, emerges again and again in the history of art. This eternal feminine principle dominates every culture, but only rarely is it so clearly and so consistently manifested in the work of a single artist. Moore has been capable of this revelation, not because he has made a conscious attempt to give his work an archetypal significance, but rather because, of all artists powerfully endowed with aesthetic sensibility, he is one of the most unsophisticated. By comparison the self-conscious peasantry of a Brancusi is manneristic.[5]

Such archetypal forms must necessarily be projected from the unconscious, and for that reason Moore has not had facile disciples. Some of the superficial characteristics of his style have been imitated, especially abroad, but in England he remains without a rival, and with no successor. The sculptor who must always be associated with him, because of her similar origins and training, is Barbara Hepworth, but the very fact that she is a woman would preclude any fundamental similarity. In fact her work, which has certain technical

113　Victor Pasmore. 1958　(*Great Britain*)

characteristics that resemble Moore's (pierced forms and stringed figures) is essentially different in style. In spite of an obvious but superficial charm, the underlying archetype is masculine, the Vertical Man rather than the Reclining Woman, and the basis of the style is geometric rather than organic. The curvilinear rhythm of many of the forms does not alter the fact – the circle is also a geometric form, and many organic forms, such as crystals and tree trunks, are geometric. The contrast I wish to make in this connection is not between organic and geometric form, but between forms that are constructive and forms that are projected. Moore's sculpture is an art of internal necessity (to use Kandinsky's phrase); Barbara Hepworth's sculpture is an art of external harmony. During the war she was in close touch with Naum Gabo, a hightly conscious Constructivist; but long before she knew Gabo or his work, in the early Torsos of 1932 and 1933, the tendency is to give the human figure a columnar construction, sexually epicene. During the war her work was consistently geometric and rarely, and then only remotely, related to the human figure. At the beginning of the postwar period we find the miraculous calm of a form like *Pelagos*, a calm evolved from a perpetual self-contained movement. The subsequent years have seen a return from time to time to anthropomorphic figures, such as the *Two Figures* of 1947–8, the colossal *Contrapuntal Forms* (H. 120 in.) of 1950 (commissioned by the Arts Council for the Festival of Britain and now owned by Harlow New Town), and the *Vertical Forms* ($65^1/_2$ in.) commissioned for Hatfield Technical College. But even in these humanistic forms, the tendency is towards a vital geometry rather than an archetypal symbol. And always the vertical reasserts itself against the horizontal – in willed opposition to recumbency. *Image* of 1951–2, a carving in Hopton Wood Stone (H. $58^1/_2$ ins.) represents the perfect fusion of humanism and geometry. Other recent works are of a strictly geometric conception – for example. the *Curved Form (Delphi)* of African mahogany, 1955 (plate 124) and the moulded *Curved Form (pavan)* of 1956.

Barbara Hepworth has always accepted the discipline of direct carving, and this technical restriction gives to her work a precision that is lacking in the moulded and cast sculpture which most of the younger sculptors in England indulgently practise. An exception is Robert Adams (b. 1917), whose work in stone, wood or metal has the same precision as Barbara Hepworth's, though the forms are less organic. He cannot be called a Constructivist because his approach is still from the figurative image; but he carries geometricisation to the limits of abstraction. Some of his recent bronzes have the tense power of early Chinese ceremonial bronzes and jades.

Adams's recent preference for metal as a material for sculpture is in line with a general tendency among the sculptors in England. In the case of Reg Butler (b. 1913, plate 125) this springs from training and experience – he was educated as an architect and during the war worked as a blacksmith. But in general (and the generalisation includes Butler)

230

this tendency is due, firstly to the example of Alexander Calder, and then (a generalisation which would include Calder) to an appreciation of the early metal sculptures of Picasso, Gonzalez and Brancusi. More recently this tendency has been diverted from its more Cubistic or Constructivist aims by the powerful influence of Giacometti, of which more later. When Butler at the end of the war turned from practical ironwork to metal sculpture, he used his material to create vitalistic images rather than geometrical constructions – in fact, now that this sculptor seems fully committed to the sensuous representation of the human form, it is easy to see that from the beginning his figures, wrought from wire and sheet metal, and insectlike rather than human, were nevertheless essentially organic. What gave a general impression to the contrary was the geometrical scaffolding of his prize-winning design for the monument to the *Unknown Political Prisoner* (1952). In the maquette for this monument, especially when reduced in scale for reproduction, the symbolic tower completely dominates the figures of three women on the rock base. But the monument was designed for a minimum height of 100 ft., and even a height of 300–400 ft. was contemplated by the sculptor. When erected, the spectator will be far more conscious of the three figures, of more than life size, standing at the base of the tower.

The fundamentally humanistic intention of the sculptor was clearly expressed in the description that accompanied the maquette. "Unlike the Cenotaph and other similar monuments to the Unknown Soldier of the 1914–18 war (this monument) is not a purely abstract solution to the problem. It consists of three elements: the *natural rock foundation* which provides a fundamentally 'natural' setting even where the monument may be sited in the centre of a city; *the three women* in whose minds the unknown prisoner is remembered and who set the whole dramatic context of the monument; and *the tower* intended as an easily identified symbol which both suggests the tyranny of persecution and the capacity of man to rise beyond it."

Further, the three women, the Watchers, "have been placed so as to establish the dramatic significance of the monument. The two outer figures are in a sense spectators, in some ways beyond the reach of the situation ... The third woman stands almost immediately beneath and certainly well within the dramatic focus of the tower, she is totally contained by the tension of the occasion, and in full correspondence with the spirit of the monument ... All three figures are intended both to establish and resolve the situation, and by their reference to human scale to develop in the spectator a sense of participation. The faces of all three women look upwards and the living spectator would by their presence be drawn into the same focus by the power and direction of their gaze."

In spite of these very clear directives, which accompanied the maquette and were published in the catalogue of the exhibition of the prize-winning entries, Butler's design was received in his own country with incomprehension, a state of mind which the critics did nothing to dispel. It was treated as a work of extreme modernism, whereas it was intended to be, and is, "a powerful, easily identifiable symbol." The monument has not yet been erected, although at the time of writing a site has been offered by the municipality of West Berlin and there seems to be a definite prospect of the work finally being realised with its intended form and scale.

Since 1952 Butler has developed in the direction of an expressionistic humanism, taking the female form as his dominant theme. His female is a "girl" rather than a mature woman, and he models her in every kind of posture, standing, sitting, bending, stretching arms above the head, legs akimbo, tumbling on her back, or caught like a chicken on a spit, in a geometrical frame (*Figure in Space*, *Study for Falling*). The sensuousness, not to say the sensuality, of these figures is their most striking characteristic. The place they occupy in modern sculpture is in the tradition of Degas and Renoir and has little to do with the contemporary work of either of his elders, Moore and Hepworth, or his contemporaries, Lynn Chadwick and F. E. McWilliam (b. 1909) or of younger men like Armitage and Paolozzi. At the same time Butler's work is in no sense retrogressive. A certain sadistic quality, an exasperated sensuality (best revealed in his drawings and lithographs) brings it into line with that development of sensibility which is characteristic of all the arts in postwar Europe. In a note written for the catalogue of the British works at the 26th Biennale (1952) I suggested that the kind of images projected by the younger generation of British sculptors belong to "the iconography of despair, or of defiance," and in this sense Butler was typical of the whole group. I described their work as "images of flight, of ragged claws, 'scuttling across the floors of silent seas,' of excoriated flesh, frustrated sex, the geometry of fear. Gone for ever is the serenity, the monumental calm, that a Winckelmann had imposed on the formal imagination of Europe; gone, too, is the plastic stress of Rodin . . . These young men express their immediate sensations, sometimes with an almost sophisticated grace (Butler), sometimes with a scorn of bourgeois 'finish' (Paolozzi). Their art is close to the nerves, nervous, wiry. They have found metal — in sheet, strip, or wire rather than in mass — their favourite medium. Picasso had anticipated them, as he has anticipated us all, but these British sculptors have given sculpture what it never had before our time – a linear cursive quality. From Calder some of them have taken the notion of movement in sculpture (Chadwick). The consistent avoidance of massiveness, of monumentality, is what distinguishes these epigoni from their immediate predecessor, Moore. They have seized Eliot's image of the Hollow Man, and given it an isomorphic materiality. They have peopled the Waste Land with their iron waifs."

I was attributing to these younger British sculptors a collective unity which they would not have acknowledged, and which perhaps they never possessed, and in the six years that

114   Ivon Hitchens. 1956 (*Great Britain*)

have passed since I wrote these words Butler has, a I have just said, emphasised the essentially plastic nature of his work. Nevertheless, he has not abandoned what I called "the geometry of fear," and in a work like the *Figure in Space* of 1956 the sensuous figure of the girl is tossed like a tortured and abandoned corpse on the geometrical grid.

Lynn Chadwick, (b. 1914, plate 126), who was awarded the International Prize for Sculpture at the 1956 Biennale, has also moved away from the linear to the massive, without, however, sacrificing the harsh and angular forms of his early work. This early work was strongly influenced by Calder, but was always more aggressive and dramatic than Calder's work, which is uniformly organic and graceful. Chadwick, like Butler, came to sculpture comparatively late in life, and like Butler had an early training in architecture. It was only at the end of the war that he decided to turn to this other art. During the war he had been a pilot in the Fleet Air Arm, and it is perhaps not too fanciful to suggest that this experience of moving in space had some influence on his conception of "mobile" sculpture. But the work that emerged was in no sense mechanical – it was intensely vital and even humanistic. There was always a suggestion of an animal form in the early "balanced sculptures," of a swordfish or a scorpion, and latterly the forms have become recognisably human. The underlying structure is always metallic – forged iron frameworks carrying, perhaps, an immense ingot of coloured glass, and latterly (from 1953 onwards) filled in with a cement made from a plastic material mixed with iron filings to form a solid angular mass. The iron frames are still evident, like stretched tendons, and articulate a human form, or an animal form, that expresses a peculiar power, a contained "presence," like the animals painted thousands of years ago by prehistoric man on the walls of the caves.

Chadwick's formal imagination is intense rather than varied, limited to the isolation and perfection of a single image (the same might be said of Giacometti's imagination). This image is not archetypal in the sense that it derives from and represents some collective experience (as do Moore's characteristic images); rather it is a concentration of instinct, a canalisation of the life force itself. Its analogies are with the "animal style" of the Scythians, with Celtic ornament, with the Rock paintings of the Bushmen and the Australian aborigines. Compared with Butler's recent sculpture it is an anti-humanist art.

The same cannot be said of Kenneth Armitage's art. Two years younger than Chadwick, he too first came into prominence at the 1952 Venice Biennale. He has worked almost entirely in bronze, and has confined himself to the human figure, usually in groups – *People in a Wind, Walking Group, Family Going for a Walk*, etc. These groups show acute observation, and witty comment. There is an element of caricature, always dangerous in sculpture, for caricature is for a quick glance, not for permanent contemplation. But Armitage, like Daumier, does not rest at the superficial level of caricature, but

234

proceeds to a formal invention of deeper significance. There is an integration of movement and mass in the walking groups which is reminiscent of Rodin's *Burghers of Calais*; and in the more recent and less recognisably human figures there is a tortured sense of stretched tendons and taut muscle which again suggests a geometry of fear. The deformations wrought on the human frame by all these sculptors are deliberate humiliations of the human or animal frame, inspired by the prevailing sense of the absurd. But as Camus has said, if I judge a thing true I must preserve it. Modern art, like existentialist philosophy, is an unceasing struggle to confront the anomalies of being without forcing, or "faking," a solution. This struggle implies "a total absence of hope (which has nothing to do with despair), a continual rejection (which must not be confused with renunciation), and a conscious dissatisfaction (which must not be compared to immature unrest) . . . The absurd has meaning only in so far as it is not agreed to."

One begins to see (in the images proliferated by these new sculptors) how this new humanism differs from the traditional humanism. The old humanism, by ignoring the anomalies of existence, could present an ideal form, a perfect frame, the Greek god-man. But as Camus points out, the very scale of the human body is inadequate. Camus takes the drama as an example of the necessary deformation that truth demands – not only the mask and the buskin, the make-up that reduces and accentuates the face in its essential elements, the costume that exaggerates and simplifies – but the physical deformation that the acting out of the passions demands, so that the stage, in *Lear* for example, becomes peopled by madmen – "no fewer than four madmen: one by trade, another by intention, and the last two through suffering – four dismembered bodies, four unutterable aspects of a single condition!"

Armitage's recent sculptures (as the recent paintings of Francis Bacon and William Scott, to which I shall presently turn) are to be considered as the unutterable aspects of the human body. The impulse to project such images is not philosophical – one might say, rather, that such an activity replaces philosophy. The problem is one of consciousness, of cognition, of presentation; to reflect on the absurd is already to veil its reality. "For the absurd man it is not a matter of explaining and solving, but of experiencing and describing. *Everything begins with lucid indifference.*"

This phrase of Camus' which I have emphasised is the key to the understanding of the art we are now concerned with. Chadwick and Armitage create their images with the necessary creative passion; but they are indifferent to the irrationality of the world they create. It is not for the artist to make sense of the world's absurdity, but to be the authentic witness to its diversity. Art is not an instrument of understanding, but of consciousness. It is the presentation of the concrete, of the sensuous, of the carnal. Armitage's later works are dramas of the flesh, conflicts of bone and flesh, of the skeletal and the visceral; and they signify nothing more than the absurdity of the body that the human spirit is condemned to occupy.

The crustacean images of Bernard Meadows (b. 1915) belong to the same climate. Meadows was for a time a pupil and assistant of Henry Moore, but though some of his early works are related to the hollowed and pierced forms of Moore, the resemblance is superficial. Meadows exploits bronze with a fantasy that is essentially baroque, and therefore playful. He is perhaps nearer to Lipchitz than to any sculptor of the earlier generation, but Picasso again (the Picasso of *The Girl with a Cock*, 1938) has been a decisive inspiration.

William Turnbull (b. 1922) and Geoffrey Clarke (b. 1924) also belong to the metallic school. Clarke's work is predominantly linear in style and his talent is not confined to sculpture – he is one of the principal designers of the stained-glass windows for the new cathedral in Coventry. With Turnbull and Eduardo Paolozzi (b. 1924) we are once more involved in images of the absurd. But their images, unlike those of Chadwick and Armitage, are not vitalistic. They have some relation to the paintings of Dubuffet or De Kooning, or to the sculpture of César or Mirko. Again the omnipresent inspiration of Picasso is present (the Picasso of the *Baboon and Young*, 1951), and as in this bronze casting, there is a tendency to make use of ready-made objects – the piece of sculpture becomes a "collage" of rubbish, as in the *Merzbilder* of Schwitters. The intention is to create "an art in which the concrete signifies nothing more than itself" (Camus).

I have mentioned eight sculptors, all born between the years 1913 and 1924. They form a significant group, a generation with diverse personalities but a coherent Weltanschauung. Its analogies are with the existentialist literature of Camus and Sartre,[6] though there is no direct link. But both embody (and one must insist on that corporeal fact) an intellectual drama, in which the artist is engaged as a living being. The drama has no lesson to teach: it is the drama of man in the midst of an inhuman universe.

There are still younger sculptors whose names should be recorded in this chronicle: Hubert Dalwood (b. 1924), Leslie Thornton (b. 1925), Robert Chatworthy (b. 1928), Anthony Caro (b. 1924).

III.

The painters of the postwar period do not present such a coherent attitude. Paul Nash, who had been the most representative English painter of his generation, barely survived the war – he died on July 11, 1946 at the age of fifty-seven. There are painters older than Nash who survived the war and are still living who have had nothing significant to contribute to postwar developments. For that reason this is not the occasion to discuss the work of Augustus John or Sir Matthew Smith. Wyndham Lewis did not, in any vital sense, survive the First World War as a painter. His best work was always graphic. "Well-equipped

115   William Scott. *Britain)*

painter that nts a fellow painter,[7] "Lewis lacked, when he did not eschew them, the qy prized as 'painterly'. His pictures have no charm, neither melancholy mood in fact. They have nothing, at any point, to do with modishness y to come round to that in the future. The marvellous precision will note loss of grace in handling paint, nor is the colour, an act of will like all etimes wonderfully fine, any more in the line of English art-loving." Th was not in the line of any "art-loving," and when he died in 1957 he had ary and resentful, hostile to all who had shared the intellectual enthusiasms is significant that his only disciples are a few academic realists of extreme s

A companio m the Vorticist period (the 1912–14 period of Marinetti and the Futurists erts (b. 1895) who has consistently developed a Cubist idiom, applied to su e as socially "realistic" as any in contemporary British painting. A simila d subject-matter suggests a comparison with Fernand Léger, and as a cohe nt the work of Roberts is worthy of such a comparison. This painter has r he recognition that is his due; alone among English painters he has conso l nical inventions of the Cubist period.

The anomalo nley Spencer (b. 1891) must also be mentioned, for he is still an active and He should perhaps be considered as a belated Pre-Raphaelite – he has the P interest in faithfully-rendered detail, a predilection for vast symbolical ca indifference to charm that can only be matched by Wyndham Lewis. Adde sterous bucolic fantasy, and a naive trust in his own quasi-mystical visio ble to ignore his work, firstly because the imagery is popular and represen traditional English "humour"; and then because its positive qualities, how g to our current aesthetic taste, insist on creating their own standards of v respect they resemble the novels of John Cowper Powys, or even the arch udi.

I shall next g a number of painters who began in the same school of lyrical Impressionism ely indebted to Whistler, influenced occasionally by Bonnard and the late essionists (through the channel of Walter Sickert, Harold Gilman and V son), but who scrarcely survived the war in any recognisable unity. Some o s Ivon Hitchens (b. 1893, color plate 114) and Claude Rogers (b. 1907) have perfectly consistent development. David Jones (b. 1895) and William Colds) have not undergone any violent change of spirit, but their production is r spasmodic. The influence of the whole group survives in the schools, and it that all English painters now serve an apprenticeship to academic Impress nly serves to emphasise the decisive break made by one of this

116 Peter Lanyon. 1957 *(Great Britain)*

group, Victor Pasmore (b. 1908, color plate 113), who now leads, both as a painter and a teacher, a movement largely inspired by the Constructivist philosophy of the Bauhaus. Pasmore's conversion to Constructivism, which occurred in the year 1948–49, has been the most revolutionary event in postwar British art. To appreciate its significance one must realise the position Pasmore had come to occupy at the end of the war. It is neatly recorded in the Penguin volume on his work, written by Mr. Clive Bell, and published in 1945. In that volume he could be welcomed, by a critic of the old school, as a promise of sensuous French virtues in a cold Anglo-Saxon climate. The influence of Bonnard was observed and welcomed and it was asserted that though his nature rebels against theory and dogma, "essentially that nature is conservative, and allows him to sympathise, without doing any violence to a priori notions, with an essentially conservative reaction." Perhaps that last phrase acted as a warning; at any rate, no sooner was this record of his early "artistic temperament" out of the way than Pasmore proceeded to "enlarge his powers of expression" in a manner that dismayed his former admirers. He underwent the typical conversion process of the modern artist, proceeding from Impressionism to analysis, from analysis to synthesis, until he attained an art of pure form, the "new reality" of Mondrian.

On his way he passed, with scarcely a nod of recognition, the position occupied by the leading abstract painter in England, Ben Nicholson (b. 1894, color plate 111). Nicholson, the son of a distinguished painter of the Impressionist school (Sir William Nicholson) was himself influenced by Mondrian, but more obviously than Pasmore, his nature has rebelled against theory and dogma. His early work does not concern us here, for already by 1945 a personal style had been formed from which the artist has never deviated, though that style is nevertheless so flexible that it can still accommodate, alongside abstractions as pure as Mondrian, drawings and paintings of natural scenes and objects. The distinction which we make between reality and abstraction is, to Nicholson, not valid, and in the two volumes that have been devoted to his work,[8] he has deliberately reproduced side by side extreme examples of both styles to demonstrate their essential unity. A tree and a mountain, a jug and a table, a square and a circle — these are all objective shapes, and the artist can use them disinterestedly (that is to say, without pronouncing on their relative values as "real" objects) as elements in a composition which creates its own values – values of spatial harmony. The only dogma is an insistence on "objectivity" – that is to say, one must not confuse the issue, which is the creation of a distinct, self-subsisting harmony, with irrelevant emotional overtones. A human head, if the painter ventured to use such a shape, would be a definite bony structure with certain characteristics of color or movement, and not "the mirror of a human soul", or any subjective or expressionistic symbol. The business of art, Nicholson would say, is not to interpret being or existence; it has no function beyond the creation of visual delight. In a statement he made in June,

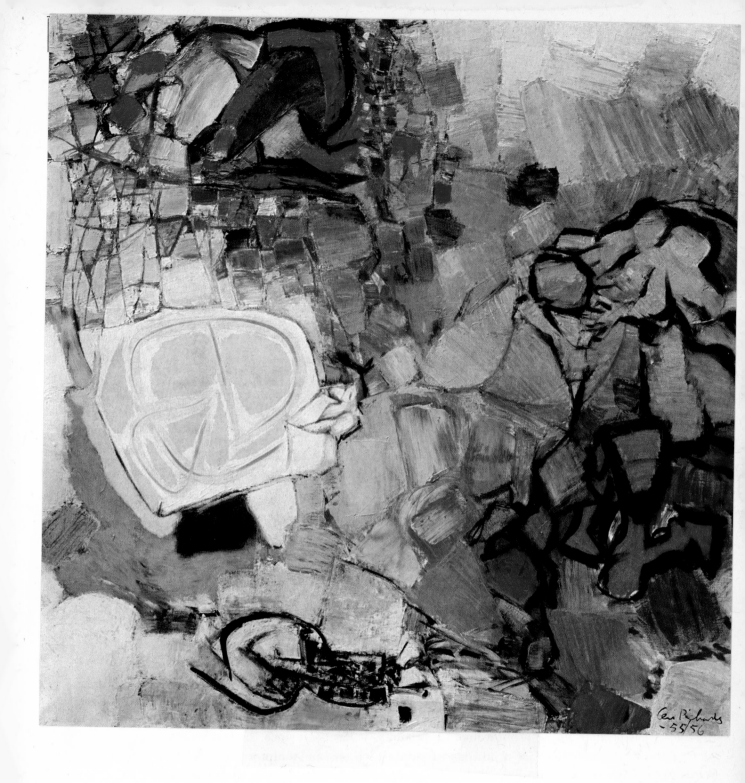

117   Ceri Richards. 1955–56 *(Great Britain)*

1948, Nicholson describes art as "a power peculiar to itself," and continues: "the kind of painting which I find exciting is not necessarily representational or non-representational, but is both musical and architectural, where the architectural construction is used to express a 'musical' relationship between form, tone and colour; and whether this visual, 'musical' relationship is slightly more or slightly less abstract is for me beside the point." In all good painting – all the paintings that he enjoys – it is "its superb organisation, its rhythm, its intensity," that make the reality in the paintings seem more alive than the life from which it springs.

"The life from which it springs" – the implication is that art, while based on observation, on life, is always an extension of life, an enhancement of vitality, an increase of the area or depth of consciousness. Certainly no art in our time has more inherent vitality than Ben Nicholson's, and if it is objected that nevertheless it has no relation to the social problems and preoccupations of our time, that it is an art of the ivory tower, the objection can be dismissed as irrelevant since, to repeat two phrases already quoted from Camus: "the concrete signifies nothing more than itself." "Creating or not creating changes nothing." The purpose of philosophy may, as Marx said, be to change the world, not to interpret it: but the purpose of art is neither to interpret nor to change the world, but to add to its concrete elements. Art is an extension, not an interpretation of experience; it is an increase in the scope of our cognition.

Since the war Ben Nicholson has been widely recognised abroad: he has exhibited in Paris, Brussels, Amsterdam, Zurich, New York, Washington, Detroit, Tokyo and San Paolo. In 1952 he was awarded the first prize for painting at the 39th international exhibition at the Carnegie Institute, Pittsburgh; he received the Belgian Critics Award in 1954 and the Governor of Tokyo award in 1955. The next year he was awarded the Grand Prix at the 4th International, Lugano, and in 1957 the newly established Solomon R. Guggenheim Award for Painting, which was presented to him by President Eisenhower. He has passed his sixtieth year with undiminished energy and zeal, and no European artist has maintained his own standards of integrity more consistently. It was many years before his own countrymen admitted the excellence of his achievement, and as often in our history, the first acknowledgement was to come from abroad.

Abstract art is perhaps not so proliferous in England as it has been since the war in other parts of the world, but there are a number of notable painters and sculptors, representing every variety of a movement, that still awaits precise classification. Few of them are Constructivists in Pasmore's now strict sense of the word, though the geometric mobiles of Kenneth Martin come into this category. They are explorations of the dynamic possibilities of matter, and of its deployment in space. They bear a superficial resemblance to Calder's mobiles, but are intellectual rather than organic in their inspiration. The abstract sculpture of Barbara Hepworth and Robert Adams has already been mentioned, and it should be reconsidered as an integral part of the abstract movement in England. This movement is still ambiguous in its ideals, and perhaps should remain so. Nevertheless, there is no possible compromise between the position occupied by Pasmore ("the ideal of imitating the experience of beauty gives way to that of creating and constructing it") and the ideal of a painter like William Scott (b. 1913, color plate 115): "I am an abstract artist in the sense that I abstract. I cannot be called non-figurative while I am still interested in the modern magic of space, primitive sex forms, the sensual and the erotic, disconcerting contours, the things of life".[9] They represent the irreconcilable extremes of art long ago demonstrated by Worringer in *Abstraktion und Einfühlung*. But even in Worringer's antithesis there was a common starting-point in nature – a movement away from nature and a movement into nature. The contemporary contrast is more uncompromising for at one extreme is a parthenogenesis, a creation from virgin sensibility; at the other extreme is a metamorphosis, a translation of visual experience into personal symbols. At one extreme the intellect itself is seeking sensuous embodiment in form and colour; at the other extreme a sensibility to form and colour is seeking an intellectual structure. Scott's paintings are a vivid illustration of the second process. No contemporary English painter has a closer sensuous relationship to the materials of his craft, or a more sensitive reaction to his environment. From this opposition (for the materials of the craft have their own life and form-values, which do not necessarily correspond to the life and form-values in nature), a synthesis emerges. The vitality of the object vibrates beneath the vital organisation of form and colour on the canvas.

There are several painters whose work is metamorphic in this sense — John Tunnard (b. 1900), John Wells (b. 1907), Clifford Ellis (b. 1907), W. Barns-Graham (b. 1912), Terry Frost (b. 1915), Bryan Winter (b. 1916, plate 129), Derek Middleton (b. 1917), Peter Lanyon (b. 1918, color plate 116), Patrick Heron (b. 1920), Peter Kinley (b. 1926), Donald Hamilton Fraser (b. 1929, plate 130), Harold Cohen (b. 1928, plate 131). They are not to be confused with another group whose work is essentially expressionistic – an emotionally charged deformation of appearances rather than a formal metamorphosis. In this group I would include Roy de Maistre (b. 1898), Ceri Richards (b. 1903, color plate 117), Robert Medley (b. 1906), Keith Vaughan (b. 1912, plate 132), Robert Macbryde (b. 1913), Robert Colquhoun (b. 1914), Louis de Brocquy (b. 1917, plate 133), and John Craxton (b. 1922). This classification is not meant to be final, and in their development the artists themselves are apt to move from one group to the other, or to belong to none. The work of a painter like Ceri Richards, which has never had the recognition it deserves, is musical and architectural in the sense that Ben Nicholson used the terms; it differs from Nicholson's work in that "musical" must be interpreted more spontaneously, and "architectural" less structurally. The result is a style nearer to Matisse than to Mondrian.

The artists of the "parthenogenetic" group are perhaps easier to identify, because they admit no compromise of any kind with natural subjects. Apart from Pasmore, they are represented by Roger Hilton (b. 1911, color plate 118), William Gear (b. 1915, plate 134), Adrian Heath (b. 1920), James Hull (b. 1921), Sandra Blow (b. 1925, plate 135), and Anthony Hill (b. 1930). But again a distinction begins to emerge, and the work of a very few of these painters (perhaps only Hill and Heath) tends towards the Constructivist extreme represented by Pasmore. Some of it, on the contrary, tends towards a type of art which is anathema to the Constructivist – to so-called "Tachiste" or "action" painting.

The British painters since the war have been cautions in their attitude to this new movement in painting: the *Times* critic described it as "essentially alien to the English tradition." Perhaps only Alan Davie (b. 1920, at Grangemouth in Scotland, color plate 119) can be regarded as a consistent Tachiste, though the recent work of his fellow Scotsman, William Gear, has been moving in this direction. Nevertheless, an exhibition of "meta-visual" painting held at the Redfern Gallery, London, in April, 1957, brought to light a surprising number of artists of this school (Dorothy Bordass, b. 1905; J. Milnes-Smith, b. 1912; Paul Feiler, b. 1918; Henry Cliffe, b. 1919; John Coplans, b. 1920; Denis Bowen, b. 1921; Gillian Ayres, b. 1930; Robyn Denny, b. 1930; Gwyther Irwin, b. 1931; Ralph Rumney, b. 1934) and to these we must add the names of Magda Cordell, Austin Cooper, John McHale, Frank Auerbach (plate 136), Frank Avray-Wilson, Richard Smith, and Norman Adams, b. 1927. It seems likely that, though belated, the Tachiste tornado will sweep over the country in the immediate future, leaving its colorful wreckage on a thousand canvases.

I have mentioned many names as yet internationally unknown, but the two names that are best known abroad have so far escaped my survey – Graham Sutherland and Francis Bacon. There is good reason for this – both artists are individualists and difficult to classify, though they have a significant relationship to each other. Graham Sutherland (b. 1903, color plate 127), began his artistic career as an etcher and book illustrator; in this phase, which lasted until 1930, he was directly inspired by William Blake and by Blake's follower, Samuel Palmer. Then from 1930 until the middle of the war he produced a series of landscapes, usually in gouache or water-colour, which he himself has called "paraphrases" – "I found that I could express what I felt only by paraphrasing what I saw." These landscapes, though they develop quite naturally from the work of Blake and Palmer, might be justly compared to the early (1910–12) "compositions" of Kandinsky. Then, whether induced by the war or not, about 1945 a new phase, characterised by emotional intensity and an almost masochistic acerbity of colour and prickliness of forms, begins to appear.

244

118   Roger Hilton. 1955 *(Great Britain)*

It received an immense impetus from the commission which he was given in 1945–6 to paint a *Crucifixion* for St. Matthew's Church, Northampton (the same church for which Moore's *Madonna and Child* had been commissioned). This masterpiece was preceded by a number of studies of other incidents of the Passion (the *Deposition*, for example) and of details of thorns and thorn-trees. The *Crucifixion* has been compared to Grünewald's, and has the same quality of morbid realism.

Soon after the war Sutherland began to spend part of each year on the Mediterranean coast, and there he found new material for his now tormented vision – the sharp pointed leaves of palm trees, tortured roots and tangled vegetation. These natural objects were always "paraphrased" into strange dream figures – reality became a "dispersed and disintegrated form of imagination." Sometimes these disintegrated forms recompose into a gruesome head, or tall totemic shapes, half-vegetal, half-crustacean. A whole world inhabited by such forms has now been created by Sutherland, and into their society he has introduced the portraits of a few distinguished human beings.

These portraits have gained Sutherland a popular notoriety that his normal work would never have brought him. They began, in 1949, with a portrait of the famous writer, Somerset Maugham; they include the most famous of all our contemporaries, Sir Winston Churchill. As to their merits, opinions differ, not least among some of the sitters. But no one denies that they are accurate representations of the physiognomies in question, or that they possess a power of their own as works of art. They are, indeed, presences as disturbingly potent as the totems already mentioned, and their very texture has the same inhuman surface. As I wrote on another occasion, these portraits "assimilate the human being to thorny, spicular forms of life, as though a first frosted sheath of crystallisation had already glazed the skin."

Sutherland's work, as Sir Kenneth Clark has observed, "represents a peculiarly English form of artistic creation – the moment of vision," and it is a form of creation that is not confined to painters, such as Blake and Palmer – it is the typical "inscape" of poets like Wordsworth, Hopkins and Hardy. A contemporary poet like Dylan Thomas offers a very close parallel, and many of Thomas's images, such as

> .... the round
> Zion of the water bead
> And the synagogue of the ear of corn . . .

or
> The dead oak walks for love
> The carved limbs in the rock
> Leap, as to trumpets. Calligraphy of the old
> Leaves is dancing. Lines of age on the stones
> weave in a flock . . .

119   Alan Davie. 1956 (*Great Britain*)

might be descriptions of Sutherland's paintings. The sensibility for landscape of this painter and this poet is almost identical.

It would be more difficult to find a literary parallel for Francis Bacon (b. 1910, plate 128), though Dostoevsky has been invoked, and since Dostoevsky owed a considerable debt to Dickens, the sinister aspects of Dickens's genius also might be relevant. If we go back to the nineteenth century, the name of Edgar Allan Poe would in my opinion be more to the point. Bacon's "figures" in their geometrical frames are pre-figured in the victim of "The Pit and the Pendulum," to whom there was "the choice of death with its direct physical agonies, or death with its most hideous moral horrors." The choice, in the case of Bacon's victims, is a death with the moral horrors. The Cardinal in some of Bacon's pictures might have been a member of the Inquisition that condemned Poe's hero. "The path of the destroying crescent," a phrase from Poe's tale, is the path of Bacon's rhythmic brush.

Many tributes have been paid to the technical skill of this painter, and in the sensitive manipulation of the paint on the canvas there is a deceptive cursive facility that may be impatient rather than intuitive. There is also a suggestion of the flash-light photograph, of the person or scene recorded in a split-second of perception, and Bacon may indeed have been influenced by the all-pervasive newspaper illustration, for there is also in some of his paintings a suggestion of smudged letterpress, of the grey actuality of our daily vision of life. Of all European artists Bacon has the most topical, and one might even say the most "existential" sense of facticity. It is difficult not to write of Bacon in existentialist terms – his work is motivated by what Sartre calls "the Look," and the best possible approach to Bacon's work is through a reading of § 4 of the first chapter of Part Three of *Being and Nothingness*, particularly the paragraphs about the "man on the lawn." The artist, like the philosopher, needs the Other in order to realise all the structures of his own being. He has therefore to confirm the existence of the Other, in order that eventually he may determine the relation of his being to the being of the Other. In philosophy the existence of the Other must be demonstrated logically, by the correct use of verbal symbols. In the visual arts the demonstration must be a correct use of images, or, since the images are incorporated in a plastic material, a correct use of icons. Bacon always seems to be engaged in defining the otherness of the man or dog, when that Other is observed without being aware of it, and is existing in a space which is not the space of the observer. "The Other," as Sartre says, "is . . . the permanent flight of things towards a goal which I apprehend as an object at a certain distance from me, but which escapes from me inasmuch as *it unfolds about itself its own distances*." This last phrase is a perfect description of the illusion created by Francis Bacon in his strange paintings.

Bacon, to the best of my knowledge, is not a philosopher: as in the case of Armitage, one might say that his painting activity replaces philosophy. I doubt if he has ever read Sartre;

120   Jack Smith. 1953 *(Great Britain)*

nevertheless, more pertinently than any other European painter, he seems to proliferate, "with lucid indifference," images of the absurdity of our being. His most recent paintings (1957) are richly coloured versions of self-portraits by Van Gogh. It is not difficult to understand why the "otherness" of this particular painter should obsess the imagination of Francis Bacon. The actual schizophrenia of the Dutchman makes him the prototype of all those who fly towards unrealisable goals.

At this point I must end my survey of British art since 1945, or the chart will become confused with unessential detail. The illustrations may include a few artists who are not mentioned in the text, but their classification will be obvious. Some of my compatriots may charge me with prejudice, in that I have not given prominence to some particular artist; and I am aware that a critic with a different taste or sensibility might have made more concessions to tradition. In particular he might have attempted to present a school of Realists, or Social Realists, represented by such names as John Bratby (b. 1928), Derrick Graves (b. 1927), Edward Middleditch (b. 1923, plate 137) and Jack Smith (b. 1928, color plate 120). These are all young artists of great talent, but in a publication that will include the work of painters in the same tendency from France, Belgium and Germany, their real character will be apparent. They do not represent a doctrinaire Social Realism such as prevails in Russia; they do not seem to me to constitute a uniform tendency of any kind. Each belongs, in an individualistic way, to a realist tradition that takes its subject matter from daily life in the Welfare State: it is socially conscious and politically exasperated like the contemporary drama of John Osborne. But as these four painters develop they separate from each other. Smith becomes more conscious of abstract values in composition, Bratby of surface textures and movement, whereas Graves and Middleditch relapse into academicism. There is no longer any collective coherence in their work, and their particular significance, as in the case of many other talented young painters, has still to be established. In general, British art since 1945 has kept to the tradition of individualism or eccentricity that has characterised its history since the Middle Ages – even groups like the Pre-Raphaelite Brotherhood were linked by idealistic sympathies rather than by artistic style. This is not in contradiction with its general emergence from provincialism to internationalism, for it is still possible to be an eccentric citizen of the world. Neither Moore nor Sutherland, Butler or Bacon, can be given the neat labels that are attached to artists in Paris or Berlin. But it could be said that every great artist is a unique artist, and that when we speak of schools or movements, we are trying to organise their followers. It is precisely in this sense that British artists refuse to be organised, to the despair of their friends abroad, and of doctrinaire critics everywhere.

The five years of the Second World War took a heavy toll among Dutch artists. Mondrian died in New York, far from his homeland, in 1944; Werkman, perhaps the greatest single artistic talent we possessed, fell victim to the Nazi terror in April 1945, just before the Liberation. Many of the painters and sculptors—among others, Gerrit van der Veen, Henk Henriet, Frits van Hall, and Johan Limpers—whose underground group was one of the most active, paid with their lives for their courage and love of freedom.

After the years of grief and anger, Dutch painting came back to life with the Liberation —weakened at first, but not broken. Many older artists had survived the years of terror, partly in exile and partly in hiding. The prewar movements that had given Dutch painting its original character were again in broad daylight: Expressionism with Sluijters, Wiegers, and Chabot; the very Dutch tradition of the Stijl group with Van der Leck; and the magic realists with Hynckes, Koch, and Willink. Furthermore, during the years of suffering, the works of several artists—especially those of the woman painter, Charley Toorop—had acquired new vigor. But all these works in effect belonged to the prewar period. As is even more apparent today, ten years after the Liberation, they were a magnificent late harvest of prewar Dutch art. After 1945, the generation which had been born between 1880 and 1900 still produced work of the highest quality, and is still producing them; but it no longer exclusively determines the character of postwar Dutch art.

The place of the older generation was taken by very young artists, born after 1920. This new generation not only pushed the old one into the background, it has also eclipsed the one directly preceding it, the generation born between 1910 and 1920, which was trained chiefly by Heinrich Campendonk, formerly professor of monumental painting at the Rijksacademie in Amsterdam. Campendonk, who is still insufficiently recognized as an artist, was an excellent teacher: he brought up a whole generation of talented young painters whose style, though influenced by his own austere, sometimes harsh, lyricism, is nevertheless independent and free from imitation, as can be seen from the works of Groenveld, Horn, Peters, Muis, and others.

The youngest generation, however, consisting of artists who were twenty-five or less at the end of the war, found its immediate precursor in the person of Ouborg, born in 1880. Before the war he was relatively unknown, having worked and lived in Indonesia for many years; comparatively few of his paintings had as yet made their way into Dutch collections. But after the war his art suddenly flowered, and he produced a number of small canvases in bright colors, highly spontaneous in composition and without reference to objects, expressions of colorful, dreamlike visions. Spontaneity of treatment, automatism of the pictorial script, and coloristic dynamism characterize these works, which first signaled a fresh departure in Dutch art, until then bounded by Expressionism on the one hand, and geometric abstraction on the other. Ouborg's period of flowering was short-lived; he soon fell ill, and died in 1954. An isolated figure to his own generation, he became an inspiration to the young artists who were decisively to influence postwar Dutch painting.

The Experimental Group—which included writers as well as painters—first came to public notice on the occasion of the so-called CoBrA exhibition at the Stedelijk Museum, Amsterdam, in 1949. At the suggestion of the Danish painter Asger Jorn (plate 142) artists from Copenhagen, Brussels, and Amsterdam (hence the name 'CoBrA') made their joint debut. The exhibition created a scandal, which many of us still recall vividly. The works were new, daring, even insolent, a cry of protest against routine and lack of inspiration. These young painters dared to couple abstraction with spontaneity, indeed, even with expressiveness, and this was too much for the majority of the public. Very few of the critics, and one or two older painters, among them Sluijters, recognized the vitality of these works. Of the new men, Appel, Brands, Rooskens, Constant, and Corneille (plate 140) were especially felt to hold out great promise.

During the ten years that followed, this minority judgment was confirmed; today, the talent of some of the new painters is no longer in question. At the same time the group has acquired distinctive features. Its center has now shifted to Paris, where its Danish, Dutch, and Belgian members have moved to join French and American artists of their generation. In the stimulating atmosphere of Paris they work intensively, and several painters who made their first public appearance at the Amsterdam exhibition, among them Jorn, Appel, Alechinsky, and Corneille, have gained international recognition. While the source of their inspiration remains the same as disclosed in the works exhibited in Amsterdam, the individual painters have developed their own styles and techniques, with occasional departures from what might be thought of as the collective idiom of the group. Some of them (for instance, Constant) have followed a different path, and become separated from the group.

How can the character of this group be defined in the light of the recent developments —in so far as one can still speak of it as a group? It seems to us that the works of these young artists, whose credo is directness and spontaneity, should be regarded as reflecting a kind of romanticism, reminiscent of the *Sturm und Drang* period, and directed against every sort of routine and academicism. Such movements recur periodically in the history of art; today it is the Dutch Experimental Group which expresses the modern protest against the smothering of spontaneity and unconscious drives by rules, taboos, conventions, and dead formulas.

Every movement of this kind bears the standard of youth, of rebellious youth. The vitality, the artistic fury which characterized the works of this group just after the Liberation, were those of overconfident young men who during the war had been compelled to hold their energies in check, and who after the Liberation wanted to build a radiant new world. It is the same impetuous temperament that manifests itself in a new form in Appel's paintings of recent years. In these works he is often successful in getting down the varied magic of his rich palette in large canvases. It is the magic of spontaneity, characteristic of all romanticism, that finds its expression in these paintings. But Appel is probably the only one among the members of the original Dutch group who has been able to sustain the vehemence of his first eruptions over the years.

After all, not everyone is capable of forever producing paintings charaterized by the elemental force which primarily arises out of the impetuousness of youth, out of the explosion of elemental artistic instincts. It is perhaps more normal that unrestrained natural forces should gradually find calmer outlets, that the current which at first plunges headlong down the steep descent should gradually smooth out in a broader channel, becoming less troubled, without becoming more shallow.

Roughly speaking, this is just what has occurred in the development of the Experimental Group. There are exceptions, as elsewhere in nature: some mountain torrents continue to rush on almost to the end of their course. But changes of rhythm, the transformation of the swift stream into a deep river, are inherent in almost every romantic movement. Eruptions, even of a volcano, are not normal phenomena of nature. Much the same may be observed of the Experimental Group. The predictions of the isolated critics and painters of 1949 have also been confirmed in this, that the talent of many of these young artists has proved invulnerable to the greatest danger that threatens youth—the passing of time. Corneille's works (plate 140)—he, too, exhibited in Amsterdam in 1949—show this change most clearly, a change that can best be described as a slow maturation. The vehement gestures, the elemental eruptions, the loud noises have now vanished from his painting; and yet he has preserved the freedom he has gained in the years of Storm and Stress. It also seems characteristic of his development that he confines himself to small canvases, which, however, he fills to the brim with intense rhythms of form and color. The rhythm of nature—the desert, and that of humanity—the city, provide him with an ever renewed source of inspiration. The freedom and lyricism of his composition derive from his artistic past; and his latest works, which were shown at the Dutch Exhibition in Paris, in April 1958, testify to a consistent individual development, an organic growth.

Thus, the general character of Dutch painting has undergone another change since 1949. The collective impetus of the group has yielded to individual development. Moreover, the original members of the group have been joined by likeminded artists, such as Wagemaeker and Bouthoorn. The task that the Experimental Group had set for itself in 1949 —liberation from routine—has been taken over by a new young generation. However, a dialectical reversal seems to have taken place: a part of the youngest generation of today seeks less an outlet for temperament than order and severity—the very laws which the generation of 1920 had negated.

Two painters, both of whom belong to the generation of 1920, are most often praised and admired by the youngest painters—Nanninga and Benner. Nanninga's small canvases take us back to the intermediary realm in which so many works of Paul Klee appear to be situated, to the play of contemplative forms only remotely suggested by nature. Reference to the object has been almost entirely eliminated from these paintings; only a faint fragrance of flags, trees, figures, survives. The figures have become signs, which, to the attentive viewer, denote a recollection of reality rather than reality itself.

Gerrit Benner (plate 141) stands apart in the panorama of contemporary Dutch painting. He belongs to an older generation (he was born in 1897), and is wholly self-taught. Before the war he led a hardworking life in Friesland, a storekeeper by day, and a painter only at night. Only after the Liberation did he come to public notice as a painter. Particularly when he moved to Amsterdam, his works took on an originality and brilliance which secure for him a place in Dutch painting. He is by nature an Expressionist; but his works cannot be labeled under any of the varieties of Dutch Expressionism, which derives primarily from the Brücke: rather, they show affinities with the Blaue Reiter in the broad rhythms of his color combinations, the clear repose of his immediate response to nature, and the musicality of his tones. Benner always takes his point of departure from nature, to whose pulse he listens attentively and humbly; and he records this rhythm, which he feels deeply, in his drawings and paintings, translating it into forms and colors. His works are like the melodies of simple songs, and for the most part they are filled with a similar emotional warmth. Recently he has come closer to the Experimental Group, and as a result of this contact his technique has been enriched; yet he seems by nature at the opposite pole from this group—a man of the countryside whose humbly contemplative and reflective manner sharply contrasts with the eruptions of temperament.

Holland has always been a country of painters; and today Dutch art is as richly diversified as ever, its character determined much more by the individualities of the various artists than by movements of international scope, which lose their tidal force in our land of many streams.

Scandinavia

To do justice to the special situation of Scandinavia, we must, first of all, deal with the historical background of the present generation.

The Second World War and the occupation of Denmark and Norway isolated Scandinavia from the West. More than that, the various Scandinavian countries found themselves completely isolated from one another. Isolation has never been beneficial to the North. Between 1939 and 1945 Scandinavia fell back on its own tradition as a source of inspiration. In discussing the development of modern art in Scandinavia since the period of realism, we must take into account not only outside influences, particularly those of Paris, but also, above all, the reaction of native to foreign elements; this reaction resulted in a synthesis, which gave Scandinavian art a distinctive turn. Paris supplanted the influence of Germany (the schools of Munich and Düsseldorf), which reasserted itself in the North only with Expressionism in painting and sculpture, and with the Bauhaus style in architecture.

The native Nordic element, which, at the end of the nineteenth century (the *fin de siècle* period) and during the first decades of the twentieth strongly asserted itself in the literature and art of Germany and other Central-European countries, and which is rooted in Nordic nature, and in the traditions, ideas, and the emotional life of the Nordic nations, also determined the special character of art in the various Scandinavian countries.

At first Iceland and Finland shut themselves off from the impetuous development of modern art more completely than Denmark, Sweden, and Norway. The painting of these two countries was in the style of a meditative lyrical realism, with a muffled, often dark palette, and related in mood to the music of Sibelius. It must be noted that Icelandic painting has no tradition at all: except for one or two artists active in the nineteenth century, all Icelandic painters belong to the last fifty years. The largest part of the works of the nearly sixty professional artists of Iceland is under the influence of the three 'pioneers'—AsGrímur Jònssen (b. 1876), Jóhannes Sveinsson Kjarval (b. 1885), and Jón Stefánsson (b. 1881). Their style is more or less topographic-realistic-lyrical, sometimes tending to Expressionism (Jón Engilberts and Karen Agneta Thórarinson), Cubism (Jón Thorleifsson and Finnur Jónsson), and a simplified Fauvism (Gunnlauger Blóndal and Jóhann Brien). All the last-named artists belong to the younger generation and the one immediately preceding it. Juliana Sveinsdóttir is influenced by Gauguin. Gudmundar Einarsson is a painter of dramatic landscapes; Finnúr Jónsson's style fluctuates between the Expressionistic and the abstract; Gunnlauger Scheving, formerly a realist, is now abstract; Johannes Jóhanesson and Karl Kvaran are inspired by Picasso.

As for Finland, it must be kept in mind that new creative impulses are always slow to reach the northernmost corner of Europe. English literary Pre-Raphaelitism asserted itself there only at the beginning of the twentieth century; the first group of Impressionists did not appear until 1914, forty years after emergence of this school in Paris. Two groups were active in Finland: the September group (founded by Magnus Enckell) and the November group, which professed subjective freedom in expression under the influence of Cézanne, Van Gogh, and Karl Isakson. Its founder, Tyko Sallinen, led a movement of which the painters Gösta Diehl, Erkki Kulovesi and Erkki Kuponen were outstanding representatives. It may be characterized as a national romanticism; later representatives of it were Veikko Vionoja and Gunvor Grönvik, who painted primarily landscapes, and whose range of color extends from the somber palette of Yrjö Saarinen to the more ecstatic one of Aimo Kanerva. From an international point of view, Helen Shjerfbeck (1862–1946), whose orientation is French, may be regarded as Finland's best-known artist of this generation.

The Norwegian character is marked by a Peer Gynt-like pathos and by strong individualism; before the Second World War these characteristics led to the flowering of monumental painting (particularly murals), in a style fluctuating between the tradition of Edvard Munch and a formalized realism with symbolic content and Constructivist form. The most important artists of this tendency were Peer Krohg (b. 1889), Axel Revolt (b. 1887), Henrik Sörensen (b. 1882), and Alf Rolfssen (b. 1895). Before the Second World War this group strongly influenced Swedish art; this influence went hand in hand with the emergence in Sweden of a naïve primitive realism and Expressionism. The only Scandinavian artist who achieved an internationally leading position was Edvard Munch, the grandmaster of Expressionism who died in 1944.

Thanks to the Scandinavian followers of Matisse, particularly the Swedish *1909 ars män* group with Isaac Grünewald (1889–1946), Leander Engström (1886–1927), Einar Jolin (b. 1890), and their Scandinavian colleagues (Jean Heiberg, Henrik Sörensen, and others), Nordic art developed in close relationship with the School of Paris. Between 1910 and 1925 Scandinavia was the home of an avant-garde, like the West and the South. The French manner which was so courageously and vigorously championed by Grünewald, Hjertén and others soon ran into an opposition led by Sven Erixson (b. 1899), with artists of the *Färg och Form* group (Eric Hallström and Giedeon Börje). Hilding Linnquist, Vera Nilsson, Otte Sköld, and others reacted similarly. The opposition asserted native against French and refined values, and since these artists also represented the new social state and its class and national consciousness, we can recognize in their reaction against the influence of Paris the new Swedish style. On the western coast, there prevailed, beside the coloristic romanticism of Inge Schiöler and Ivan Ivarson, the influence of Gösta Sandel's sensibility. If we add to these names those of Ivan Aguéli, influenced by Gauguin, Nils von Dardel, and Carl Kylberg (1878–1951) whose manner was related to Rouault, we will get a fairly complete picture.

The Danes, whose aesthetic tradition is more sensitive than that of the Swedes, found it

256

easier to assimilate the French manner, particularly Fauvism, which became an integral component of their artistic consciousness. Particularly effective in Denmark was the influence of the Swede Carl Isakson (1879-1943), who was very conscious of Cézanne. Among his followers were Holger J. Jensen and Albert Gammelgarrd. After an interval of Cubism (Olaf Rude, b. 1886, and William Scharff, b. 1886; and others) the more or less Romantic tradition, with emphasis on landscapes, won the upper hand (Niels Lergaard and Jens Søndergaard). Social art never enjoyed great popularity in Denmark: John Christensen (1896–1940) was its chief exponent. A strongly accented colorism is typical of Danish art. This feature leads us without break of continuity from Impressionism and Intimism to the latest developments in abstract art. Love of color and brightness as well as humor earned for Copenhagen the name of the Nordic Paris.

The difficulties encountered by Surrealism (the Swedish Halmstad group 1929, with Stellan Mörner and Erik Olsson), and Cubism and abstract art (Aage Storstern, b. 1900, and the Swede Otto G. Carlsund) are indicative of the special position of Nordic countries in contemporary art. It was only the renewed contact with the West and the powerful unfolding of Abstract art (Abstract Expressionism and Surrealism, Tachisme, Action Painting) that touched off a new wave of modernism in the Nordic countries after the Second World War. At this point the abstract movement not only asserted itself, but achieved considerable influence.

Formerly the Swede Viking Eggeling (1880–1925) achieved international recognition thanks to his abstract films; now such recognition has been won by Richard Mortensen, a Dane who lives in Paris (b. 1910, member of the Linie group, 1934), by the Danish sculptor Robert Jacobsen (b. 1912), by Nina Tryggvadottir, a native of Iceland living in London (b. 1913), and by the Norwegian Anna-Eva Bergmann (b. 1909, plate 144) who lives in Paris. Quite important in Sweden is Endre Nemes (b. 1909, plate 143), a master of many techniques, and, in his capacity as director of the Valand School (1947–1955) the educator of a whole generation of artists. Nemes's art evolved from a Baroque Cubism and a Symbolism with Surrealist accents to a colorful Abstractionism of great vitality. Nemes was one of the founders of the Minotaur group (Adja Junkers, and others) and of the periodical *Prisma*. The most important abstract painter of Iceland today is Thorwaldur Skúlason. Other abstract artists there are: Svavar Gudnasson (b. 1909), Valtyo Peturson, and Gudmunda Andresdottir. The Icelandic avant-garde artists exhibit with the September-Syningen group. Kristjan Davidsson paints in the manner of Dubuffet.

In Sweden, the Concretist group was the first to assert itself (Lennart Rohde, P. Olofsson, and others); their absolute Abstractionism was opposed by another group, which based its art on visual reality (Evert Lundqvist, painting in the Expressionist manner; Roland Kempe, in the classical, harmonious manner; Olle Petersen, in reaction against Fauve colorism). The Surrealist vision finds its exponents in a southern Swedish group (Max Walters, b. 1912; C. O. Hultén, b. 1916, and Lars Engström, b. 1914).

In Finland, too, abstract art has asserted itself. Its most important representatives are Ole Kandelin (d. 1947), Birjer Carlstedt (b. 1907), and Lars Gunnar Nordström. Otto Mäkila (b. 1904), the only Surrealist, has turned to abstraction. Among the Danish artists, we may mention Francisca Clausen (b. 1899), Knud Nielsen, Richard Winther, and Carl Henning Pedersen.

Among the Norwegian figurative painters, after the death of Edvard Munch, Kaj Fjell (b. 1907), a lyrical painter inspired by folk art, and the dramatic-monumental Arne Ekeland have particularly distinguished themselves. Hannah Ryggen (b. 1894) makes use of the stylistic experiences of modern painting in her weaving art. Finn Faaberg (b. 1902) represents an emotional experimentalism, and Alexander Schulz (b. 1901) the tradition. Only among the youngest painters does nonfigurative art strongly assert itself; we may mention Harald Aas (geometric abstractionism), Thore Heramb (lyrical abstractionism) and Halvdan Ljösne. The first exhibition of abstract art in Sweden was held in 1933; and before 1949 there was only one other exhibition of abstract art in Scandinavia, in Oslo. Today the best of the young generation are abstract artists.

After its isolation, Scandinavian art has rejoined the current of living art, and its contemporary achievements are noteworthy.

121   Henry Moore. 1952–53 *(Great Britain)*

122   Henry Moore. 1947 *(Great Britain)*

123   Henry Moore. 1953–54 *(Great Britain)*

124   Barbara Hepworth. 1955 *(Great Britain)*

125 Reginald Butler. 1954 (*Great Britain*)

126   Lynn Chadwick. 1956 *(Great Britain)*

127   Graham Sutherland. 1946 *(Great Britain)*

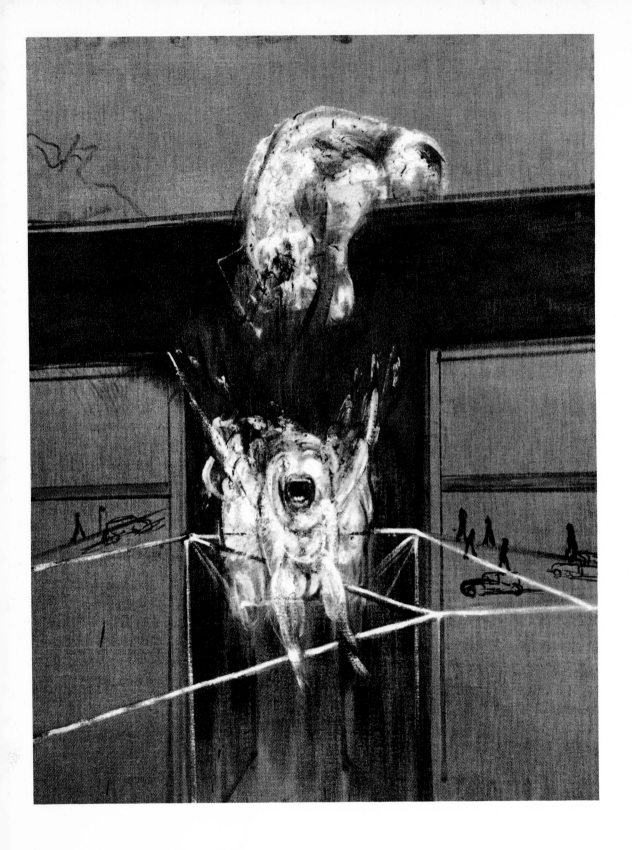

128   Francis Bacon. 1950 *(Great Britain)*

129   Bryan Winter. 1956 *(Great Britain)*

130   D. Hamilton Fraser. 1957 *(Great Britain)*

131 Harold Cohen. 1955 *(Great Britain)*

132   Keith Vaughan. 1946 *(Great Britain)*

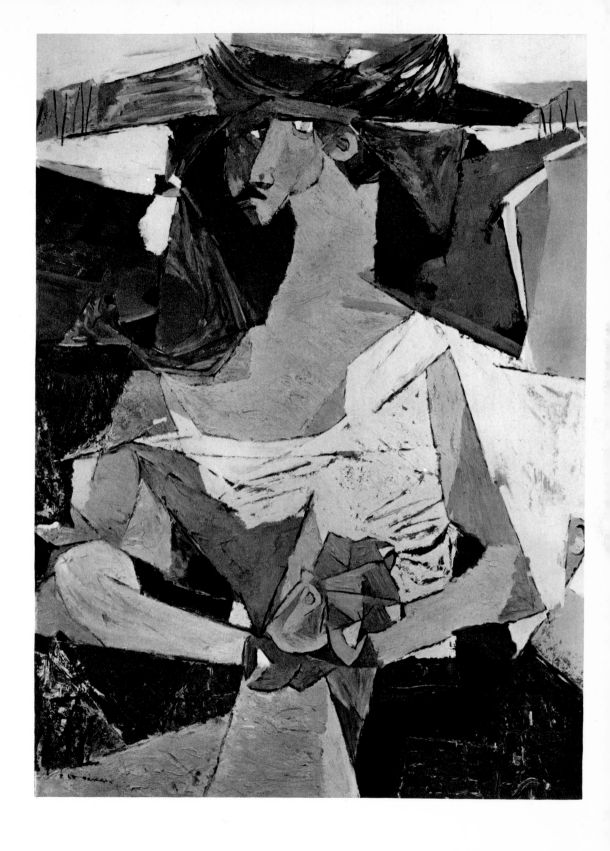

133   Louis le Brocquy. 1948 *(Great Britain)*

134   William Gear. 1955 *(Great Britain)*

135 Sandra Blow. 1957 (*Great Britain*)

136 Frank Auerbach. 1955 *(Great Britain)*

137　Edward Middleditch. 1953–54　(*Great Britain*)

138   Lucien Freud. 1958 *(Great Britain)*

139   S. W. Hayter. 1949 (*Great Britain*)

140   Corneille. 1958 *(Nederland)*

141   Gerrit Benner. 1954 (*Nederland*)

142   Asger Jorn. 1956–57 *(Danmark)*

143   Endre Nemes. 1956 *(Sverige)*

144　Anna-Eva Bergmann. 1956　*(Norge)*

A well-known advanced painter of the older generation concluded a recent lecture on the state of contemporary American art with the words: "The avant-garde is dead; long live the avant-garde!" This wry turn of phrase calls attention to a situation that has been apparent to many observers for some time: a small, dedicated band of innovators, who began to come before the public eye during the war, have in the past several years so captured the imagination of younger artists that they now find themselves the unwilling high-priests of a massive, new orthodoxy. Working principally in New York, and known as Abstract Expressionists or "action painters," these new artists are recognized as the founders of an original school of painting; their styles and those of their followers dominate the American art scene. An imageless painting, antiformal, improvisatory, energetic and free in its brushwork, is the staple of university and many independent art school teaching programs, of national exhibitions, and of those private gallery showings which receive the major share of thoughtful critical attention.

Until very recently, it had been customary to point with pride to the wide diversity of American painting, on the assumption that the opposing currents of realism, Expressionism, a traditional romanticism and abstraction were of equal validity. Now, however, serious questions are being raised about the relevance and integrity of *passéiste* modes. The Abstract Expressionists have decisively set their stamp on the epoch, throwing into sharp relief the emptiness and sentimentality of some of the more inflated native reputations; their example makes the strongest possible case for European modernism as the continuing and sole basis for the most vital contemporary creations.

The shrinking spectrum of American styles still includes much estimable achievement outside the abstract expressionist circle, however. Edward Hopper's romantic realism, Ben Shahn's poetically heightened poster art, Morris Graves' ardent, moon-struck symbols of religious contemplation, Stuart Davis' (plate 157) masterful, abstract color rhythms, and the severe geometric abstraction of Fritz Glarner, all have won a secure place in the scheme of contemporary American art. But they are the exception rather than the rule, and over the past decade only Davis has shown signs of significant development or growth. In more numerous instances, painters working independently of the Abstract Expressionists have been devastated by the rising reputation of the advanced generation, either losing conviction within their own styles or becoming shallow imitators of the newest tendencies. It would seem that the avant-garde now has nothing to fear but its own success and the pressures of conformity that arise from an astonishing record of conversions.

The artists responsible for this revolution nevertheless entertain few illusions about their victory, and put little faith in the changing fashions of taste. An intensive five-year campaign in the nation's most influential art magazine, and a succession of published articles, monographs and museum exhibitions and purchases have enhanced their prestige, and make their work eagerly sought after by a small but discriminating group of collectors. Their paintings still generate strong and violent reactions among the general public, however, and celebrity is mixed with a notoriety that has always attached itself to the more drastic innovations of modern art.

Despite a growing success, the avant-garde artist has not forgotten the rejections of the past, nor must he be reminded of the high mortality rate of modern movements in America. Recognition has eased his isolation, but it has only confirmed his resolve to stand apart, and intensified an aggressive spirit of self-determination. He enjoys the irony of his acceptance in a form of painting which is motivated by a spirit of revolt, by the need for direct expression, by the renunciation of anything reminiscent of the "finished" work—a style whose most profound commitment is to remain disaffiliated from schools, movements, indeed, from style itself. He feels that his painting is defined by a general climate of vitality and a spontaneous ideal of freedom rather than by any prescribed technical procedures, shared subject matter, program, or master-disciple relationships. Hence, his reluctance to accept such labels as Abstract Expressionist or action painter (neither of which is entirely illuminating in any case), and his distaste for critical formulations which link him with a collective impulse. Hence, too, the suspicion troubling many of its outstanding members that the very idea of the avant-garde as a opposition group, and as a standing protest against "things as they are" has lost its leverage, since nothing now seriously blocks its way.

The most resolute spirits of the older generation, however, have succumbed neither to the more facile forms of appreciation and flattery, nor to the pressures toward uniformity and mannerism that their imitators exert on them. A certain troubled sense of existence, poetically transcended in the act of creation, remains the profound note of their most significant work; and a stubborn mistrust of everything but the immediately given in experience assures an authenticity and freshness of expression. As the poet-critic Harold Rosenberg observed in the important article in which he originated the epithet "action painters": "The artist accepts as real only that which he is in the process of creating."

There is a certain quality of heroism in the Abstract Expressionists' renunciations of traditional authority, and in their obsession with the problem of freedom. An unprecedented liberty of gesture has now become the sign of the artist's personal identity, for only the self that is securely rooted in its own existence can do without the support of systematic certainties and be free. The new works represent rough tentatives and vital approximations leading to a new artistic definition of the contemporary problem of individual freedom. They end with an open question, since it is now through the *act* of creating rather than in the finished painting product that the artist must "grasp authentic being," in Karl Jaspers' phrase. "To maintain the force from settling anything, he (the artist) must exercise in himself a constant No," wrote Mr. Rosenberg in his influential article. The action painters, or Abstract Expressionists, have conferred forthright and positive values on their renunciations, inventing significant new expressive forms which meet, finally, aesthetic criteria of harmony and order.

The strenuous "existential" mood and atmosphere of crisis which characterize action painting are as difficult to sustain as they are to pass on to a younger generation whose sense of urgency is compromised by the changed and more congenial circumstances of the progressive artist in America today. Quite appropriately, too, the younger artist finds himself preoccupied with technical matters, for his painting problem in the beginning is to command the expressive means, to acquire artistic culture rather than unload it. It is small wonder, then, that the pioneering generation now casts occasional anxious glances over their shoulders, for they see their drama of struggle and doubt parodied in the quick aptitude and mannered facility of their imitators, and their own moral earnestness translated into the careless paganism of youth.

Yet, like the Dadaists before them (whose destructive spirit shows many affinities with their own), the Abstract Expressionists have discovered that they cannot escape from historical process. What began as a limited but intense wrecking enterprise directed against the "good taste" and shallow eclecticism of provincial art culture has become the climate of an epoch and produced a dynamic new aesthetic, unsystematic perhaps but capable of general assimilation. If it accomplished nothing else—and, surely, it has done much more—the radical new painting has taught a whole generation in America how to "think" directly in paint, and administered a valuable lesson of sensuality. (American art has suffered chronically from a puritanic poverty of means.) The Abstract Expressionist adventure resumes a repeated pattern in the progress of modern art: an isolated experimental venture, initiated by a few stubborn, non-conforming individualists, has acquired a programmatic value and become the basis of a widely accepted method of working. The new painting now directly conditions even our view of the past, disclosing fresh expressive values in the late Monet, in the calligraphic signs of oriental art, in Soutine, in Rodin. Abstract Expressionism in America, and the corresponding Tachiste tendencies abroad, have installed themselves at the center of contemporary artistic sensibility and significantly altered our ways of seeing.

There were many factors that contributed to the renascence of a vital advanced art, which took place in America during the war. Not the least of them was the concentration of expatriate genius in New York as a direct result of the international conflict. After 1942, Peggy Guggenheim's Art of This Century gallery became the first exhibiting center for the young American vanguard, and for a large group of European abstractionists and Surrealists, many of whom had taken refuge in America. Between 1943 and 1946, Miss Guggenheim not only gave Jackson Pollock, Robert Motherwell, William Baziotes, Hans Hofmann, Mark Rothko and Clyfford Still their first New York one-man shows, but helped stimulate the exchange of ideas between the emerging young Americans and many of the more impressive reputations of Paris. Some of the Europeans who found themselves in New York at this time and directly affected American painting, ideologically as well as pictorially, were Matta, Tanguy, Ernst, Léger, Mondrian, and Masson. The migration of European intellectuals and artists to these shores renewed vital artistic contacts that had lain moribund for many years, and helped free American artists of their provincial diffidence. New York had not known such a cosmopolitan, international atmosphere since the period immediately following the Armory Show of 1913 when Duchamp and Picabia had played an important role in the formation of the Stieglitz milieu.

In this connection, two outstanding figures should be mentioned, the art critic Clement Greenberg, and the influential teacher and painter Hans Hofmann. In Greenberg's many penetrating reviews and articles in *The Nation* and *Partisan Review* the avant-garde found their first sympathetic response. If Greenberg was an unreserved enthusiast of the new work, he also insisted on measuring it against the strict aesthetic standards of European modernism. More than any other independent writer on art, he was responsible for breaking down the provincial prejudices and the general suspicion of modernism that infested so many sectors of American art at that time. His early recognition and championship of many New York artists, and particularly of Jackson Pollock with whom he struck up a close friendship, helped create and understand the new era in American painting before its pattern was complete.

Hans Hofmann (color plate 146) began conducting art classes in New York, on a permanent basis, in 1933, after a period of frequent visits to this country from Munich, where his school of painting had acquired an international reputation. Now seventy-six, Hofmann worked in Paris in the great revolutionary years preceding World War I, and had been on intimate terms with Delaunay, Matisse, Picasso, Braque, and other leaders of modern French painting. To young New York artists who began to flock to his painting classes at the end of the thirties and in the early forties, he brought a wide culture of modern art, and a dynamic conception of space, given expressive articulation by intense color. In his own paintings, Hofmann abandoned a fauvish and intermittently representational mode in the early forties for an explosive abstract style: schematic planes of brilliant hue disintegrated into a freely moving color flux under the impact of a swift and agitated brush. He held his first entirely abstract exhibition at the Art of This Century in 1944.

It is futile to try to assign priorities in the development of the radical abstract styles, which emerged as a collective and spontaneous eruption of new energies; but Hofmann was surely one of the principal figures in this suddenr evival. Equally important was his activity as a teacher, and his insistence on the importance and transforming function of pure plastic values. Writing in 1947, Clement Greenberg assessed the role of the important

145 Mark Tobey. 1948 *(USA)*

German modernist: "Hofmann's presence in New York has served to raise up a climate of taste among at least fifty people in America that cannot be matched for rigor and correctness in Paris or London. No matter how puzzling and ugly the new and original will appear—and it will indeed appear so—the people who inhabit this climate will not fail to perceive it and hail it."

Reflecting the revived spirit of internationalism, Robert Motherwell (color plate 150), a key figure in the development of the new ideas of the avant-garde, some time later wrote: "Every intelligent painter carries the whole culture of modern painting in his head. It is his real subject, of which anything he paints is both a homage and a *critique*, and anything he says a gloss. It is the visual expression of the modern mind, subtle, rich, sensual; who lacks the culture of modern painting is without a great human experience, new, adventurous and pure with the intensity of mystical experience, but secular in background."

Such remarks, with their warm, emotional identification of individual experience and the radical forms of modern European art would have been inconceivable even in the late thirties, a period whose prevailing mood was set by the aggressive regionalist sentiment of Thomas Hart Benton and John Stuart Curry, and the neo-primitivism of Grant Wood. By contrast, the characteristic advanced painting of that era was severely intellectual, rationalist and doctrinaire in spirit, being largely derived from the geometric abstraction of Mondrian and the Constructivists.

Of all the modern artistic influences converging on New York during the early forties, however, Surrealism was perhaps the most consequential—not the Surrealism of Dali's "hand-painted dream photographs," but the automatism of Masson, of Miró, and Picasso's metamorphic transpositions of form. To the closed world of geometric abstraction, Surrealism proposed the alternative of romantic spontaneity, of unpremeditated impulse, and gave a new primacy to creative freedom. A number of Americans were quick to seize on this alternative and used it to enlarge and deepen the expressive possibilities of their art. But they adopted mainly the formal side of Surrealism, disregarding its literary symbolism, hermeticism and conception of art as a calculated, formidable mystification designed to unsettle the bourgeoisie. Eventually, they subordinated Surrealist intuitions completely to their own artistic needs, creating an art of abstract forms and concrete pictorial sensations, rather than one of bizarre fantasy and dream. Even today, however, the new art continues to acknowledge its debt to Surrealism in the physiological and visceral qualities of its shapes and movements, its explosive energies and its mood of aggression.

The impact of Surrealist liberties on the American avant-garde was sharp if somewhat oblique. Pollock (color plate 147, plates 158, 159) was undoubtedly affected by the milieu around Peggy Guggenheim, and he relied on automatism and a motor violence in his application of pigment to a large degree. Later he wrote: "The source of my painting is the Unconscious. I approach painting the same way I approach drawing, that is, directly, with no preliminary studies . . . When I am painting, I am not much aware of what is taking place; it is only after that I see what I have done." Arshile Gorky, a virtuoso in figurative and abstract modes during the thirties, was in the early years of the next decade directly influenced by the unstable forms and molten space of Matta. Later André Breton claimed Gorky for the Surrealists with the suggestion that he treated nature "as a cryptogram." The earliest paintings of the period by Baziotes, Rothko, Still and Gottlieb were all in varying degrees concerned with the "primitive," and these artists worked in a form of symbolic, Surrealist-tinctured abstraction. With Motherwell and Hofmann, they all relied on chance effects of pigmentation, harmonious or disruptive in effect, to give vitality and tension to their creations. The American aesthetic of the accidental descends in a direct line from the Surrealists' lucky find, and the appeal to chance.

Finally, Picasso's wide inventive capacity, particularly in his more fantastic phases, was a decided influence. His radical adventures in form also became a symbol for the young Americans of a felt need to push beyond the furthermost limits of art, and the self, into the unknown. There was a conviction abroad in American art during the war years that life and art must be conquered dangerously, each by means of the other.

While many individuals and many influences contributed significantly to the new atmosphere of vitality and confidence in vanguard painting during the early forties, it was Jackson Pollock's first one-man show at the Art of This Century gallery in 1943 that most decisively called attention to the new mood. In the next five years, he emerged as the symbolic painter of a generation that had come forward to claim its liberation. His influence was as much a matter of the intense drama he brought to the act of creation, as it was of his actual formal innovations, for Pollock conceived of the abstract painting as an elementary expression of belief, rather than a source, primarily, of harmonious sensation. In the beginning, he made the painting a vehicle of intense feeling, using abstraction to reach a new depth in himself. To the structural aesthetics of modernism, Pollock added a new quality of autobiographical obsession, but he identified his emotion with a purely pictorial means. His aggressive search for new pictorial liberties and his abundant animal energies carried him safely through a period of *Sturm und Drang*, during which he adapted many of the more violently expressive devices of Surrealism to convey a deepening sense of disorder. In the end, he overcame his own tormented romantic spirit, creating an art of sober objectivity and breadth, powered by its own internal dynamism.

In the early thirties, Pollock had painted under the influence of Thomas Hart Benton's "American Scene" realism, giving a more vehement emotional emphasis to Benton's commonplace, regional themes and uniform rhythms. At the end of the decade, he was affected, in rapid succession, by the violent Expressionism of the Mexican muralists, Orozco and Siqueiros, and the radical forms of European modernism. By 1942 he had arrived at an original and forceful abstract style, tinctured by Surrealist symbolism, and influenced particularly by the aggressive phantasmagoria of Picasso and Miró. Pollock's lavishly pigmented surfaces were magnetized in a new direction, however, by an erratic, energetic overwriting, a spontaneous linear invention, which soon became the entire substance of his pictorial content.

Totem I of 1944 reveals the crude and vital fantasies, and half-human, half-inhuman forms with which Pollock wrestled in his more turgid, early style. He has retained fragments of Picasso's anatomical imagery, and distorted memories of the Surrealist bestiary, all within a scheme of flowing arabesques which seem to arise spontaneously and remind us of the automatist invention of Miró or Masson. Yet Pollock's accents and motifs have an evenness of expressive emphasis that robs them of much of their symbolic power and identifies them with a realm of abstract space. Ultimately, they function as concrete signs which give tectonic definition to the picture plane. Even in the beginning, the architectural logic of surface took precedence over the logic, or illogic, of the Unconscious in Pollock's work.

Something of the charging energy and conflicting moods which characterize these first abstract pictures, however, remained in Pollock's later paintings, giving them a special emotional tension and presence. The labyrinthian coils of his "drips" and whipped lines in the paintings of 1947–1950 seem to heave and bulge, as if some invisible beast, trapped within their depths, were seeking desperately to free itself. Whatever his style, each picture for Pollock became the representation of a moment of stability in a drama of conflict. The metaphor, or self-image, his paintings suggest is that of the storm-tossed sailor seeking the still center of a hurricane. Pollock's surfaces are in continuous spatial movement, but they also have a way of reaching momentary arrest and calm, in a split-second equilibration of contending forces. Similarly, his more violent, expressive devices have a way of reversing themselves, and can reveal, simultaneously, a rococo delicacy of rhythmic phrasing.

A key year in the development of Pollock's style was 1946, when he committed himself decisively to a purely abstract means. *Shimmering Substance* (plate 158), a small panel, shows the energetic, scrolling brushstrokes, expanding in widening arcs from a central core, which Pollock adopted in order to intensify and unify his surfaces. A violent motor activity in handling is contradicted and opposed by the sculptured relief of paint textures and the monolithic unity of a uniformly accented surface. Such oppositions, and a quality of ambiguous, fluctuating spatial depth, keep the surface in dynamic formal operation and draw it into another gravitational sphere where a whole new stirring drama of space can unfold. In 1947, Pollock's rapturous lyricism was intensified and given an epic range with the introduction of his radical drip methods (color plate 147). A this time he temporarily abandoned

146   Hans Hofmann. 1955 *(USA)*

conventional painting procedures and began to work by spreading his canvases on the floor and swinging a loaded brush or a dripping, paint-dipped stick over his surfaces in intricate figures, as a skillful cowboy twirls his lariat. His applications of aluminum paint and commercial enamels gave an industrial texture to his work, in further and more extreme defiance of the traditional integrity of medium and "noble" means. But it also allowed him to expand his style and elaborate an entirely new expressive form, built on free rhythms, in paintings which one writer has aptly described as "unframed space." Pollock's dynamic structures often took form on immense surfaces, as if he were prepared to invade and compete with our natural environment in its own spatial domain. His new style pulverized the painting's material surface, allowing it to compose and decompose freely into particles spinning in an infinitely permeable, limitless space. If organic life, with its poetry of growth and change, and the mechanical movements of the machine had provided the two main visual metaphors for modern abstract art, Pollock invented a third: the effort of dynamic matter to overcome chaos and attain determinate form.

In 1951, Pollock reduced his palette to black and white alone, and returned to the compact anatomical schemes of his earliest abstract style. Such paintings as *Echo* rely on a purely linear invention and elaboration, although they are architectural in scale. In related works of the period, an explicit and recognizable figurative imagery emerged. Perhaps this limited return to image suggestion and anatomical forms acknowledged the forceful impact of Willem de Kooning, who had revived a naturalistic imagery, beginning in 1949, with a series of variations on the theme of "Woman." These disquieting and powerful forms, whose terrible, grinning masks recalled the grotesque seated figures Picasso had painted around 1927, were known and had a wide influence among the New York avant-garde even before they were shown publicly for the first time in an exhibition of 1953. But even Pollock's earlier non-objective manner had carried with it a vague halo of ideas and near-images, and intermittently uncovered in its depths some residual ties to natural reality. A curse hung over Pollock's fragmentary and disordered figuration, as if the pull of tradition represented a terrible bondage which impinged on the artist's dream of absolute freedom. At other times, however, it was clear that Pollock looked on his titanic abstract inventions, of 1949 and 1950 particularly, as a lonely and inhuman world, a splendid creation existing in a void. Tradition, art history and cultivated memory, no matter how peripheral their role, or how distorted the images that embodied them, emerged as essential human forces, counteracting the anonymous powers of Pollock's universe of non-being.

After 1952, Pollock returned to a more dense, material expression and refulgent color, painting more conventionally with brush and tube pigment. His last two years before the fatal automobile accident which in 1956 took his life, at the age of forty-four, were a period of prolonged inactivity. He seemed at the mercy of some unspoken, solitary anguish, and a growing celebrity only caused him embarrassment. It is idle to speculate whether his creative powers would have revived if death had not cut him off. Pollock's sudden passing only served to make him more of a heroic figure for a younger generation of artists, and dramatized his impressive role as an innovator.

Because Pollock's techniques were unconventional and extreme, and his manner of executing the modern painting, in an athletic and frenzied dance-movement, had distinct publicity value, he received a good deal of attention and notoriety in the press. For fellow-artists, his committed search for pictorial liberties and his aggressive spirit of revolt made Pollock into something of a creative demiurge. He supplied perhaps the conclusive example in his generation of the artist engaged by painting as a *total act*. His expressive freedom, implemented by the spatializing powers of his brushwork and of his later cursive "writing" in paint, helped give the contemporary American artist a new *modus operandi*: it identified passion with an abstract means and gave these means the power to express directly certain phases of human consciousness.[10]

In the Pacific Northwest, Mark Tobey (born 1890, color plate 145, and plate 160) had, by the early forties, independently arrived at an automatic, calligraphic form of abstraction. While his graceful, runic script constitutes a minor lyrical episode in the development of contemporary abstraction, and he cannot be regarded either as a member of, or an influence upon, the New York School, his viewpoint does to a degree illuminate their work. Like the Zen Buddhist artists, Tobey considers the brushstrokes "the symbol of the spirit." Pollock and his allied contemporaries in New York showed no spiritualist inclinations, but they shared with Tobey a conviction that an abstract means could deliver intense, lyrical emotion, and, ultimately deal with problems of existence. It was the concrete power and compelling plastic qualities of Pollock's surfaces that placed him, unlike Tobey, in the mainstream of modern Western painting, and gained him an impressive force in American art.

No greater contrast to Pollock's savage, and explosive style can be found than that of Arshile Gorky, emphasizing again that despite the manifest links between the radical abstract painters in New York, it was the differences that mattered. To American abstraction Gorky brought a new elegance of device, a wealth of assimilated culture, and a complex and subtle intellect. Born in a village on Lake Van in Turkish Armenia in 1904, Gorky came to America in 1920. By the late twenties and early thirties, he was working in a neo-classic style, under the influence of Picasso. He also emulated, and often in conversation expressed his regard for, the supple graces of Ingres' line. A freely moving, disembodied contour line of extraordinary refinement in time became the most characteristic element of his art. In the figure paintings of the late thirties, areas of Gorky's representational forms and of their empty backgrounds are isolated, and the edges of these detached shapes are subtly connected in a network of undulating lines that play over the surface musically. Such figurative paintings as the seductive and gracious *The Artist and His Mother* of 1926–36, in the Whitney Museum, have many links with his later style; the interplay and delicate fusion of the background, with its partitioned spatial areas, and the flattened volumes of the figures create an impression of weightless suspension. This device remained central to the later entirely abstract phases of Gorky's art. A subdued palette, whose enameled buffs, pale grays and blues may have been inspired by Ingres' understated hues, was the source of the tinted backgrounds against which Gorky later set his vivacious color spottings.

After painting still lifes in a heavy, mortar-like impasto and somber hues, and thus following Picasso's lead during the middle and late thirties, Gorky, around 1940, released his shapes and colors in a more fluid, organic manner, under the influence of Miró. Until 1943 his art seemed dominated by obvious Parisian influences, although, in retrospect, the artist's own distinct individuality now emerges more clearly. If Gorky was in a sense still educating himself at this time, he also was instrumental in raising the level of painting around him, and his work had an especially forceful impact on his intimate friend, Willem de Kooning. It is probably true that Gorky's obsession with the devices of Picasso and Miró was one of the most critical factors during the fermenting thirties and early forties in establishing the aesthetic foundations of the new abstraction, and in bringing American painting back into the mainstream of modern art which stemmed from Cubism and Miró. It is important to note that today the derivative aspects of Gorky's work of the period are far less disturbing or apparent; his inventive metamorphoses of shape, his voluptuous color and linear refinement tend to separate him more and more from his models.

An important turning point in Gorky's art took place in the summer of 1943 when he went with his wife to her parents' farm in Virginia. Here he worked from nature and created a series of studies in pencil and colored crayon that were tumultuous, ardent and far freer in invention. James Johnson Sweeney later wrote of an exhibition based on this new departure: "Gorky's latest work shows his realization of the value of literally returning to the earth . . . last summer Gorky decided to put out of his mind the galleries of Fifty-Seventh Street and the reproductions of Picasso, Léger and Miró, and look into the grass, as he put it. The product was a series of monumentally-drawn details of what one might see in the heavy August grass, rendered without a thought of his fellow-artists' ambitions or theories of what a picture should be. And the result of this free response to nature was a freshness and personalization of idiom which Gorky had never previously approached, and a new vocabulary of forms on which he is at present drawing for a group of large paintings."

Out of this experience evolved the morphological paintings of Gorky's last period, with their lyrical profusion of floral-visceral shapes. André Breton two years later claimed the

147   Jackson Pollock. 1947 *(USA)*

new paintings for Surrealism. In a catalogue introduction to the one-man show of 1945, Breton described Gorky's repertory of shapes as "*hybrid* forms in which all human emotion is precipitated." Gorky's language of form, Breton declared, linked and synthesized natural phenomena, childhood memory and art history. "It is my concern," he wrote, "to emphasize that Gorky is, of all the Surrealist artists, the only one who maintains direct contact with nature—sits down to paint *before her*. Furthermore, it is out of the question that he would take the expression of this nature as an end in itself—rightly he demands of her that she provide sensations that can serve as springboards for both knowledge and pleasure in fathoming certain profound states of mind. Whatever may be the subtle ways by which these states of mind choose to express themselves, they stem from the wild and tender personality which Gorky hides, and share the sublime struggle of flowers growing toward the light of day. Here for the first time nature is treated as a cryptogram. The artist has a code by reason of his own sensitive anterior impressions, and can decode nature to reveal the very rhythm of life."

The Waterfall, painted somewhat under the influence of Kandinsky, and of Matta's volcanic landscapes, shows Gorky's gifts of poetic transmutation of natural forms and events, in this case with a pictorial paraphrase of the play of water over rocks. It is futile to seek too close a relationship between the artist's invention and natural phenomena, for the painting is conceived as an autonomous esthetic creation. However, it does establish analogies with, and is amplified by, those qualities of flux and movement which measure the rhythmic pulse of nature.

The Surrealists had taught Gorky a more vivid appreciation of automatism, and his accidental spatters and color diffusions paid tribute to their unpremeditated methods. Something of the hermetic quality of Surrealist art also touched his work; one encounters in his paintings a cultivation of mystery for its own sake, unusual conjunctures of forms and pictorial events, an unaccountable, hyperactive principle of analogy and metamorphic transposition that does not always disclose its motivation. Gorky's work contains a secret, which seems to represent the convergence on an exceptionally plastic and impressionable temperament of what the artist himself described as "the invisible relations and phenomena of this modern time." Like Matta, who was perhaps his strongest influence after 1943, he sought pictorial correspondences for the hidden forces in modern experience that govern our lives. Technically, his eruptive, brilliant color and vaporous backgrounds reveal an even more direct debt to Matta, and in his last years Gorky's composite, free fantasies on anatomical forms, often with explicit erotic content, seemed to follow closely the development of Matta's demonic iconography.

The differences between the two artists are even more significant, howerer. Expression for Gorky was not simply a matter of literary-symbolic invention, and his engagement in the painting was more than visual. Despite their residues of a subconscious imagery, Gorky's paintings are essentially concrete; they must be experienced as objects of sensation, and they embody rather than "illustrate" their themes. If Matta was an influence, then Pollock and de Kooning were even more fundamental conditioning factors in Gorky's more direct, late style. A new spontaneity and expressiveness in terms of the painterly means themselves are the new factors in the art of Gorky's last four years. It was in these years that such remarkable works as *Water of the Flowery Mill*, *The Liver Is the Cockscomb*, *The Diary of a Seducer*, *The Plow and the Song*, *The Calendars*, *Agony*, and many smaller related oils and drawings were created. Between 1943 and 1948 Gorky's art achieved its maximum tension and pictorial substance in a climactic burst of painting.

Early in 1946, fire destroyed Gorky's studio in Sherman, Connecticut, and with it, some twenty-seven paintings, including the major portion of the precious year's production. The fire was the first in an ineluctable chain of disasters which overtook the artist: the following month he underwent an operation for cancer, and a year later suffered a broken neck in an automobile accident. In the summer of 1948, the artist took his own life, at the age of forty-four. A tragic atmosphere of conflict haunts many of Gorky's paintings, both before and after fortune began to conspire against hin. This mood is as characteristic of the somber grisaille, *The Diary of a Seducer*, as it is of the opulent and fiery *Agony* (color plate 148). Whatever violent instincts reached awareness in Gorky's turbulent forms or feverish color schemes, they submitted to, and were transformed by, his masterful control of a subtle and refined pictorial means; it is this controlled elegance and equipoise that finally define Gorky's genius.

Mistakenly identified for many years as a Gorky protégé and imitator, Willem de Kooning emerged in his first one-man show of 1948 as an artist of significant and independent stature. He has extended the range of abstract devices to include a wider variety of formal solutions, drawing on both modern and traditional antecedents. At a time when Pollock was taking the abstract picture beyond the reach of his contemporaries, de Kooning provided a more viable pictorial means for many of his fellow abstract painters, and gave a new momentum to the Abstract Expressionist tendency. There is no single figure who has exerted greater influence on American painting over the past decade; he is directly responsible for the general physiognomy of much of the painting of a rising younger generation.

In 1947 and 1948 Pollock had begun to atomize form more drastically by his drip techniques, and extend the theater of his operations over larger surfaces. His paintings became more homogeneous and uniform in appearance, and more inimitable; the progressive neutralization of the material means left only the narrowest basis on which these paintings might be reconstructed as "style" or "manner." Whereas Pollock, in the interests of freedom, unloaded the identifiable, traditional features of his art, even to the extent of denying his forms weight, mass and gravity, de Kooning implemented his own abstract expression with disembodied fragments of traditional art, thus acknowledging the existence of the past. If Pollock emptied and atomized space, de Kooning anatomized, reinstating mass and solidity. His fleshy, opulent brush gave a new corporeality to the abstract picture, and a certain rhetorical presence as well, since it invited comparison with the virtuoso brushwork and rhythmic phrasing of the grand manner.

Despite their air of assimilated culture, de Kooning's paintings, like Pollock's, address themselves to the drama of matter, transformed and transfigured in the act of creation; his images show visble evidence of the route traversed in their making. Intelligible forms are wrested free from the seething of anonymous matter and achieve a momentary stability, but in the process they are often warped and mutilated almost beyond recognition, as in the case of the terrible masks of his cult-image, "Woman." For an artist of de Kooning's painterly reponses and attainments, figurative tradition is not so easily set aside. He would feel as uncomfortable and dispossessed in the vast free spaces of the modern fantastic as Pollock felt ambivalent toward a revived naturalistic imagery. Yet, curiously, each artist met the other halfway—Pollock by returning to anatomical schemes and recognizable figuration in his last works; and de Kooning, by embarking on a more explosive and fragmentary mode of abstraction in his most recent phase.

If Pollock's paintings sometimes remind us of the cosmic drama of van Gogh's night skies, de Kooning's recall the massive upheavals and titanic struggles of his fields and landscapes, or even more appropriately, point to the tragic identity of paint and flesh in Soutine's passionate brushwork. De Kooning's stubborn attachment to the real and the tangible is indicated by a statement he made in 1951:

"The argument often used that science is really abstract, and that painting could be like music and for this reason, that you cannot paint a man leaning against a lamp post is utterly ridiculous. That space of science—the space of the physicists—I am truly bored with by now. Their lenses are so thick that seen through them, the space gets more and more melancholy. There seems to be no end to the misery of scientists' space. All that it contains is billions and billions of hunks of matter, hot or cold, floating around in darkness according to a great design of aimlessness. The stars *I* think about, if I could fly, I could reach in a few old-fashioned days. But physicists' stars I use as buttons, buttoning up curtains of emptiness. If I stretch my arms next to the rest of myself and wonder where my fingers are—that is all the space I need as a painter."

Although de Kooning now is one of the seminal forces in American painting, it is well to keep the atavistic sources of his art in mind. He was born in Holland in 1904 and lived there until the age of twenty-one, serving as an apprentice in a painting and decorating firm, and later studying painting at the Academy of Fine Arts in Rotterdam, the Brussels

148   Arshile Gorky. 1947 *(USA)*

Academy and a school of design in Antwerp. He came to America in 1926 and went to work first as a house painter, and then as a commercial artist. In Holland, de Kooning has stated, the two great admirations of art students in his youth were van Gogh and Mondrian, and to a native their antagonistic moods and styles did not seem irreconcilable. Something of van Gogh's passionate intensity, and transfiguration of matter, and of Mondrian's structuralism are fused in de Kooning's paintings. And his method of establishing shapes may very well derive from the sign-painter's technique of "cutting in" background areas while reserving the foreground image. In 1945 a full-page color illustration depicting a Dutch genre scene was published in *Fortune* magazine by the Container Corporation of America over de Kooning's name; for all its picturesque anecdote, it is a swashing, vigorous abstract structure, and demonstrates very clearly the artist's debt to a commercial technique of utilizing "negative" background space to limit and fix the oscillation of foreground shapes.

This method, it must be noted, is also closely related to the technical procedures of Arshile Gorky during the thirties when he was working in a neo-classical style, and later when he executed his Picassoid abstractions. In the latter, Gorky's unoccupied background spaces seemed to advance into the picture plane as positive shapes, reversing the function of those shapes which clearly defined form as mass. It is worth elaborating on this device at some length since it suggests the main source of ambiguity in de Kooning's art, and touches on the very core of his sensibility: an ability to play on multiple responses, and to set loose opposing forces on the canvas surface, which, in analogy, seem to capture the complex quality of lived experience. Out of the reciprocal interplay of depth and flatness, and the polyvalent qualities of his forms derive the whole tension of his art. Without such co-ordinated ambiguities de Kooning's paintings would either harden into flat decoration or simply become a barbarous and distastefully ugly expressionism. The vitality of his abstract means, their organic complexity of movement which follows the dilation of the mind itself in the act of conceptualizing, supply him with almost unlimited occasions for pictorial invention.

De Kooning (plate 161) did not hold his first one-man show until 1948, although he was a well-known and admired figure in the avant-garde throughout the early forties. He had worked during that period alternately in a neo-classical and fluid, curvilinear, abstract idiom, sharing Gorky's preoccupation with shallow spatial depth and the mystery of relationship between flattened foreground volumes and their backgrounds. From this period he has retained, and from time to time reactivated, many pictorial forms: disembodied rectangles, bulging globes, and a loose, mobile structure of hooked, calligraphic lines. In his later work, these forms seem to have passed into another atmosphere where, moving at greater velocity, they begin to disintegrate and fuse more integrally with the picture plane. Similarly, de Kooning's investment of energy in the mystery of the human figure in relation to its pictorial environment was too great for him to dispense with recognizable representation completely. Like some obsessive reality, the figure returned to his art about 1949 in the beginning series of his violent and inspired variations on the theme of "Woman" (color plate 149).

It is particularly important to define the powerful originality of de Kooning's artistic contribution; his influence, in terms of the actual number of painters who have been formed by his art, is without parallel in recent American painting history. Although Gorky's painting hinted at some of the spatial and plastic problems he himself would wrestle with, de Kooning's solutions have been more "plastic." A residue of eclecticism remained in many of Gorky's paintings; his own wide artistic culture prevented him from a total commitment to the more radical implications of his methods. And in moments of hesitation, he fell back on form of tinted drawing, exquisitely controlled in nuance and metamorphic elaboration. Gorky's spatial divisions were schematic rather than organic, creating at times the impression of an art of dismembered parts, unified by skillful handling and luxuriant color.

De Kooning's unities have been more vital, complex and aggressive, and far less attached to a linear scheme. Where Gorky refined and eliminated in the interests of harmony, de Kooning has implemented his plastic devices and loaded his surfaces—often to the point where a disturbing cacophonous effect results. He has dragged his paintings through a kind of sluggish mud, so to speak, assuring them an immediate and unequivocal physical presence. At the same time, he has tried to salvage from the restless movement which characterizes the painting style of the epoch certain traditional qualities of permanence. Few of de Kooning's contemporaries can compete with his power to beget durable forms, without subsiding into some closed and systematic rigidity of manner that denies the dynamic premises of Abstract Expressionist painting. In the face of Gorky's exquisite attenuations, with their echoes of French painting cuisine, and Pollock's atomized surface, de Kooning has given the abstract picture a more substantial painterly flesh, and a renewed plastic vigor.

From 1949 to 1953, he also made an attempt to concentrate and unify the abstract means around the human figure, but did so neither in a retrospective mood nor simply in order to revive humanistic sentiment. The "Woman" was an experiment, in a sense, made to test the inclusiveness of the variety of oppositions and dualisms de Kooning, like a supreme juggler, kept in operation during the act of creation. It was as if the artist had asked himself if it might be possible to evokes human image, whose essential features were determined not by nostalgic memory, association or simple representational intent, but by the dynamic events of the creative act itself. This effort to approach representation from the reverse side of creation, by giving full scope to impulse and accident, rather than by submitting to the control of objective reality, was a magnificent failure—as imagery. As paintings, the "Woman" series are among the artist's most powerful and successful inventions. De Kooning now feels that his imagery was "too terrible" to endure, and he has in recent years returned to a nonfigurative expression.

But a quality of *terribilità*, fused with an elation in execution and paint manipulation, continues to inhabit de Kooning's expression. Like fish battling upstream, his shape-complexes assert themselves against the flux of a continuously moving space, which threatens them with extinction. The identity of individual forms, and the integrity of each canvas must be snatched dangerously from an engulfing chaos of brushstrokes. By awarding disorder a major role as pictorial environment, and by denying his forms a more determinate and stable order of existence, de Kooning externalizes one of the root experiences of modern man: the precariousness of the individual fate in a world without transcendence. Through his poetic creation, however, the artist is enabled to transcend meaningless experience, and, in a sense, redeem existence. His work seems to represent a heroic attempt to assert himself in the region of the *nihil*.

It would be difficult to determine how far de Kooning might credit such an interpretation. He has taken a stand, in an artists' symposium of 1950, to the effect that no art, of the past or the present, can be abstractly categorized or considered apart from the effort, struggles and hesitations of its creator. In so doing, he seemed to give sanction to the view that an enlightened uncertainty, and with it, a sharp awareness of the limits of rational knowledge, is an important condition for the making of modern art. In the midst of a discussion which opposed the clarity of geometric shapes to the mystery of automatic invention of a free form character, de Kooning stated: "I consider all painting free. As far as I am concerned, geometric shapes are not necessarily clear. When things are circumspect or physically clear, it is purely an optical phenomenon. It is a form of uncertainty; it is like accounting for something. It is like drawing something that then is bookkeeping. Bookkeeping is the most unclear thing." Somewhat later, in the same context of the discussion, he said: "Mondrian is not geometric, he does not paint straight lines. A picture to me is not geometric—it has a face . . . It is some form of Impressionism."

William Seitz has pointed out in his scholarly essa yon Abstract Expressionism that de Kooning's anguished sensibility finds release through the orgiastic gaiety of his paint manipulation. The anguish in the artist's work is not a matter of sentiment or mood so much as conflicting energies: a ferocious assault on imagery, alongside the unrepentant hunger for stable reality, which takes the form of identifiable, intelligible fragments of representation. Pain and struggle are given vivid expression in material medium. In this connection, Mr. Seitz quotes Jean-Paul Sartre on a famous Venetian crucifixion, eloquently suggesting how de Kooning's disquieting emotion is delivered through the concrete paint-

149　Willem de Kooning. 1952　*(USA)*

ing means. In *What Is Literature* Sartre writes: "Tintoretto did not choose that yellow rift of sky above Golgotha to *signify* anguish or to *provoke* it. It is anguish and yellow sky at the same time. Not sky of anguish or anguished sky; it is an anguish become thing, an anguish which has turned into yellow rift of sky, and which is thereby submerged and impasted by the proper qualities of things, by their impermeability, their extension, their blind permanence, their externality, and that infinity of relations which they maintain with other things."

A European sense of style, based on School of Paris taste, in collision with alternately lyrical and violent gusts of native American feeling characterizes the art of Robert Motherwell (born 1915), one of the most significant intellectual figures in the "first wave" of Abstract Expressionism. In the early and middle forties, Motherwell was an outstanding and articulate spokesman of the avant-garde, and he has been an editor and a penetrating writer, as well as a painter whose natural gifts are indisputable. To Gorky's studio professionalism, Pollock's elemental vehemence, and de Kooning's powerful and skilled artisanship, Motherwell added a new image of the contemporary American artist: that of the gifted amateur of sensibility, steeped in the literary romanticism of Baudelaire and Rimbaud, and sensitively aware of the great issues of individual freedom at stake in modern art. He was the first native artist to propound to the American vanguard Surrealism's attitudes of revolt, although his acceptance of the Surrealist viewpoint was limited and never doctrinaire. Writing in the magazine *Dyn* in 1944, he ascribed the "crisis" of the modern artist to his "rejection *in toto* of the values of the bourgeois world," and declared that "modern artists form a kind of *spiritual underground*."

Despite his intense literary and speculative interests, Motherwell has shown a richly developed painterly intelligence. Modern art for him was not a casual seduction, but a serious and deep commitment. However, it is significant that he assimilated modern art culture with such rapidity, for he began to paint seriously only in the early forties with almost no previous training; his informal directness and non-professional attitudes could only have gained expressive force within the context of a style which admitted wide inclusions, and one in which sensibility, temperament and a preoccupation with one's own inner processes were at a premium.

A certain flavor of boyish romanticism and autobiographical obsession characterizes Motherwell's work, giving it an appealing intimacy and freshness; such qualities achieve the tension of art because they are supported by a sureness in handling and general knowledgeability. In his awareness of the crucial expressive function of medium as such, whether in oil paintings or in his masterful collages, Motherwell associates himself with the new abstract generation. Like his fellow artists, he, too, has relied on the appeal to accident, on a romantic spontaneity and on a multi-evocative imagery. He draws apart from his contemporaries, however, in his attachment to Parisian taste and hedonism, his intellectuality and, technically, in his extremely sensitive handling of collage.

Motherwell's earliest work of the forties seemed to derive in part from Picasso's Constructivist paintings, and in part from the Dada collages of Schwitters and Arp. Such paintings as *Western Air* and *The Painter*, both of 1947, show a skillful manipulation of silhouetted ovoid and geometric forms within a segmented spatial grid, recalling Picasso's "studio" paintings of 1929; *Pancho Villa Dead or Alive*, of 1943, is one of his very beautiful collages, elegant and terse, rich in psycho-sexual symbolism despite a schematic bareness of elaboration. In paintings of the late forties, Motherwell's instinctive taste for voluptuous color brought him at times closer to Matisse than any other influence.

Despite their obvious sources, and the occasional direct quotations in his work, Motherwell's paintings and collages achieve a direct force and originality. His expressive manner is stamped with an individual sense of style. Within a somewhat conventional structural schema there were evident in his earliest paintings interesting oppositions of strict forms and amorphous shapes. The dominant shapes and relationships, established by aggressive linear boundaries, were constantly in danger of being undermined by a deliberate aimlessness in the activity of minor forms, as if reverie and elegiac poetic sentiment could not be separated entirely from even his most decisive artistic gestures. The multiple logic of Motherwell's devices, and their capacity for promoting new and unexpected morphologies of form, helped loosen the compact structuralism of his early linear designs.

For Motherwell, it is the imprecise and undefined margins of pictorial reality that lead to new and unknown structures. The artist guards that area of his sensibility which to the general public may seem simply vague, indecisive and uncommitted as one of the most precious sources of his inspiration. In a foreword introducing an exhibition of "The New York School," and in support of his own view of modern painting, Motherwell quoted Odilon Redon, who had written at the turn of the century that his symbolist paintings "*inspire* and are not meant to be defined. They determine nothing. They place us, as does music, in the ambiguous realm of the undetermined. They are a kind of metaphor. . ."

To bring off a unified and dramatic abstract configuration within a loose and shifting structural organization was Motherwell's feat in his earlier work. His pictorial emotion was concentrated, and focused, by the concrete challenge of medium, and by the wealth of associations certain colors and forms set poetically vibrating in his mind. "The 'pure' red of which certain abstractionists speak," he once stated, "does not exist, no matter how one shifts its physical context. Any red is rooted in blood, glass, wine, hunters' caps, and a thousand other concrete phenomena. Otherwise we should have no feeling toward red or its relations, and it would be useless as an artistic element."

305 Motherwell's elegiac emotion found effective and freer pictorial form in the group of stark "wall paintings" begun in 1949. *The Voyage* (color plate 150) belongs to this series of monumental designs, grave and subdued in palette, almost stoical in their unadorned surfaces and elementary forms. In the years since, Motherwell has alternated between mural-size paintings, which utilize nonaggressive, flowing forms, and collages, or torn paper compositions, of great verve and freedom.

In the hands of a number of other fine American artists of Motherwell's generation the collage has achieved a new freedom and expressiveness. Pollock executed a limited number of collages in the late forties, staining and spattering rice paper with water color and building up dense layers of wafer-thin, torn and cut segments of these papers; the effect was of veiled, translucent depths, teeming with delicate life. De Kooning has used collage elements in his paintings to dislocate his formal unities, forcing a new regrouping of forms in contact with the obstruction of materials alien to the oil medium. He has also made collages exclusively, achieving a miraculous richness and massiveness with his flattened segments of cut and pasted colored papers. Another gifted manipulator of texture and surface is Esteban Vicente; he has demonstrated a controlled articulation of small, rather uniform units of torn paper, which synthesize the Cubists' formal rigors with a more spontaneous and fluid elaboration of shape. For many artists the collage has provided a useful resistance to the restless movement of Abstract Expressionist paintings. It serves to crystallize in distinct form some of the ambiguities of the new genre of painting: its paradoxical confrontations of structure and free-form, placement and movement, chaos and order, measure and impulse.

One of the most interesting resolutions of the simultaneous interplay of an ordered formalism and spontaneous, expressive gesture was made by Bradley Walker Tomlin (1899–1953, color plate 151). Tomlin's artistic temper was not unlike Motherwell's, in its civilized restraint and essentially European standards of taste; but it was the outgrowth of an entirely different education. Whereas Motherwell's youthful ardor and rebelliousness, in contact with the Surrealists, set him on the high road to freedom at the very beginning of his career, Tomlin was a gradualist who had to find his way more cautiously, overcoming an instinctive distaste for the more violent manifestation of freedom in contemporary painting. He came to abstract painting in mid-career, tentatively in 1944 and with complete authority four years later. By then he was forty-nine, with a little less than five years of creative activity remaining, for he was to die of a heart attack in the spring of 1953. In the brief period of his mature style, Tomlin produced an impressive body of work, of an astonishing creative vigor and breadth for an artist who had previously been associated only with sensitive but rather mild paintings, clearly Cubist in derivation.

The artistic energies, or simply aggression, that Tomlin seemed unable to release in his earlier paintings are markedly present from 1947 onward, a period when he was in in-

150   Robert Motherwell. 1949   *(USA)*

timate contact with and eventually became a leading member of the New York avant-garde. His first significant ventures in the new manner were his "automatics" of 1948, a form of spontaneous, Surrealist-tinctured "writing" in alternately white or vivid confetti colors on flat, black grounds. *Number 3, 1948* is a brilliant example, and one of his most dramatic and vehement paintings. In it, and in a number of other works of the same year, there is a new demon of impulse at large, agitating Tomlin's surfaces and routing his more precautionary instincts. At the time, Jackson Pollock, Gorky, and possibly de Kooning (whose freely written alphabetical characters in such paintings of 1947 as *Zurich* may have come to Tomlin's attention) were very much on his mind. He was both impressed and disturbed by the "Expressionist" violence of the new abstraction. For, if the new painting gave Tomlin a taste for the dynamic and expanded his appreciation of the elementary potencies of medium, it also soon generated an opposing reaction.

In the following year, the explosive release of the "automatics" was supplanted by a renewed emphasis on formal order. What emerged was Tomlin's most characteristic style, a kind of open, elastic pictorial architecture that contained and utilized the free calligraphic energies of his preceding paintings within a system of rectlinear grids. The "constructed" aspect of these works provided resistance and traction for his wide, flowing ribbons of paint, which in turn lost their emblematic character and functioned as pure plastic signs.

Tomlin's insistence that an essentially Constructivist ordering of form could be merged creatively wirh the contemporary addiction to a more flowing, homogeneous pictorial means is indicated by his statement: "Geometric shapes can be used to achieve a fluid and organic structure." The structuralism of Cubism and Mondrian's syncopated rhythms in his last New York phase have more pertinent affinities than Pollock to the rationalist spirit of *Number 20, 1949*, a work that is remarkable for its free play of energies within a clearly demarcated and limiting formal structure. A tension between strict forms and free movement marked all of Tomlin's best work. The hectic tempo of his charged script was also offset by the classical restraint of his palette, whose muted olives, siennas, tans and off-whites are curiously American in their mellow sobriety.

Tomlin later employed more sensuous and luxurious chromatic schemes; in his final, and more Impressionistic works, his colors were bright, gay, lyrical, a chromatic distillation of a harlequinade, almost as if the illusion and artifice of the circus, or the theater, were his own private metaphors for the artistic life. Behind the façade of motley, behind the festive hedonism and dainty rococo flourishes, however, one sensed the obsessive reality of all fine artists for whom painting is nothing if it is not a total commitment. This is the quality that gives a jolting immediacy and fundamental simplicity to his best work. His emblematic devices and mannered gestures (which the eighteenth century would classify as "gallant invention") became expendable in the pursuit of more significant aesthetic objectives. In open defiance of his instinctive finesse and tact, Tomlin allowed the raw, heavily worked surfaces of many of his paintings to stand, a candid admission that the work issued from a process of trial and error. That admirable tension of measure and impulse which Tomlin finally achieved is embodied in only a handful of major works, but with the passage of time these paintings increasingly assume the aspect of classics in their genre of abstraction.

Thus far, all the artists considered have been allied in the intense activism of their surfaces, no matter how widely separated by temperament and formal repertory. Another equally significant group of artists has emerged among the so-called Abstract Expressionists, however, whose paintings are characterized by relative immobility and "non-action," by the stern suppression of explosive movement. The co-ordinated ambiguities that emerge in the forms of Pollock and de Kooning, as they operate at high speed and under high energy pressure, can also be extracted from shapes and forms that function under an opposite principle of deceleration, and at low energy. As the Surrealists long ago discovered, inertia and immobility can be as magical and poetic transforming agencies as the Futurists' headlong rush into the time-space continuum. Such American artists as Mark Rothko (born 1903, plate 164), Clyfford Still (born 1904, color plate 152) and Barnett Newman (born 1905) have in their separate and distinguished ways created a more solemn and hieratic art of resonant color sensation. The nervosity and restless linearity of Pollock and de Kooning are eliminated, or subdued, by a massive equilibrium of broad, undetailed flat masses, of color. The intensity of these artists' color expression, the interplay of shapes, whether geometric and rigorously ruled with straight lines, or free, and the variety of means they have invented both to unify and dissociate their component colored forms, give their works a direct impact comporable to the more readily identifiable "action" styles. Quiet and ordered though their surface may appear at first glance, the paintings aggressively envelop the observer in immense fields of burning hue of such intensity that they begin to act as a total and immediately experienced environment. They achieve architectural scale through magnified color sensation, as the paintings of Pollock and de Kooning achieved it through magnified and continuous movement.

Both Still and Rothko conceive of their work as revelatory, or mediumistic, to a degree. In conversation, Still has defined his painting not as a way of "seeing," but as a mode of "being within a revelation." And Rothko, in the effort to penetrate beyond existing artistic categories and break new ground, has quite consciously tried to rehabilitate the transcendental. "The familiar identity of things," he has written, "has to be pulverized in order to destroy the finite associations with which our society increasingly enshrouds every aspect of our environment." As in the case of Still, Rothko's search for universals and for some immaterial absolute is conducted in and through the expressive means; no matter how intense or exalted his emotion, it is embodied directly in concrete pictorial sensation.

In the transition to their present styles, both Rothko and Still shared, during the early forties, an interest in ritualistic subject matter and archaic forms. It is another aspect of the regenerative processes at work in American painting a decade and a half ago that many artists were preoccupied with "myth" and the primitive. In their different ways, William Baziotes (born 1912, plate 162) and Adolph Gottlieb (born 1903), as well as Newman, Rothko and Still, sought a new freedom in terms of the totemic imagery of the primitive arts. Gottlieb's "pictographs" of the period (plate 163) fused simplified cuneiform signs with subtle color and textural modulation and an emphatic feeling for the frontal plane. In more recent years, he has experimented widely in a purely abstract idiom. Baziotes has retained his totemic images, suspending them against indeterminate backgrounds of subtle tonal modulation. His shapes are multi-evocative symbols of both immediate consciousness and nostalgic reverie. Newman also passed through a primitivistic phase before arriving at his severely rectilinear abstractions.

The enigmatic mood of the new abstraction was conveyed indirectly be Newman's comments in a catalogue introduction for an exhibition of American Indian art, held in 1947: "The abstract shape he [the Kwakiutl Indian artist] used, his entire plastic language, was directed by a ritualistic will towards metaphysical understanding . . . To him a shape was a living thing, a vehicle for an abstract thought-complex, a carrier of awesome feeling he felt before the terror of the unknowable. The abstract shape was, therefore, real rather than a formal 'abstraction' of a visual fact, with its overtone of an already known nature. Spontaneous, and emerging from several points, there has arisen during the war years a new force in American painting that is the modern counterpart of the primitive art impulse . . . Here is a group of artists who are not abstract painters, although working in what is known as the abstract style."

Again and again, one encounters in the statements of these artists the repudiation of purist abstraction, and the identification of an abstract means with emotion, fantasy and the inner drama of the self. The urge toward the primitive was a transitional phase in the development of new expressive forms, which also represented new modes of awareness. For Rothko, the art of primitive peoples arose from their need for "transcendental experience," and were projections of the profound forces that governed their lives. In defense of the archaic and primitivistic inspiration of his own paintings at the time, the artist in 1947 wrote: "Without monsters and Gods, art cannot enact our drama." It is interesting to note that, with the exception of Baziotes, all the artists under discussion abandoned recognizable subject matter and image suggestion by the end of the decade. The abstract painterly means rather than symbolism became the carrier of content. Despite the rigorous purification of means, however, certain mythical residues and an atmosphere of mystery clung to their work for a time.

151   Bradley Walker Tomlin. 1950 *(USA)*

The direction Rothko's painting was to take is foreshadowed by elements in his very earliest painting, although there was then no way of anticipating the unprecedented pictorial means he finally created. His style has evolved with a kind of massive calm and gravity from a modified Expressionism in the thirties to the monumental inventions of the present day. Largely self-taught, in the middle and late thirties he painted urban scenes of modest pretension that are especially interesting for their unconventional handling of figures in space. In a series of paintings of underground subway stations, the artist set slender, stylized figures in an architectural network of pillars, and bathed them in a dissolving, grayed light. The pervasive and subtle illumination seems to eat away space, and much of the substantial bulk of his flattened forms; even within the flexible conventions of the period's dominating realism-cum-expressionism, there was an unusual emphasis on abstract qualities of design and on the expressive possibilities of bare spatial areas. His isolated human figures had a studied unreality and qualities of self-containment, as if, in anticipation of Giacometti's attenuated and alienated humanity, they had lost contact with each other and surrendered their powers of communication.

Later, Rothko described the traditional past as a deserted square occupied by figures making vacant and futile gestures in a charade of human frustration. The paintings of the past that engaged him were those "of the single human figure—alone in a moment of utter immobility." The monumental humanity of great traditional art, however, was unable to escape the isolation which had become a condition of their identity. "The solitary figure," he wrote, "could not raise its limbs in a single gesture that might indicate its concern with the fact of mortality and an insatiable appetite for ubiquitous experience in face of this fact. Nor could the solitude be overcome. It could gather on beaches and streets and in parks only through coincidence, and, with its companions, form a *tableau vivant* of human incommunicability."

To break "this silence and solitude" Rothko first sought liberation through the dislocations of Surrealism, and finally by purifying the pictorial means themselves. His first exhibition at Peggy Guggenheim's Art of This Century showed the influence of Masson's automatism and Ernst's hybrid organic-anatomical forms. There was even then, however, something expedient and provisional in Rothko's adaptions of Surrealist devices; his fanciful forms seemed to melt and coalesce in a tonal atmosphere which dispersed and muffled their separate intensities. Predatory events and forms were softened and transmuted by light, as if seen through depths of water. Soon after, Rothko's shapes lost any relationship or semblance to organic life, to waving grasses, ferns or submarine growth, and became accents in a purely abstract scheme of fine lines, with delicate sprays and diffusions of color.

By the end of 1947, the artist abandoned linear elaboration entirely, building his surfaces of irregular color zones, high in key. These brilliant red and orange cores of light asserted themselves more aggressively, and their indistinct edges and backgrounds of reduced intensity gave them an ominous power; each luminous center suggested a sun moving through layers of fog, whose color intensity was only a hint of its blinding light under conditions of full visibility. The chemical brilliance of Rothko's hues, and the cacophonous juxtapositions of hot colors created an atmosphere of magical incandescence: matter became sublimated into light, or in another analogy, the material elements which comprised the painting, like some miraculous fuel, seemed to consume themselves in the act of creation, giving off some purer, poetic substance.

In 1950, Rothko began to work in broad, rigorously parallel bars of color, extending them from the lateral limits of the canvas rectangle. Or he would set one or two solid flat masses of brilliant hue in a homogeneous field of closely related color. By giving a thinner density and increased luminosity to his blunt, blocky masses at their edges, and by a subtle internal modulation of area, he preserved a quality of weightless suspension. The lack of a clear point of termination in the boundaries of shapes created an ambiguous interplay of advance and recession, and a multiple logic of movement; Rothko's flat color masses can be read, alternately, as forward plane or background void. A rigorous frontality, symmetry and rectilinearity, however, give his paintings an extraordinary architectonic power (color plate 153). It is difficult to think of any modern paintings in which such an intensified coloristic expression has been combined with such an insistent pictorial architecture, unless it be in such works of Matisse as *The Blue Window* and *Red Studio* of 1911, both of which hang in the Museum of Modern Art, New York. There, too, space expresses itself simultaneously as flattened, suspended mass and orphic color, all within the limits of a few simplified planes. It is interesting to note that Matisse at the time spoke of his desire to find a scheme of "absolute" color. (In this connection the name of Milton Avery must be brought up; one of the few contemporary American painters directly influenced by Matisse, Avery was an early and persisting admiration of Rothko.) To Matisse's schemes of the 1911 period Rothko has added his own ardor, purity and monumentality, and of course radically altered them by his invention of an original pictorial means.

Unlike Matisse, Rothko is impelled by a sense of grave ethical purpose. His progress from individualized definition of forms in his early work to a more encompassing unity based on free rhythms and slab-like color mass, held in a delicate tension of balance, has been part of an acknowledged and continuing search for transcendental reality. While it is totally unrelated to Mondrian's Neo-Plasticism, or to his mood and methods, Rothko's painting has absorbed something of the great Dutch artist's exalted concept of art. Mondrian's injunction, "We must destroy the *particular* form," provided the most drastic modern liberation from naturalism and was a step on the path to an absolute art which in Mondrian's words would "reveal, as far as possible, the universal aspect of life." These aims, it would seem, have found a forceful contemporary application in Rothko's work.

It is only fitting to add that Rothko himself finds any comparison with Mondrian misleading: he feels that his own art deals directly with human emotion, and often with tragic forces. The differences with Mondrian's chaste expression are obvious and important. Rothko's forms are both more emotional in impact and less determinate; color, shape and edge do not neutralize each other in their interplay, to the end of achieving a refined equilibrium of plastic forces. Each chromatic block retains its autonomy, and a concrete material presence. Yet Rothko's paintings also permit associations with varied moods, with a menacing hostility, a pan-like lyricism, or an ideal calm. Although the primary significance of these paintings is as concrete objects of aesthetic contemplation, they are colored by a vision, alternately angelic and demonic, of a world disembodied in human inwardness. A sensitive critic of the artist's work has applied the word "voodoo" to Rothko's most recent paintings, which are dominated by unrelieved blacks and resonant browns of majestic, sullen power. It is impossible to ignore the pressures of the many emotional atmospheres created by the artist's expressive color, and by his abstract imagery of light and darkness, vacancy and splendor, quiescence and vibration.

Rothko's work suggests a polarity of types in the new genre of abstraction which significantly enlarges the more restricted definition implicit in the term "action painting." It also leads us to a more detailed consideration of the scheme of values and the viewpoints that the new American paintings represent, for their most profound claim to seriousness arises ultimately from their content. The division of Abstract Expressionist painting into two dissimilar but related categories was first suggested by the well-known art historian Meyer Schapiro in a lecture, "The Younger American Painters of Today," delivered in England two years ago, and reprinted in *The Listener*. Dr. Schapiro is an enthusiast of the new movement and has now emerged as one of its principal aesthetic theorists, although he only rarely writes about the individual painters within it. In his lecture Dr. Schapiro described the painting of Pollock and de Kooning as an art of "impulse and chance," and opposed it to the painting of Rothko with its emphasis on sensation. "Each," he declared, "seeks an absolute in which the receptive viewer can lose himself, the one in compulsive movement, the other in an all-pervading, as if internalized, sensation of dominant color. The result in both is a painted world with powerful, immediate impact; in awareness of this goal, the artists have tended to work on a larger and larger scale—canvases as big as mural paintings are common in the shows in New York and, indeed, are the ones which permit the artists to realize their aims most effectively."

Adopting Dr. Schapiro's illuminating distinction, we may go on and discover other significant characteristics which separate the two generic types of abstract painting, and draw

152   Clyfford Still. 1949 (USA)

some conclusions about the differing viewpoints revealed by each. The energetic, linear style of Pollock, or the endless spatial movement of de Kooning derive from Surrealist automatism, but can also be related to what might be called an existential view of things. The artist takes responsibility for his actions and at critical moments intercedes and gives direction to the pictorial events that seem to arise spontaneously on his canvas surface. His permissiveness is limited, and is a means rather than an end, a way of tapping new creative powers in himself. For these two artists, and for a vast number of others whose work is also characterized by the free play energies, the revealed dynamics of the painting process have assumed the character of a significant and *vital* action. The artist finds his identity, and proves his own existence to himself, in effect, through his actions on the canvas surface, although, of course, memory, response to tradition and to other contemporary creations also play an important determining role in what finally emerges. More than ever before, the painting becomes a kind of denuded, structural exposure in time and space of the self engaged in a chain of critical episodes of choice and decision, acting under the flood and stress of immediate feeling. The artist "paints blind," Franz Kline has said. Some time before the epithet "action painting" was invented, another painter of this group, William Baziotes, wrote: "Whereas certain people start with a recollection of an experience and paint that experience, to some of us *the act of doing it becomes the experience;* so that we are not quite clear why we are engaged on a particular work."

The special qualities of urgency in action painting do not necessarily mean that it tends to be subjective or "confessional" in character. Indeed, the strict limits put upon the expression fantasy and psychological content, and the intense concentration on the concrete expressive means return all the data of feeling to the aesthetic process. We are left finally with a form of painting that suggests a vivid metaphor for a general dynamism and energy, and with a pictorial reality that like ourselves is involved in a constant and never-finished process of movement, development, and change.

In the painting of Pollock and de Kooning free rein is given to impulse, fancy and a mineral flow of the material evidence of the raw, untransformed painting process. Such painting suggests an "impure" attitude of mind which accepts life, change, and action. The appeal to chance, the activity of the free brush, the sense conveyed of the drama of matter define an art that is multiple, changing, bound to time and duration and to the contingencies of living. Despite its dynamism and the apotheosis of the creative process as an occasion for free and sovereign action, however, there is a sobering strain of pessimism in the new work. Its drastic rejections, rawness, frequently violent eruptions and mania for totality suggest a suppression of individualized feeling, and an exaggerated regard for an unconstrained expressiveness. But this emotional atmosphere is perhaps also characteristic of certain aspects of the American temper. The symbolic repudiation of authority, and some ideal dream of unlimited freedom are still firmly implanted in the American's myth of himself, no matter how sharply the harsh realities of material existence press on his consciousness. In many ways, Walt Whitman is the figure most prophetic of the new spirit of contemporary American painting, the Walt Whitman who found an idealistic promise in the brute energies of the raw American environment:

> In this broad earth of ours,
> Amid the measureless grossness and slag,
> Enclosed and safe within its central heart,
> Nestles the seed perfection.

One must add that if the art of Pollock and de Kooning seems to oppose taste and the more cultivated uses of the painting medium, it has also introduced us to a new order of artistic reality so compelling that we do not miss the felicitous, transforming qualities of traditional art.

At the opposite pole is the art of such painters as Rothko and Clyfford Still, a type of painting based on purer and more absolute attitudes. Derived, as we have seen, from "symbolist" modes, their art admits the accidental and the random only marginally, and seeks instead a more hieratic style that stands above fatality, chance, and the laws of the world: a more controlled, starkly simplified and stable art, exempt from the contingent and the accidental. Playing on resonant color sensations, which induce associations with symbolist color reveries, these artists seem to wish to make contact with a transcendental reality, a sphere of Otherness beyond the self. Indeed, the painting even threatens to become an instrument of occult knowledge, or at least an instrument of revelation. Whereas the art of Pollock and de Kooning is one of particulars, of furiously animated details, and emphasizes the multiplicity of Being, that of Rothko and Still presents a single magnified sensation, and an undifferentiated continuum, suggesting the unity of Being. Matter is refined into a luminous suspension which becomes a vibrant sign of some secret, inner harmony; the painting defines itself as a phase in the effort to cultivate a permanent openness of the spirit to mystery. Exalted through splendid color, the senses develop strange powers and mysterious antennae which reach beyond the self into the regions of the Ideal.

Here, the example of Mallarmé provides support and illumination. Very much to the point in evoking the atmosphere of the paintings of Rothko and Still is Marcel Raymond's description of a poem by Mallarmé: "The subject is reduced to virtually nothing, the poem's starting point is infinitely transcended, but a great dream-like effervescence is born of this whisper that is so close to silence." Rothko's disembodied sheets of colored atmosphere are sensuous, spatial envelopes; yet they give an impression of a curious detachment and their space belongs to a sphere beyond the human. They are the unappeased, voluptuous embodiments of pure mind, which may never be entirely reconciled with the immediate necessities of living:

> O intoxication! Space quivers
> Like a great kiss
> Which frantic at being born for no one,
> Can neither spring forward nor be appeased.

If the painting of de Kooning and Pollock may be termed one of commission, in which the artist does not hesitate to reveal himself, that of Still and Rothko is an art of omission, where more is suggested than stated. In Still's work there is an elaboration of "biomorphic" shapes and empty areas of negative space that evoke the nullities, voids and general mood of negation of Dada. This inspiration has been expanded, of course, and his surfaces assert themselves as total presences, within an autonomous aesthetic whole. Rothko's sensuousness is more traditional and positive, although his artistic means are actually far more radical. At its solemn and deep best, Rothko's art, like that of another modern painter who challenged the Absolute, Piet Mondrian, is informed by a sense of great tasks and moves on the heights.

Since 1951 Philip Guston (born 1912) has provided a vital, new alternative to, and in some respects a synthesis of, the two opposing tendencies of action painting and the more absolutist aims of Rothko and Still. Guston's canvases forcefully testify to their maker's active presence in the work. The assertive material textures and the rudimentary expressiveness of the pigmented surface identify the painting as a phase of a continuing creative impulse rather than a pat finished product. His work embodies a primitively direct consciousness of creation itself, and comes to birth at the point where determinate artistic reality and indeterminate matter intersect. Artistic form is revealed at the source, in the very process of achieving existence and order. The drama of Guston's paintings is bound up with their intimate disclosure of the events of the creative act, and they comprise a concrete representation of the unities of mind in naked and luminous contact with the unformed paint matter. To adopt Paul Valéry's discerning comment on the nature of modern poetry, Guston's painting "enjoins us to come into being . . ."

Unlike de Kooning and Pollock, Guston has avoided the more explosive manifestations of artistic freedom, and accepts the property of inertia in matter. In his earlier paintings, he built up and maintained his surface with many, small uniform accents of melting, intense color; more recently, he has worked with irregular opposing shapes of indeterminate character. In either case, the movement of a weighted brush is deliberately checked and controlled, as if its free activity were subject to imponderable forces and grave obstructions.

153　Mark Rothko. 1957　*(USA)*

With its underlying stabilities, unhasting rhythms and heightened color sensations, Guston's painting achieves, finally, the unity of a single, optical pulsation not dissimilar in effect from the splendid sonorities of Rothko's color structures. As an artistic temperament, Guston is impulsive, volatile and lyrical, however; the material function of his pigment is more explicit than Rothko's, and he seems to paint out of immediate, existential needs rather than out of ideal drives.

Guston's early abstract paintings have been referredto as "Abstract Impressionist" due to their quality of atmospheric permeation, their high-keyed palette, and a fluent brushstroke that superficially suggest the late Monet. But they had little to do with passive optical perception in Monet's terms, and their cumulative color strokes functioned to give tectonic definition to the picture plane. Guston's seductive surface perhaps obscured for some the underlying structuralism of his work. From 1950 to 1954, he massed dense clusters of crisscrossing color strokes against thinly painted background areas and scattered touches; the predominantly vertical and horizontal accents seemed related to Mondrian's plus-and-minus drawings, although Guston's scheme was looser and did not depend on a linear elaboration of form. Indeed, there was an intentional blurring of any pictorial elements that might tend to suggest an explicit formal order, as if structure had become implicit in the activity of the pigment itself and no longer required the support of an externalized schema.

Between 1954 and 1956, Guston moved even more boldly from a "constructed" to an intuitive ordering of form, which in itself constitued a *new* structure. Painting primarily in a variety of reds, and wielding a broader and more fleshy brush, he grouped his irregular color masses in asymmetric compositions, far up, far down, or to one side of the canvas rectangle. His shapes began to act on each other in unexpected ways, as they were released from the tightly woven web of crisscrossing color strokes, and to assert their individual identities. They took their positions on the canvas according to their secret affinities or repulsions, and formed an isolated nuclear center of activity, set against an empty background, for the larger spatial areas of the canvas were often left unaccented and virtually bare. In the place of Pollock's drips and de Kooning's whipped brushstroke, Guston had introduced a new pictorial unit: the checked flow of pigment, palpable in its material density but tremulous still with motion.

Another distinguishing mark of Guston's style has been its wayward Epicureanism, which breaks out unexpectedly in the midst of an essentially formal pictorial environment. While his handling is direct, positive and vital, there is a quality of romantic readiness and receptivity in his work. It is a matter largely of tone and mood, an emanation. Perhaps it is best defined by Keats' expression "negative capability," which the English poet explained as the condition of the man who "is capable of being in uncertainties, mysteries, doubts, without any irritable reaching after truth." For Keats the surrender to passive unconscious life was a source of poetic power; similarly Guston's paintings, which are in form and tempo the opposite of the more strenuous varieties of action painting, demonstrate the power and vitality of a principle of non-action. By a process of alternately enriching and impoverishing his surfaces, Guston achieves both an immediate splendor and its weakened echo, the direct heat of passion and the cooling, remembered ecstasy. The elegiac quality of his lyricism is the persisting link to an earlier representational style of the forties, so apparently dissimilar in every other way. There clings subtly and tenaciously to his paintings a subversive atmosphere of voluptuousness, pointing to the romantic sensibility. However, a taste for luxurious sensation only forms the threshold of an undertaking whose successful realization has little to do with the seductive possibilities of medium.

For Guston the act of painting is an onerous task which proceeds, often painfully, from the habitual and the customary to the unfamiliar, from old recognitions to new and unforeseen encounters, a complex creative progress toward a more meaningful goal of freedom. The elusive state of freedom must be *achieved* and won, yet it cannot be possessed by a mere show of force or simple energy. Guston has described his complex experience before the evolving picture in simple and eloquent language:

"What is seen and called the picture is what remains—an evidence. Even as one travels in painting towards a state of 'unfreedom' where only certain things can happen, unaccountably the unknown and the free must appear. Usually I am on a work for a long stretch, until a moment arrives when the air of the arbitrary vanishes and the paint falls into positions that feel destined. The very matter of painting—its pigment and spaces—is so resistant to the will, so disinclined to assert its plane and remain still. Painting seems like an impossibility, with only a sign now and then of its own light. Which must be because of the narrow passage from a diagramming to that other state, a corporeality. In this sense. to paint is a possessing rather than a picturing."

It is clear that his concept of creation is identified both with the aesthetic ideals of modern art, and with the contemporary crisis of the spirit. In conversation Guston has pointed out that since Cézanne and the Cubists, the first principle of the modern aesthetic has been "to give existence to the plane," that is, to the picture plane. But the emphasis on the aesthetic autonomy of the work of art does not mean that it is divorced from human reality. On the contrary, Guston insists that the "plane" also takes on a subjective aspect, becoming "a mirror of the self," and it functions finally as a symbol of lived experience as well as a set of plastic signs. "When the unities I seek are achieved," the artist has explained, "I am aware of something like surprise, since the picture looks both familiar and new. I feel that I have not invented so much as revealed, in a coded way, something that already existed. Now, while I am talking about form, I am also talking about myself. As an artist I have no way of finding my identity except through such a highly formalized experience." This reiteration of self, and of the human condition, in and through the act of painting comprises, to Guston's mind, the only "true painting." The rest he describes as "facile gesture," which has to do with "too quick a summation of how one would like to appear in the world." In the kind of painting he has in mind, Guston has asserted, "you don't care how you appear; you have given that up." The artist concedes that the phrase "true painting" has the ring of modern religious utterance, with its renunciations, sense of obstacle and anguished sense of individual responsibility. He finds his own objectives illuminated by the following quotation from Kafka's notebooks: "The true way is along a rope that is not spanned high in the air, but only just above the ground. It seems intended more to cause stumbling than to be walked along."

If there is a certain grim, the chips-are-down atmosphere in these remarks, there is also the same tension of belief which informs the best New York abstract painting. In character with the drastic tone of Guston's remarks, a new and even somewhat forbidding mood has invaded his most recent paintings. His forms have become harsh and aggressive, his rhythms more emphatic, and his palette far more somber. The result has been some of the most dramatic and expressive paintings of his career (color plate 154, and plate 165). Despite their liberal use of areas of black, their impressive scale and intensity, these paintings do not overpower, but continue to insinuate their presence in a curiously disembodied way. They are not so much demonstrations of some "action" principle as they are luminous signs of moments of consciousness, moments which have their source in great depths and bear their own mysterious charge of poetry. They penetrate beneath the level of cultivated assurances and deal directly with that nagging sense of uncertainty which preys on the most serious modern minds. At times, almost as a relief from the mortification of the act of painting, a dark, sardonic humor breaks out, and spreads throughout the painting surface like some sudden, atmospheric disturbance, leaving a wake of tumbled shapes and disorder, and precipitating a whole new chain of formal metamorphoses. Although his painting means are radically different, Guston feels a strong sympathy for Surrealism, not so much as program but as an *état d'esprit*. The goal of Surrealist expression indicated by the critic Jacques Rivière perhaps defines the single most important aspect of Guston's aims: "To grasp our being before it has yielded to consistency; to seize it in its incoherence, or better, its primitive coherence, before the idea of contradiction has appeared and compelled it to reduce and construct itself; to replace its logical unity, which can only be acquired, by its absurd unity, which alone is innate."

For many artists, seeking the self in the act of painting is as dangerous as it is unnatural. To turn every encounter with the paint substance into an occasion for asserting the authority of man's consciousness over dumb matter can be folly for all but the sternest spirits;

322

154 Philip Guston. 1957 (*USA*)

to stay aware constantly of the problem of the real, as if it were an open wound, is to inhabit an obsession. There are other equally valid considerations for contemporary painting, values of aesthetic harmony, order and coherence, the ideal of beauty, if you will. Such criteria are inherent in the language of painting itself, nor do they exclude elements of a more metaphysical sensibility. James Brooks (born 1906, plate 166) is an artist whose instinctive lyricism directs him towards objective values. He has also felt the impact of the vital paintings of his period in America, and contact with such artists as Pollock and de Kooning served to deepen and concentrate the expressive powers of his art.

During the thirties Brooks was an outstanding genre realist, or "American Scene" painter, in keeping with the social preoccupations of art in that period. In the early forties he began to work in an elegant, muted semi-abstract manner, under the modified Cubist influence which then had such wide currency among the avant-garde. Then, around 1948, he felt the influence of the vital, new abstract painting which had begun to emerge in New York; his own art was transformed, much as that of Bradley Walker Tomlin and Philip Guston had also changed between 1947 and 1949. In 1950 he showed his first abstract paintings in the new manner in a one-man show. Brooks painted from a light palette, and at times with silvery grays, thinned blacks and off whites only, setting rapidly developed shapes of an amorphous character in movement around a focal center and employing "drips," color stains and whipped lines in a manner reminiscent of Pollock. His new work was immediately noticed for its unmistakably individual qualities—for its refined lyrical accents and exquisite tonalism.

For all their finesse, however, these paintings showed a tough, springing strength in the interplay of overlapping forms and taut paint-drip paths. Brooks' pictorial world had the quality of a group of shapes swimming in and out of focus, vague and amorphous at one moment, and of a crystalline clarity the next, as if the tangible and the ephemeral were the opposing faces of the same coin. His dark, active foreground shapes could also be read as non-active, background voids, thus pushing the reserved areas between them into the forward plane as active protagonists in a drama of fluctuating movements. In this connection, the artist has said that the subject of a painting "is carried in its relationships, and the shapes and colors and things in it exist not as separate identities but as carriers. The impulse they transmit through the painting is its spirit and its meaning."

"The arts," he continues, "have brought man today to the threshold of a new view of his existence, where the process of change is more real than the idea of static permanence." Brooks' oscillating patterns of movement revolve gently like a slow kaleidoscope creating on the background of consciousness, amorphous, evanescent figures whose destinies are mysteriously bound up with the affective stirrings of the self. "There is no more forthright declaration," he has written, "and no shorter path to a man's richness, nakedness and poverty than the painting he does." Nonetheless, whatever their origins or associations in the artist's own mind, his emergent forms have surrendered any subjective function or meaning, and operate in objective pictorial space as purely aesthetic signs. A masterfully controlled ambiguity of movement in shallow depth is the real content of his work. The enjoyment of sensuous color for its own sake, the unimpeded flow of spatial movement and an inexhaustible faculty for elaboration give Brooks' paintings a quality of noble decoration. If the implication is that he adopts and applies, rather than invents, expressive conventions, that must not be construed as a criticism of his art.

Around 1953, Brooks began to employ heavier and more clumsy masses, and resonant colors, darker in key, under the acknowledged influence of de Kooning's weighted forms and lavish palette. His shapes showed a more stubborn resistance to the flow of continuous spatial movement, and kept a more vigorous grip on their individual identities. New elements of tension and friction made themselves felt in his space. In the years since he has continued experimenting with extremely personal chromatic harmonies, from muted earth tones and neutrals to brilliant, bursting complexes of spectral color (color plate 155). Whenever his predilections of the moment, and his repertory of shape, stroke and hue have seemed to approach repetitive formulas, he has not hesitated to introduce unexpected changes, relying, with notable success, on such strategies to revive qualities of freshness and creativity. His art of the past several years is remarkable, if not for sudden, dynamic growth, then for its unswerving integrity of purpose, capacity for renewal and evenness of quality.

Jack Tworkov (born 1900), like James Brooks, has cultivated and consolidated the ground won by some of his more celebrated contemporaries, rather than extending the range of painting's possibilities. Such an activity is no mean accomplishment, and by its very nature contributes to the existence of a general art culture. Without such sensitive and gifted eclectics as Tworkov, recent American painting history would be a matter of a few isolated individuals of breath-taking talent. It is unlikely that they could have sustained their collective impulse, lacking the support of a responsive and vital surrounding milieu. In any case, Tworkov is a fine artist in his own right, with an unerring instinct for ordered structure and light, lyrical color. At one time closely associated with de Kooning, he has recently broken away to make more decisive and personal artistic statements. In his work, a natural feeling for the paint paste and for subtle color modulation leads to a form of structural Impressionism. Tworkov's palette is now composed of reds and blues mainly, ranging from tints of a rococo delicacy to notes of full resonance and brilliancy. He builds form with loose, sweeping color strokes which incline steeply in one diagonal direction, until his surface begins to burn like a windswept prairie fire. His structures seem to achieve maximum tension just as they are about to sink into an insignificant chaos of warring color accents. A tough, central core of bright, tensely articulated strokes, with diminishing intensities and a die-away quality at the edges of his surfaces, characterizes this refined lyricism (color plate 156).

The first wave of Abstract Expressionism broke violently on the American painting scene between the years 1943 and 1948. To this period belongs the rediscovery, and drastic transformation, of Surrealist impulses; the revived interest in "myth" and primitivistic sources of inspiration; and a growing sense of the autonomy of native tendencies. During these years such artists as Jackson Pollock, Hans Hofmann, Robert Motherwell, Adolph Gottlieb, William Baziotes, Mark Rothko and Clyfford Still held their first one-man shows. After 1948 emerged Willem de Kooning, Franz Kline, Bradley Walker Tomlin, Philip Guston, James Brooks, Jack Tworkov, Esteban Vicente and a whole new generation of younger painters. The major innovators among the older figures themselves began to change and expand their styles after 1948, working in larger format and substituting, in their varied ways, monumental scale and more abstract qualities for an earlier concern with chimerical subject matter. A fantasia of the Unconscious gave way to a more objective dynamism, identified with the abstract means alone, turgidity to transparency, and the private obsession was dissolved in an epic lyricism.

Beginning in 1948, the successive one-man shows of Willem de Kooning had an incalculable impact on painters both of his own and the younger generation, renewing in a refreshing, painterly manner the old antagonism to naturalism and doctrinaire abstraction. After 1950, however, de Kooning's "Woman" series provided sanction for the reintroduction of the natural image and figuration. De Kooning's more "Expressionist" effects carried weight with the many painters who had begun to look to him for leadership; strong, violent sensations and many of his mannerisms of paint application began to manifest themselves in contemporary painting. The virtual suppression of color in de Kooning's first show, and in paintings of an earlier period by Pollock, Gorky and Still, found a sympathetic and even more drastic echo in the black-and-white canvases begun by Robert Motherwell in 1950, and then in the dramatic first one-man show of Franz Kline (born 1910) in 1951.

Kline's exhibition represented perhaps the most radical departure in American painting since the earlier exhibitions of Pollock, Rothko, Still and de Kooning. He has since proved himself one of the most impressive and concentrated talents on the American painting scene. If any of the group of painters under discussion should be known as *the* action painter, it is Kline. The term seems almost to have been invented for his athletic, black-and-white gestures in paint, which essentialize and project the abrupt and powerful driving movements of the body, under the muscular and psychological tension of action (plate 167). At the same time, his drastic black grids are effectively ordered plastic structures.

155 James Brooks. 1956 (*USA*)

Unlike the calligraphy of the East with which they have so often been compared, Kline's paintings utilize the reserved white areas of background space as positive forms; these white, rectangular intervals function in a space of their own making, obstructing, refracting or amplifying the thrust of his solid bars of black. Usually, too, the white backgrounds are solidly established in paint, giving a further material presence to the total formal configuration.

Kline's forms are materialized velocities and energies, released at collision point by broad, skidding, arm's-length brush-strokes. In his art a whole new spatial dynamism has declared itself quite miraculously without the resource of color, depending solely on the weighted stroke, the thick or thin, mat or glistening streaks of black and white pigment. With Philip Guston's show of the same year, Kline's exhibition in 1951 defined perhaps the last significant *new* extensions of the radical abstract styles of the decade.

Many other painters have, of course, refined on the innovations of the immediate past with great individual distinction, and there is a rising group of younger painters among whom revolutions may yet be born. Thus far the livelier young artists have been intent mainly on assimilation, although a number have completed their artistic education and emerged as distinct, fully formed personalities. They can be divided, generally, between a vast majority who work directly under de Kooning's influence, and a group of mavericks, some of whom have felt the impact of Clyfford Still and Pollock. In the first group are Milton Resnick, who at the age of forty-one actually belongs to the older generation although he is identified with the younger artists, Grace Hartigan (born 1922), Joan Mitchell (born 1926), Alfred Leslie (born 1927) and many other extremely talented young artists too numerous to list. Despite certain basic assumptions and mannerisms of handling that link them with de Kooning, they represent a variety of moods.

Resnick is a powerful, almost deliberately clumsy artist who trowels paint on canvas in lavish slabs (plate 168). Behind his blunt force and elementary simplicity is a well-stocked artistic memory and a sensitive, responsive intelligence. Grace Hartigan also manages a certain *gaucherie*, as if a cultivated refinement were a threat of some kind; she is a brilliant and exquisitely original colorist, however, and one of the few younger artists who unapologetically leaves evidence on her surfaces of systematic composition and structure (plate 170). Joan Mitchell's controlled, attenuated webs of brush strokes have a somewhat repetitive quality, as if method were its own reward, but, within the strict limits she sets herself, she has shown a strong inventive capacity. Temperament and sensibility are everywhere in evidence in Leslie's work, and his touch is unusually swift and sure; but he too often depends on the lucky find to resolve a merely promising chaos. All these artists are notable for their painterly ambition, their mastery of large surfaces and their fluency of idiom. With the exception perhaps of Grace Hartigan, none has shown a distinctly new note in his work.

156   Jack Tworkov. 1954 (*USA*)

Perhaps more original are the paintings of Sam Francis (born 1923) and Helen Frankenthaler (born 1928), although no invidious comparison with the first group on the basis of quality is intended. Francis has made an impressive reputation in Paris, his place of residence over the past several years. He was one of a number of students who studied with Clyfford Still when that artist was teaching in San Francisco during the late forties; many of his students have since made names for themselves in New York galleries. Francis paints in large, flat, loosely massed areas made up of a multitude of kidney-shaped forms, which run down the canvas in slow trickles, drips and smears of thinned oil medium. His immense surfaces throb with alternately brilliant and dark, sullen tones, like a black pool of water over which an oil slick has spread and erupted in prismatic colors. More recently, Francis has released his nuclear chains of amoeba shapes in simplified loops and arabesques, laying them into a shallow depth on large, unsized surfaces, and leaving vast areas entirely bare (plate 169).

Helen Frankenthaler allows her paint to run less systematically, and varies her exploding, fan-like trails of thinly washed pigment with sudden obstructions and firmly planted, flat shapes. If flux is her subject matter, her sensibility is firmly rooted in an intuitive elaboration of rhythmic structure. In a distinctly personal and feminine manner, she conveys such abstract poetic ideas as unfolding, enfolding and reaching; her paintings have the quality of some delicate, nameless organism, which opens and closes almost imperceptibly beneath our gaze, with the expansiveness and dilation of time itself.

Grace Hartigan was one of a number of artists who, following de Kooning's lead, have in the recent past tried, with some success, to renew natural imagery and representation while still retaining the spontaneity of expression and the improvisatory surfaces of Abstract Expressionism. Most other young artists who returned to the object and to a limited form of representation, however, have found their path beset with obstacles: they seemed unable to avoid a certain self-consciousness about their counter-revolution, nor could they overcome the derivative echoes of one or another *démodé* styles of the past which invariably crept into their work. The repudiation of abstraction has been isolated and without program, however; it would seem less an index of some positive new painting alternative than a limited, conservative reaction on the part of a few painters in whom the new idioms had not struck deep roots. For the time being, we may assume that the styles of Pollock and de Kooning on the one hand, and of Rothko and Still on the other, continue to define the antipodes of advanced American painting.

Whatever the ultimate evaluation of the past fifteen years of American painting, it is clear that a bold and original movement has come to birth. Its originality becomes even clearer if this new painting is compared with the related Tachiste tendencies which have arisen independently abroad, and to a more limited degree in Canada. The art of the Canadians

Paul-Emile Borduas (born 1905, plate 171), of Jean-Paul Riopelle (born 1923), living in Paris, and the young William Ronald (born 1926, plate 172), who makes New York his place of residence, provides instructive parallels and divergences. All three Canadians have covered large canvases with spontaneous, rapidly developed forms, which can be reduced in the case of Borduas and Riopelle to a continuous field of uniform accents. Ronald works with isolated shape complexes and lavishly pigmented masses, which run at their edges and fuse with a non-active background, giving no clear sense of demarcation between space and form. There is a rhythmically sustained flowing movement, a struggle against limitation and containment, and a quality of explosive release and excitement in the work of each of these three artists that link it with contemporary American painting. Yet, by comparison, the painting of any one of the Americans under discussion must seem far more "raw," direct and physical, deficient in professional surface, and without the air of studio manufacture to be found in comparable Canadian or Parisian work. That in itself is cause neither for alarm nor for self-congratulation, although some American artists feel impelled to identify art with the repudiation of all civilized values, and some Europeans insist on seeing American artistic culture as elementary and barbaric, no matter how much evidence can be marshaled to the contrary.

The plastic vigor of American Abstract Expressionism stems from a heightened consciousness of the act of creation. It is an art of origins, young, intense, harsh and new; its emotional force derives from the identification of an abstract means, of the painting process itself, with passion, with disquiet, with problems of existence and being. In a stern and disapproving letter to a fellow writer, Charles Maurras once expressed the distaste of the classicist for a romantic primitivism: "You have seen the primal being . . . But you have stopped there. You have not seen the order of the earth and the heavens blossom from the mixtures of this universal mud. And you have done nothing to hasten the birth of lights and harmonies . . . No origin is beautiful, true beauty is at the end of things." The new American painters would violently dissent in this opinion.

True beauty, they would say, will be found at the beginning of things, and only in the full awareness of "this universal mud" are we today capable of grasping the "order of earth and heaven." For them traditional authority no longer commands blind and uncritical allegiance. However, they see the destruction of traditional values not as a source of despair but of power, and as an occasion of new growth. They argue that only the artistic self which is certain of its identity, since it knows that its existence can be proved through the act of creation, is able to be free, and can dispense with the armor of systematic certainties. These American artists have found new modes of awareness by returning to their creative beginnings. In so doing, they have introduced an original expressive physiognomy and unprecedented forms into modern painting.

Notes

[1] To commemorate the assassination of over 400 Italian hostages by the Nazis. (p. 92, 97)

[2] Socialists living in exile in France. Their assassination was attributed to Fascist henchmen, and was a cause célèbre in the 1930s. (p. 102)

[3] In 1946 its title became the Arts Council of Great Britain. (p. 222)

[4] *Paul Nash*, by Anthony Bertram. London, 1955, p. 278. (p. 224)

[5] For a detailed analysis of the archetypal significance of Moore's work, see Erich Neumann. (p. 228)

[6] I am aware that Camus does not claim to be an existentialist philosopher, and that there are important differences between his philosophy and Sartre's; nevertheless both writers belong to the same climate of opinion, to which also belong the artists I am describing. (p. 236)

[7] William Townsend in *The Burlington Magazine*, Vol. XCIX (June, 1957), p. 203. (p. 238)

[8] *Ben Nicholson: Paintings, Reliefs, Drawings*. With an introduction by Herbert Read. London (Lund Humphries) 1948; *Ben Nicholson: Work since 1947*. With an introduction by Herbert Read. London (Lund Humphries) 1956. (p. 240)

[9] Quotations from *Nine Abstract Artists: their work and theory*. Edited by Lawrence Alloway. London (A. Tiranti), 1954. (p. 243)

[10] In the Museum of Modern Art catalogue introduction for the Jackson Pollock retrospective exhibition of 1956, the author spoke of the suggestions Pollock "found in Picasso's paintings of the thirties that abstraction could be more than a language of pure aesthetic relation, and could embody its creator's fancies, disquiet and passions." For the further development of these and related ideas, he is greatly indebted to William C. Seitz's important, unpublished doctoral dissertation, *Abstract-Expressionist Painting in America: An Interpretation of the Work and Thought of Six Key Figures* (Department of Fine Arts and Archeology, Princeton University, 1955), which he has since read. Mr. Seitz restricts his study to six contemporary abstract artists and does not give Pollock major consideration; this document nevertheless remains perhaps the most comprehensive and illuminating interpretation of the styles and ideals of the new painting that has yet been written. (p. 293)

157 Stuart Davis. 1951 (*USA*)

158　Jackson Pollock. 1946　*(USA)*

159   Jackson Pollock. 1953 *(USA)*

160 Mark Tobey. 1951 *(USA)*

161   Willem de Kooning. 1956 *(USA)*

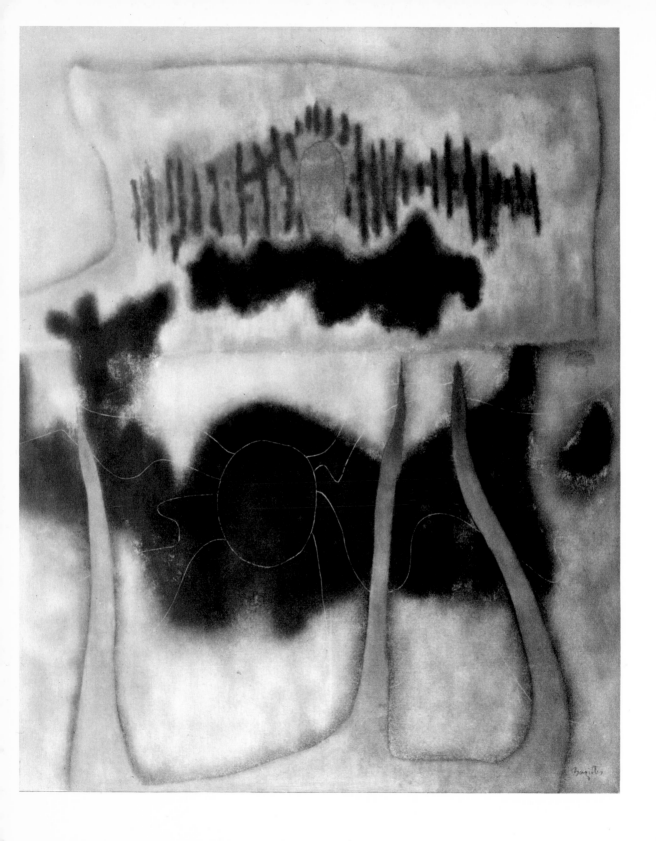

162 William Baziotes. 1955 *(USA)*

163   Adolph Gottlieb. 1946 *(USA)*

164   Mark Rothko. 1956   *(USA)*

165 Philip Guston. 1953–54 *(USA)*

166   James Brooks. 1957 (USA)

167   Franz Kline. 1955 *(USA)*

168   Milton Resnick. 1957 *(USA)*

169 Sam Francis. 1957 *(USA)*

170   Grace Hartigan. 1957 *(USA)*

171   Paul-Emil Borduas. 1948 (*USA*)

172 William Ronald. 1957 *(USA)*

Bibliography

Reference Works

H. Vollmer. Allgemeines Lexikon der bildenden Künstler. Leipzig 1953.
Dictionnaire de la peinture moderne. Paris 1954.
Knaurs Lexikon moderner Kunst. München 1955.
Dictionnaire de la peinture abstraite. Paris 1957.

General

M. Seuphor. L'art abstrait. Paris 1949.
L. Degand. Témoignages pour l'art abstrait. Paris 1952.
Masters of Modern Art. Ed. A. H. Barr, Jr. New York, 1954.
Premier bilan d'art actuel (Le soleil noir), ed. R. Lebel. Paris 1953.
A. C. Ritchie. The New Decade: 22 European Painters and Sculptors. New York 1955.

France

M. Brion. Art abstrait. Paris 1956.
M. Ragon. L'art abstrait. Paris 1956.
J. Bouret. L'art abstrait. Paris 1957.

Italy

J. Th. Soby. Twentieth-Century Italian Art. New York 1949.
G. Ghiringhelli. Pittura moderna italiana. Turin 1949.
U. Apollonio. Pittura moderna italiana. Venice 1950.
G. Marchiori. Panorama dell'arte italiana. Turin 1951.
L. Venturi. Otto pittori italiani. Rome 1952.
Giovanni artisti italiani. Mostra organizzata dal quotidiano il Giorno. Milan 1958.

Germany

O. Domnick. Die schöpferischen Kräfte in der abstrakten Malerei. Stuttgart-Bergen 1947.

G. Händler. Deutsche Malerei der Gegenwart. Berlin 1956.
Junger Westen. Deutsche Kunst nach Baumeister. Introduction by Schultze-Vellinghausen. Recklinghausen 1958. Kataloge der Kestner-Gesellschaft Hannover. New series 1948.

Britain

H. Read. Art Now. Enlarged Edition. London 1948.
H. Read. Contemporary British Art. Harmondsworth 1951.
A. C. Ritchie. Masters of British Painting. New York 1956.

USA

J. Th. Soby. Contemporary Painters. New York 1948.
Contemporary American Painting. University of Illinois 1948.
J. J. Sweeney. Younger American Painters. New York 1954.
New Art in America. 50 Painters of the 20th Century, ed. by I. H. Baur. Graphic Society, New York 1957.

Periodicals

Art d'aujourd'hui. Paris 1949—.
Aujourd'hui, art et architecture. Paris 1955—.
Art News. New York 1902—.
Biennale. Venice 1950—.
Cahiers d'art. Paris 1926—.
Cimaise. Paris 1953—.
College Art Journal. New York 1941—.
Das Kunstwerk. Baden-Baden and Krefeld 1946—.

Jackson Pollock. Drawing. Collection Mrs. L. K. Pollock, New York

350

The data, whenever available, are given in the following order: title, date, medium (omitted when it is oil on canvas), dimensions, and location.

■ *refers to color plates*

FRANCE

■ 1 Edouard Pignon
b. Marles-les-Mines (Pas-de-Calais), 1905

Paysage. 1957. $59 \times 36^{1}/_{2}''$. Galerie de France, Paris

■ 2 Nicolaes de Staël
b. Petersburg, 1914; d. Antibes, 1952

Les Martigues. 1952. $32^{1}/_{2} \times 39^{1}/_{2}''$. Galerie Änne Abels, Cologne

■ 3 Maria Elena Vieira da Silva
b. Lisbon, 1908

La bibliothèque. 1955. $32 \times 39^{1}/_{2}''$

■ 4 Maurice Estèves
b. Culan, 1904

Tacet. 1956. $36^{1}/_{4} \times 22''$

■ 5 Serge Poliakoff
b. Moscow, 1906

Composition en rouge, jaune, et noir. 1954. $46 \times 35''$. Moderne Galerie Otto Stangl, Munich

■ 6 Jean Bazaine
b. Paris, 1904

Marée basse. 1955. $55^{1}/_{4} \times 76^{3}/_{4}''$. Galerie Maeght, Paris

■ 7 Alfred Manessier
b. Saint-Ouen, 1911

Plain-chant. 1955. $21^{1}/_{4} \times 32''$. Galerie Änne Abels, Cologne

■ 8 Richard Mortensen
b. Copenhagen, 1910

Peinture. 1957. Galerie Denise René, Paris

■ 9 Hans Hartung
b. Leipzig, 1904

T. 56–21. 1957. Galerie de France, Paris

■ 10 André Lanskoy
b. Moscow, 1902

Composition. $39^{1}/_{2} \times 28^{3}/_{4}''$. Galerie Beyeler, Basel

■ 11 Gérard Schneider
b. Sainte-Croix (Switzerland), 1896

Composition. 1957. $63^{3}/_{4} \times 51^{1}/_{4}''$. The Kootz Gallery, New York

■ 12 Pierre Soulages
b. Rodez, 1919

Composition. 1954. $31^{1}/_{2} \times 23^{1}/_{4}''$. Moderne Galerie Otto Stangl, Munich

■	13 Jean-Paul Riopelle b. Montreal (Canada), 1924	*Rencontre.* 1956. 39^1/$_4$ × 32″. Wallraf-Richartz-Museum, Cologne
■	14 Gaston Bertrand b. Wonck (Belgium), 1910	*Italie.* 1956. 38^1/$_4$ × 64^1/$_2$″
	15 Georges Braque b. Argenteuil, 1882	*L'oiseau et son nid.* 1956. 51^1/$_4$ × 68^3/$_4$″
	16 Léon Gischia b. Dax (France), 1903	*Le grand arbre.* 1956. 18^1/$_4$ × 12^3/$_4$″
	17 Gustave Singier b. Warneton (Belgium), 1909	*Solitude, oliviers et la mer.* 1956. 21^1/$_2$ × 22^3/$_4$″. Galerie Änne Abels, Cologne
	18 Roger Bissière b. Villeréal, 1888	*Composition.* 1957. 18 × 21^1/$_2$″. Galerie Änne Abels, Cologne
	19 Pierre Tal Coat b. Montroig (Spain), 1905	*Peint sur le rocher.* 1955. 50 × 61^1/$_2$″. Galerie Maeght, Paris
	20 Mario Prassinos b. Constantinopel, 1916	*La lune de l'arbre.* 1957. 76^3/$_4$ × 68^3/$_4$″. Galerie de France, Paris
	21 Jean Deyrolle b. Nogent-sur-Marne, 1911	*Bala Huc.* 1956. 39^1/$_2$ × 32″. Galerie de France, Paris
	22 Victor Vasarely b. Pécs (Hungary), 1908	*Cintra.* 1955–56. 51^1/$_4$ × 63^3/$_4$″. Galerie Denise René, Paris
	23 Alberto Magnelli b. Florence, 1888	*Tranquillité sidérale.* 1950. 39^1/$_2$ × 32″. Galerie de France, Paris
	24 Camille Bryen b. Nantes, 1907	*Hollande (Paysage No. 30).* 1957. 36^1/$_4$ × 25^1/$_2$″
	25 Jean Fautrier b. Paris. 1898	*La mare aux Grenouilles.* 1957. 45^3/$_4$ × 32″

26	Jean Dubuffet b. Le Havre, 1901	*L'éjaculeur*. 1951. 37 × 29″. Collection Frua de Angeli
27	Zao Wou Ki b. Peking, 1920	*Stéle pour un ami.* 1956. 63³/₄ × 45″. Moderne Galerie Otto Stangl, Munich
28	Alberto Giacometti b. Stampa (Switzerland), 1910	*Peinture.* 1956. 25¹/₄ × 20³/₄″. Galerie Maeght, Paris
29	Bernard Buffet b. Paris, 1928	*Nature-morte, bouteille et verre.* 1951. 14³/₄ × 23³/₄″
30	Christian d'Orgeix b. Foix, 1927	*Cathedrale de Cologne.* 1954. 37¹/₄ × 33⁷/₈″. Galerie Springer, Berlin
31	Claude Georges b. Fumay (Ardennes), 1929	*Rouge et noir.* 1958. 36¹/₂ × 28³/₄″. Galerie Änne Abels, Cologne
32 a	Georges Mathieu b. Boulogne-sur-Mer, 1921	*Magnificence de Bon Duc de Borgogne à son banquet de voeux.* 1957. 30 × 80″
32 b	Jaroslaw Serpan b. Prague, 1922	*Poogendij (Peinture No. 511).* 1957. 47¹/₄ × 81¹/₂″. Galerie Änne Abels, Cologne

BELGIUM

33	Pierre Alechinsky b. Brussels, 1927	*Peinture.* 1957. 63 × 55¹/₈″
34	Raoul Ubac b. Malmédy, 1910	*Mur.* 1956–58. 52¹/₄ × 58³/₈″. Galerie Maeght, Paris
35	René Margritte b. 1898	*L'empire des lumières.* 1955. 63⁷/₈ × 51¹/₄″
36	Paul Delvaux b. Antheit (Belgium), 1897	*La Mise au Tombeau.* 1951. 60¹/₄ × 105¹/₂″

37	Lismonde b. Brussels, 1908	*Ruines I.* 1953. Chalk, $28^3/_4 \times 41^3/_8''$
38	Anne Bonnet b. Brussels, 1908	*Sacre oriental.* 1956. $63^7/_8 \times 51^1/_4''$

ITALY

▪ 39	Giorgio Morandi b. Bologna, 1890	*Fiori.* 1944. $8^1/_4 \times 7$
▪ 40	Renato Guttuso b. Palermo, 1912	*Paese del latifondo siciliano.* 1956. $42^1/_8 \times 30^3/_4''$
▪ 41	Atanasio Soldati b. Parma, 1887–1953	*Composizione.* 1952. $39^1/_2 \times 25^1/_2''$
▪ 42	Renato Birolli b. Verona, 1906	*Le Cinque Terre.* 1955. $29^1/_8 \times 41^3/_4''$
▪ 43	Antonio Corpora b. Tunis, 1909	*Pittura.* 1958. Galleria La Bussola, Rome
▪ 44	Ennio Morlotti b. Lecco, 1910	*La colazione sull'erba.* 1956. $59 \times 45''$
▪ 45	Bruno Cassinari b. Piacenza, 1912	*Paesaggio.* 1957. $39^1/_2 \times 31^1/_2''$
▪ 46	Giuseppe Santomaso b. Venice, 1907	*Rossi e gialli della mietura.* 1957. $63^3/_4 \times 45''$
▪ 47	Emilio Vedova b. Venice, 1919	*Lettera aperta.* 1957. Tempera on cardboard, $67 \times 53^1/_4''$
▪ 48	Osvaldo Licini b. Monte Vidon Corrado (Italy), 1894	*Angelo.* 1951. Oil on cardboard, $13 \times 15^3/_4''$

354

■ 49 Giuseppe Capogrossi
b. Rome, 1900

Superficie. 1957. $37^3/_4 \times 57^1/_2''$

■ 50 Fausto Pirandello
b. Rome, 1899

Natura morta. 1955. $39 \times 31^1/_2''$. Private collection, Rome

51 Giulio Turcato
b. Mantua, 1912

Composizione. 1958. $39^1/_2 \times 37^1/_2''$

52 Achille Perilli
b. Rome, 1927

La minaccia. 1957. $45 \times 57^1/_2''$

53 Piero Dorazio
b. Rome, 1927

Supernova. 1958. $39^1/_2 \times 32''$

54 Renato Birollo
b. Verona, 1906

Espansione. 1957. $39^1/_2 \times 22''$

55 Afro (Afro Basaldella)
b. Udine, 1912

Ombra bruciata. 1956. $39^1/_2 \times 59''$. Galleria d'arte moderna, Rome

56 Marro Reggiani
b. Modena, 1897

Composizione in azzuro. 1955

57 Enrico Prampolini
b. Modena, 1896

Anatomie concrete. 1950. $55^1/_8 \times 31^1/_2''$

58 Alberto Burri
b. Città di Castello, 1915

Combustione legno. 1958.

59 Luigi Spazzapan
b. Gradisca, 1890

La nuit tombe dans le lac transparent. 1957. $79 \times 39^1/_2''$. Galleria La Bussola, Rome

60 Alberto Brunori
b. Perugia, 1924

Mare bleu. 1957. $45 \times 57^1/_2''$

61 Mattia Moreni
b. Pavia, 1920

Incendio. 1957. $51^1/_4 \times 63^7/_8''$. GalerieÄnne Abels, Cologne

62   Lucio Fontana   *Conzetto spaziale.* 1958
      Rosario Santa Fé/Argentina, 1899

63   Gianni Dova   *Ucello alla finestra.* 1957. $28^1/_4 \times 23^1/_2''$.
      b. Rome, 1925   Galleria Blu, Milan

64   Roberto Crippa   *Consistenza sicura.* 1958
      b. Monza (Italy), 1921

65   Zoran Music   *Paysage.* 1954
      b. Gorizia, 1909

66   Franco Gentilini   *Figure e tavoli.* 1957. Collection Luigi de
      b. Faenza, 1909   Luca, Rome

SPAIN

67   Antonio Tapies   *Painting.* 1958. $77^1/_2 \times 52''$
      b. Barcelona, 1923

68   Antonio Saura   *Marta.* 1958. $25^3/_4 \times 20^1/_2''$
      b. Cienca, 1930

69   Juan Josè Tharrats   *Morte d'incanto.* 1957. $32^1/_4 \times 39^1/_4''$
      b. Gerona, 1918

70   Rafael Canogar   *Painting Nr. 2.* 1957. $12^1/_2 \times 16^1/_4''$
      b. Toledo, 1934

71 a Luis Feito   *Painting Nr. 4.* 1958. $15^3/_4 \times 23^1/_2''$
      b. Madrid, 1929

71 b Vicente Vela   *Painting.* 1958. $13^1/_4 \times 15^3/_4''$
      b. Jerez de la Frontera, 1931

YUGOSLAVIA

72 Edo Murtić
    b. Velika Pizanica/Croatia, 1921

Persistenza. 1958

73 Lazar Vujaklija
    b. Vienna, 1914

Composition. 1954

POLAND

74.a Tadeusz Kantor
    b. 1915

Painting. 1958

74.b Wladyslaw Strzeminski
    b. near Minsk, 1893; d. Lodz, 1952

Composition. 1948. $28^3/_8 \times 24''$

GERMANY

- 75 Willi Baumeister
    Stuttgart, 1889–1955

Zwei Laternen. 1955. $25^1/_2 \times 21^1/_4''$

- 76 Theodor Werner
    b. Berlin, 1903

In Bewegung. 1957. Oil with tempera on cardboard. $19^3/_4 \times 28^3/_4''$

- 77 Fritz Winter
    b. Altenbögge, 1905

Komposition. 1956. $53^1/_4 \times 57^1/_8''$. Collection Klaus Gebhard, Wuppertal

- 78 Ernst Wilhelm Nay
    b. Berlin, 1902

Diamant rot. 1958. $46^1/_2 \times 35^1/_2''$.

- 79 Wols (Wolfgang Schultze)
    b. Berlin, 1913; d. Paris, 1951

Komposition. 1950. Watercolor and pen, $7^1/_4 \times 9^1/_8''$. Collection Klaus Gebhard, Wuppertal

- 80 Werner Gilles
    b. Rheydt, 1894

Fischer am Strand von Ischia. 1954. $12^1/_4 \times 25^1/_4''$

81	Heinz Trökes b. Hamborn, 1913	*Staccato*. 1952. Tempera. $27^1/_2 \times 34^1/_2''$. Collection Klaus Gebhard, Wuppertal
82	Bernhard Schultze b. Schneidemühl, 1915	*Torsyt*. 1958. $39^1/_2 \times 31^1/_2''$
83	Georg Meistermann b. Solingen, 1911	*Glasfenster*. 1958. House of Ströher, Darmstadt
84	Woty Werner b. Berlin, 1903	*Harlekinade*. 1956. Tapestry. $58^3/_8 \times 26''$
85	Max Bill b. Winterthur, 1908	*Transmutation*. 1955. $37^3/_4 \times 12^1/_2''$
86	Karel Appel b. Amsterdam, 1921	*Zwei Köpfe*. 1953. $39^1/_2 \times 56^3/_8''$
87	Alexander Camaro b. Breslau, 1901	*Morgen am Fluss*. 1953
88	Werner Heldt Berlin, 1904–1955	*Oktobernachmittag*. 1952. $22 \times 30^3/_4''$. Galerie Springer, Berlin
89	Rolf Nesch b. Oberesslingen/Württ., 1893	*Fridolin*. 1954. $22^1/_2 \times 16^1/_8''$
90	H. A. P. Grieshaber b. Schloß Rot, 1909	*Fest*. 1957. Woodcut
91	Werner Scholz b. Berlin, 1898	*Zirkusreiterin*. 1950. $35^1/_2 \times 34^1/_2''$
92	Friedrich Karl Gotsch b. Preis/Schleswig, 1900	*Im Sturm*. 1956. $39^1/_2 \times 31^1/_2''$
93	Max Ernst b. Brühl, 1891	*Portugiesische Nonne*. 1950

| 94 | Richard Oelze | *An einer Kirche.* 1949–54. $31^1/_2 \times 39^1/_2''$ |
| | b. Magdeburg, 1900 | |

| 95 | Josef Fassbender | *Dionysos.* 1957. $55^1/_8 \times 79''$ |
| | b. Cologne, 1903 | |

| 96 a | Eduard Bargheer | *Città meridionale.* 1956. $31^1/_8 \times 51^1/_2''$ |
| | b. Hamburg, 1901 | |

| 96 b | Margherita Russo | *Oberflächen.* 1957–58. $82^3/_4 \times 78^3/_8''$ |
| | b. Munich | |

| 97 | Karl Otto Götz | *AGDE.* 1957. $23^1/_2 \times 27^1/_2''$ |
| | b. Aix-la-Chapelle, 1914 | |

| 98 | Hann Trier | *Engpass II.* 1957. $51^1/_4 \times 32''$ |
| | b. Kaiserswerth, 1915 | |

| 99 a | Max Ackermann | *Bajamar.* 1957 |
| | b. Berlin, 1877 | |

| 99 b | Julius Bissier | *Painting 4.8.1958* |
| | b. Freiburg, 1893 | |

| 100 | K. R. H. Sonderborg | *Flying Thought.* 1958 |
| | b. Sonderborg on Alsen, 1958 | |

| 101 | Winfred Gaul | *Schwarz und Weiss.* 1957. Oil on paper and canvas. $39^1/_2 \times 25^1/_2''$ |
| | b. Düsseldorf, 1928 | |

| 102 | Gerhard Hoehme | *Durchbruch des Violett.* 1958. $39^1/_2 \times 31^1/_2''$. Galerie 22, Düsseldorf |
| | b. Greppin, 1920 | |

| 103 | Emil Schumacher | *Barbaros.* 1957. $52 \times 67''$. Collection Miller, Bodensee |
| | b. Hagen, 1912 | |

| 104 | Fred Thieler | *S–X–57.* 1958. $39^1/_2 \times 25^1/_2''$ |
| | b. Königsberg, 1916 | |

105	Rupprecht Geiger b. Munich, 1908	*E 245.* 1957
106	Rudolf Mauke b. Magdeburg, 1924	*Orten.* 1958. $31 \times 40^1/_2''$

AUSTRIA

107a	Josef Mikl b. Vienna, 1929	*Resurrection.* 1957. Stained-glass, Church in Salzburg-Parsch
107b	Fritz Hundertwasser b. Vienna, 1928	*Cette fleur aura raison des hommes.* 1957
108a	Carl Unger b. near Znaim, 1915	*Composition.* 1957
108b	Karl Anton Wolf b. Vienna, 1908	*Composition.* 1958

SWITZERLAND

109	Varlin b. Zurich, 1900	*Portrait of Manuel Gasser.* 1955. $76 \times 34^1/_2''$
110a	Walter Bodmer b. 1903, Basel	*Wire painting.* 1951. Öffentliche Kunst- sammlungen, Basel
110b	Fritz Glarner b. Zurich, 1899	*Relational Painting, 80.* 1954. $24^1/_2 \times$ $24^1/_2''$. Collection W. Loeffler, Zurich

GREAT BRITAIN

111	Ben Nicholson b. near Uxbridge, 1894	*Blue Trevose.* 1957. $48 \times 30''$

- 112 Graham Sutherland
  b. London, 1903

  Three Standing Forms in a Garden. 1952. 43 × 40″. Collection Mrs. Graham Sutherland

- 113 Victor Pasmore
  b. Chesham, 1908

  Relief Construction in White, Black, Brown and Maroon. 1958. Painted wood. 29 × 27″

- 114 Ivon Hitchens
  b. London, 1893

  Dahlias and Poppies. 1956. 22 × 33″. The Redfern Gallery

- 115 William Scott
  b. Greenoch, 1913

  Orange and Blue. 1957. 34 × 44″. The British Council, London

- 116 Peter Lanyon
  b. St. Ives, Cornwall, 1918

  Coast Wind. 73 × 50″. 1957

- 117 Ceri Richards
  b. Swansea, 1903

  Cycle of Nature. 1955–56. 50 × 50″. Collection F. E. Williams

- 118 Roger Hilton
  b. Northwood, 1911

  Painting June 1955. 49³/₄ × 40″

- 119 Alan Davie
  b. Grangemouth/Scotland

  Sacrifice. 92 × 126″. 1956

- 120 Jack Smith
  b. Sheffield, 1928

  Child Walking. 1953. 62 × 48″. The British Council, London

121 Henry Moore

King and Queen. 1952–53. Bronze, h. 5 ft. 4¹/₂″. Collection W. J. Keswick, Glenkiln/Scotland

122 Henry Moore
b. Castlefort, 1898

Reclining Figures. Sketches for Sculptures. 1947. Chalk, pencil and water color. 10³/₄ × 9″. Collection Mrs. Henry Moore

123 Henry Moore

Reclining Figure (external forms). 1953–54. Bronze. l. 7 ft.

124	Barbara Hepworth b. Wakefield/Yorkshire, 1903	*Curved Form (Delphi)*. 1955. Carved Nigerian scented guarea, h. 42″
125	Reginald Butler b. Buntingford, 1913	*The Manipulator*. 1954. Bronze, h. 68″
126	Lynn Chadwick b. London, 1914	*Maquette for Two Winged Figures*. 1956. Iron, h. 22$^1/_2$″
127	Graham Sutherland b. London, 1903	*Estuary with Rocks*. 1946. Watercolor and gouache. 8$^1/_4$ × 10$^3/_4$″. The British Council, London
128	Francis Bacon b. Dublin, 1910	*Fragment of a Crucifixion*. 1950. 54 × 42″. Collection Mrs. Helen Grigg
129	Bryan Winter b. London, 1915	*Lost City*. 1956. 56$^3/_4$ × 44$^3/_4$″
130	D. Hamilton Fraser b. London, 1928	*Landscape (City III)*. 1957. 48 × 36″. Gimpel Fils Gallery, London
131	Harold Cohen b. London, 1928	*Seated Figure*. 1955. 48 × 32″. Gimpel Fils Gallery, London
132	Keith Vaughan b. Sesley Bill, 1912	*Figures by a Torn Tree Branch*. 1946. 21 × 31 cm. Private collection, London
133	Louis de Brocquy b. Dublin, 1916	*The Last Tinker*. 45 × 32$^1/_2$″. 1948
134	William Gear b. Fife/Scotland, 1915	*Structure White Element*. 1955. 21$^1/_4$ × 25$^1/_2$″. Gimpel Fils Gallery, London
135	Sandra Blow b. London, 1925	*Painting*. 1957. 54 × 42″. Gimpel Fils Gallery, London

136	Frank Auerbach b. Berlin, 1931	*Head of E.O.W.* 1955. Oil on cardboard. Collection Julius Fleischmann, Ohio, USA
137	Edward Middleditch b. Chelmsford, 1925	*Pigeons in Trafalgar Square.* 1953–54. 6 ft. × 4 ft. Beaux Arts Gallery, London
138	Lucien Freud b. Berlin, 1922	*Portrait of Stephen Spender.* 1958. Collection Stephen Spender, Esq.
139	Stanley William Hayter b. London, 1901	*Orpheus.* 1949. $74^3/_4 \times 59^7/_8''$. Kunsthalle Basel

HOLLAND

140	Corneille (Cornélis van Beverloo) b. Liège, 1922	*Spanish City.* 1958. $32 \times 45^3/_4''$
141	Gerrit Benner b. Leeuwarden, 1897	*Farmhouse.* 1954. $23^1/_2 \times 31^1/_2''$

SCANDINAVIA

142	Asger Jorn b. Vejrun, 1914	*Letter to my Son.* 1956–57. $51^1/_4 \times 76^3/_4''$
143	Endre Nemes	*Insects and Vegetal Forms* (detail). 1956. $275^3/_4 \times 98^1/_2''$
144	Anna-Eva Bergmann b. Stockholm, 1909	*Composition.* 1956

USA

145	Mark Tobey b. Centerville/Wisconsin, 1890	*Tropicalism.* 1948. Tempera. $26^1/_2 \times 19^3/_4''$. Willard Gallery, New York

146	Hans Hofmann b. Weissenburg, 1880	*Exuberance*. 1955. 50 × 40″. Albright Art Gallery, Buffalo, N. Y.
147	Jackson Pollock b. Cody/Wyoming, 1912 d. East Hampton 1956	*Cathedral*. 1947. Duco and aluminum paint on canvas. 71 × 35″. Dallas Museum of Fine Arts, Dallas, Texas
148	Arshile Gorky b. in Armenia, 1904 d. New York, 1948	*Agony*. 1947. 40 × 50$^1/_2$″. The Museum of Modern Art, New York
149	Willem de Kooning b. Rotterdam, 1904	*Woman II*. 1952. 59 × 43$^1/_4$″. The Museum of Modern Art, New York
150	Robert Motherwell b. Aberdeen, USA, 1915	*The Voyage*. 1949. Oil and tempera on paper, 48 × 94″. The Museum of Modern Art, New York
▪ 151	Bradley Walker Tomlin b. Syracuse/N.Y., 1899	*Nr. 9: In Praise of Gertrude Stein*. 1950. 49″ × 8′6″. The Museum of Modern Art, New York
▪ 152	Clyfford Still b. Grandin/North Dakota, 1904	*Number 2*. 1949. 91 × 69″. Collection Ben Heller, New York
▪ 153	Mark Rothko b. Dvinsk (Russia), 1905	*Black over Reds*. 1957. 95 × 81$^1/_2$″. Collection Edgar Mermann, Baltimore, Maryland
▪ 154	Philip Guston b. Montreal, 1913	*The Mirror*. 1957. 68 × 60$^1/_2$″. Collection Bliss Parkinson, New York
▪ 155	James Brooks b. St. Louis/Missouri, 1906	*Karrig*. 1956. 79$^1/_8$ × 73$^1/_2$″. Stable Gallery, New York
▪ 156	Jack Tworkov b. Biala/Polen, 1900	*Pink Mississippi*. 1954. 60 × 50″. Stable Gallery, New York

157	Stuart Davis	*Owh! in San Pao.* 1951. $52^3/_8 \times 42''$. Whitney Museum of American Art, New York
	b. Philadelphia, 1894	
158	Jackson Pollock	*Shimmering Substance.* 1946. $30 \times 24''$. Collection Mrs. Emily Walker, Ridgefield/Connecticut
159	Jackson Pollock	*Four Opposites.* $72^1/_4 \times 5^1/_4''$. Collection Boris and Sophie Leavitt, Lana Lobell, Hanover, Pa.
160	Mark Tobey	*1951.* Tempera. Collection Joseph R. Schapiro, Oak Park/Illinois
161	Willem de Kooning	*Easter Monday.* 1956. $96 \times 74''$. The Metropolitan Museum of Art, New York
162	William Baziotes	*Pompeii.* 1955. $60 \times 48''$. The Museum of Modern Art, New York
	b. Pittsburgh, 1912	
163	Adolph Gottlieb	*Voyager's Return.* 1946. $37^7/_8 \times 29^7/_8''$. The Museum of Modern Art, New York
	b. New York, 1903	
164	Mark Rothko	*Yellow over Purple.* 1956. $69^1/_2 \times 59^1/_4''$. Collection Morton G. Neumann, Chicago.
165	Philip Guston	*Zone.* 1953–54. $46 \times 48''$. Collection Ben Heller, New York
166	James Brooks	*Ainlee.* 1957. $85 \times 66''$. The Metropolitan Museum of Art, New York
167	Franz Kline	*Wanamaker Block.* 1955. $6' 6^1/_2 \times 71''$. Collection Richard Brown Baker, New York
	b. Wilkes-Barre/Pennsylvania, 1910	
168	Milton Resnick	*Rubble.* 1957. $40 \times 46''$. Poindexter Gallery, New York
	b. 1917	

169	Sam Francis b. San Malteo/California, 1923	*Summer Nr. II*. 1957. 6 ft. × 8 ft. Martha Jackson Gallery, New York
170	Grace Hartigan b. Newark/New Jersey, 1922	*Billboard*. 1957. 6 ft. × 7 ft.. Tibor de Nagy Gallery, New York
171	Paul-Emil Borduas b. Hilaire, Rouville County, 1905	*Morning Candelabra*. 1948. $32^1/_4 \times 43''$. The Museum of Modern Art, New York
172	William Ronald b. Stratford/Ontario, 1926	*Chieftain*. 1957. $50^1/_2 \times 60''$. Collection Peter Rübel, Cos Cob/Connecticut

Index

Aalto 89
Aas, Harald 258
Abeele, Remy van den 56
Accardi, Carla 110, 120
Acht, René 194
Ackermann, Max 174, *pl. 99 a*
Adams, Norman 244
Adams, Robert 230, 243
Adolf, Erich 101
Afro (Basaldella) 97, 116, *pl. 55*
Agam 37
Aguéli, Ivan 256
Aizpiri 17, 18
Ajmone 120
Albers, Josef 155, 156
Albini, F. 89
Alechinsky, Pierre 48, 59, 185, 190, 252, 253, *pl. 33*
Allaux, J. P. 30
Altdorfer, Heinrich 186
Andresdottir, Gudmunda 257
Apollinaire, Guillaume 28
Apollonio, Umbro 110, 118
Appel, Karel 185, 252, 253, *col. pl. 86*
Archipenko, Alexander 226
Armitage, Kenneth 232, 234, 235, 236, 248
Arnal 47
Arp, Hans 92, 98, 101, 127, 158, 168, 186, 194, 305
Astengo 89
Atlan 22
Attardi, Ugo 110
Auerbach, Frank 244, *pl. 136*
Avery, Milton 313
Avray-Wilson, Frank 244
Ayllon, José 122
Ayres, Gillian 244

Bacon, Francis 235, 244, 248, 250, *pl. 128*
Badosi 93
Baj 120
Bargheer, Eduard 174, *pl. 96 a*
Barisani 101, 120
Barns-Graham, W. 243
Baroni 102
Barré 44
Bartel, Kurt 188
Battke, Heinz 182

Bauchant 28
Baudelaire, Charles 304
Baumeister, Willi 155, 158, 160, 161, 162, 164, 166, 169, 172, 174, 185, 193, *col. pl. 75*
Baumgarten, P. 166
Bazaine, Jean 22, 24, 25, 114, *col. pl. 6*
Baziotes, William 285, 289, 310, 316, 326, *pl. 162*
Beaudin, André 14
Beauvoir, Hélène de 26
Bechtold, Erwin 188
Beck, Gustav K. 193
Becker, Walter 181
Beckett, Samuel 174
Beckmann, Max 155, 157, 158
Bell, Clive 240
Bellegarde 25
Bellmer, Hans 158, 182
Bendini 120
Benn, Gottfried 193
Benner, Gerrit 254, *pl. 141*
Benton, Thomas Hart 288, 289
Berçot, Paul 26
Bergmann, Anna-Eva 22, 257, *pl. 144*
Berke, Hubert 157
Berlewi, Henryk 127
Bertini, Gianni 120
Bertrand, Gaston 58, *col. pl. 14*
Bill, Max 157, 158, 194, 195, *col. pl. 85*
Birolli, Renato 93, 106, 110, 112, 114, 116, *col. pl. 42, pl. 54*
Bissier, Julius 174, *pl. 99 b*
Bissière, Roger 24, *pl. 18*
Blake, William 221, 244, 246
Bloc, André 36
Blöndal, Gunnlauger 255
Blondel 28, 29
Blow, Sandra 244, *pl. 135*
Bluth, Manfred 182
Boccioni, Umberto 85, 102
Bodart, Roger 57
Bodmer, Walter 194, *pl. 110 a*
Bogliardi 106
Bombois 28
Bona 33
Bonnard, Pierre 53, 182, 190, 238
Bonnet, Anne 59, *pl. 38*

Bordas, Dorothy 244
Borduas, Paul-Emile 47, 331, *pl. 171*
Börje, Giedeon 256
Borés, Francisco 20
Bosch, Hieronymus 54, 56
Bouthoorn 253
Bowel, Jessie 104
Bowen, Denis 244
Brancusi 98, 101, 231
Brands 252
Braque, Georges 12, 53, 125, 126, 164, 286, *pl. 15*
Bratby, John 250
Brauner, Victor 33
Brayer, Yves 16
Breker, Arno 101
Breton, André 289, 294, 296
Brianchon, Maurice 16
Brielle, Roger 33
Brien, Jóhann 255
Brignoni, Serge 194
Brocquy, Louis de 243, *pl. 133*
Brooks, James 324–326, *col. pl. 155, pl. 166*
Brossa, Juan 121
Bruegel 54, 57
Brunori, Alberto 120, *pl. 60*
Brüning, Peter 188
Brussens 54
Bruycker, Jules de 57
Bryen, Camille 46, 47, 186, *pl. 24*
Brzozowski, Tadeusz 128, 129
Buchheister, Carl 174, 185
Bueno, Vicente Perez 121
Buffet, Bernard 17, *pl. 29*
Burri, Alberto 118, *pl. 58*
Burssens, Jan 59
Bury, Pol 37, 53, 56
Busse, Jacques 22
Butler, Reginald 230, 231, 232, 234, 250, *pl. 125*

Cagli, Corrado 118
Caillaud 29
Calder, Alexander 37, 231, 232, 234, 242
Calò, Aldo 101
Camaro, Alexander 157, 158, 178, 180, 181, *pl. 87*

Campendonk, Heinrich 251
Campigli, Massimo 92
Camus, Albert 235, 236, 242
Camus, Gustave 53, 54
Canogar, Rafael 122, *pl. 70*
Capogrossi, Giuseppe 118,
  col. pl. 49
Capello, Carmelo 101
Carlsund, Otto G. 257
Carlstedt, Birjer 258
Caro, Anthony 236
Caro, Anita de 44
Carra 92
Carrade 44
Carzou 30
Casorati 92
Cassinari, Bruno 106, 110, 112,
  118, *col. pl. 45*
Cavael, Rolf 174
Cavaillés, Jules 16
Celebonovic, Marko 125, 126
Celic, Stojan 126, 129
Cerni, Vicente Aguilera 122
César 236
Cetin, Mire 126
Cézanne, Paul 85, 94, 121, 125,
  161, 256, 257, 321
Chabot 251
Chadwick, Lynn 232, 234-236,
  pl. 126
Chagall, Marc 12, 156
Chapelain-Midy 16
Chapoval, Jules 42
Char, René 172, 186
Chardin, Jean-Baptiste Siméon
  126
Chastel, Roger 21
Chatworthy, Robert 236
Chessa, L. 93
Chighine, Alfredo 120
Chilida, Eduardo 122
Chirico, Giorgio de 56, 85
Chirrino, Martin 122
Christensen, John 257
Churchill, Sir Winston 246
Ciarocchi 108
Cirlot, Juan Eduardo 121, 122
Clark, Sir Kenneth 224, 246
Clarke, Geoffrey 236
Clausen, Francisca 258
Clavé, Anton 18

Cliffe, Henry 244
Coester, Otto 182
Cohen, Harold 243, *pl. 131*
Coldstream, William 238
Colquhoun, Robert 243
Conde, Manolo 122
Consagra, Pietro 92, 97, 100, 108
Constant 252
Cooper, Austin 244
Coplans, John 244
Cordell, Magda 244
Corneille 252, 253, *pl. 140*
Corpora, Antonio 97, 108, 112,
  114, 116, *col. pl. 43*
Cossio, Francisco 121
Courteline, Georges 29
Coutaud 32
Cox, Jan 53
Craxton, John 243
Crépin 28
Crippa, Roberto 102, 119, *pl. 64*
Curry, John Stuart 288
Cuixart, Modest 121, 122, 124

Dahmen, Karl Fred 188, 190
Dali, Salvador 57, 121
Dalwood, Hubert 236
Damme, Suzanne van 57
Dardel, Nils von 256
Davidsson, Kristjàn 257
Davie, Alan 244, *col. pl. 119*
Davis, Stuart 283, *pl. 157*
Debré, Michel 40
Déchelette 28
Degas, Edgar 172, 232
Delacroix, Eugène 12, 188
Delahaut 53, 58
Delaunay, Robert 34, 170, 286
Delhaye, José 56
Del Marle 36
Delvaux, Paul 30, 54, 57, *pl. 36*
Demonchy 28
Denny, Robyn 244
Desnoyer 16
Despierre 16
Dewasne 38, 58
Deyrolle, Jean 34, 38, *pl. 21*
Diaz, Daniel Vazquez 121
Dickens, Charles 248
Diehl, Gösta 256
Dix, Otto 158

Dmitrienko 42
Doesburg, Theo van 36, 58, 158,
  194
Domela, César 37, 58
Dominguez, Oscar 33
Donatello 96
Dorazio, Piero 108, 110, 120,
  pl. 53
Dostoevsky, Fiodor 248
Dova, Gianni 119, *pl. 63*
Dubosq, Jean 56
Dubuffet, Jean 48, 236, 257,
  pl. 26
Duchamp, Marcel 37, 286
Dudant, Roger 58
Dufour, Bernard 22
Duthoo 44

Eble, Theo 194
Echevarria, Juan de 121
Eddington 166
Eggeling, Viking 257
Einarsson, Gudmandur 255
Einaudi, Luigi 104
Einstein, Albert 162
Einstein, Carl 164
Eisenhower, Dwight David,
  President 242
Eliot, T. S. 232
Ellis, Clifford 243
Elno 53
Enckell, Magnus 256
Engilberts, Jòn 255
Engström, Lars 256, 258
Ensor, James 53, 57, 58
Epstein, Jacob 226
Erixson, Sven 256
Erni, Hans 194
Ernst, Max 12, 32, 56, 119, 156,
  158, 182, 184, 286, 312, *pl. 93*
Estève, Maurice 21, *col. pl. 4*
Eve 28

Fabbri, Agenore 101
Fabian, Gottfried 193
Fabritius, Carel 14
Farreras, Francisico 124
Fasberg, Finn 258
Fassbender, Josef 174, *pl. 95*
Fautrier, Jean 48, *pl. 25*
Fazzini, Pericle 97, 108, 112

Fédier, Franz   194
Feiler, Paul   244
Feininger, Lyonel   155, 168
Feito, Luis   122, 124, *pl. 71 a*
Ferrant, Angel   122
Fietz, Gerhard   178
Fini, Léonore   32
Fischer, Klaus   188
Fischli, Hans   194
Fjell, Kaj   258
Fontana, Lucio   100, 119, *pl. 62*
Fontené, René   34, 36
Fougeron, André   17
Fous, Jean   28, 29
Francis, Sam   186, 330, *pl. 169*
Franchina, Nino   92, 97, 98, 100,
   112, 116
Frankenthaler, Helen   330
Fraser, Donald Hamilton   243,
   pl. 130
Freud, Lucien   *pl. 138*
Frobenius, A. L.   162
Frost, Terry   243
Fuhr, Xaver   181
Fürst, Albert   188

Gabo, Naum   36, 158, 230
Galente   104
Gammelgaard, Albert   257
Gardella, I.   89
Garelli, Franco   101
Gaudi   238
Gauguin, Paul   121, 160, 255,
   256
Gaul, Winfried   160, 188, 190,
   192, *pl. 101*
Gear, William   244, *pl. 134*
Gebser   166
Geiger, Rupprecht   186, *pl. 105*
Geitlinger, Ernst   174, 178
Generalic, Ivan   127
Gentilini, Franco   119, *pl. 66*
Georges, Claude   *pl. 31*
Gerardi   97
Ghiringelli   106
Giacometti, Alberto   32, 33, 231,
   234, 312, *pl. 28*
Gierowski, Stefan   128, 129
Gilles, Werner   157, 158, 160,
   178, 180, *col. pl. 80*
Gillet   44

Gilman, Harold   238
Gischia, Léon   22, 114, *pl. 16*
Glarner, Fritz   158, 194, *pl. 110b*
Gogh, Vincent van   94, 160, 250,
   256, 298, 300
Goller, Bruno   182
Gonzales   231
Gorin   36
Goris, Karl   192
Göritz, Mathias   122
Gorky, Arshile   289, 293, 294,
   296, 297, 300, 301, 304, 308,
   326, *col. pl. 148*
Gottlieb, Adolph   289, 310, 326,
   pl. 163
Gotsch, Friedrich-Karl   181, 182,
   pl. 92
Götz, Karl Otto   174, 185, 186,
   192, *pl. 97*
Graverol, Jane   56
Graves, Derrick   250
Graves, Morris   283
Greco, Emilio   97
Greenberg, Clement   286
Greffe, Léon   28
Gregorio, de   120
Greis, Otto   188, 190, 192
Grieshaber, H. A. P.   178, 181,
   pl. 90
Gris, Juan   20, 121, 164, 178
Groeneveld   251
Grönvik, Gunvor   256
Gropius, Walter   88
Grosz, Georg   158
Gruber, Francis   17
Grünewald, Isaak   256
Grünewald, Mathias   246
Gudnasson, Svavar   257
Guggenheim, Peggy   285, 288,
   312
Guerrier   18
Guerrini   101, 110
Guinovart, José   122
Gullon, Riccardo   122,
Guston, Philip   318, 320, 321,
   322, 324, 326, 328
   col. pl. 154, pl. 165
Guttuso, Renato   93, 94, 98, 104,
   110, 112, 114, 116, *col. pl. 40*

Hall, Fritz van   251

Hallström, Eric   256
Hardy, Thomas   246
Hartigan, Grace   328, 330, *pl. 170*
Hartung, Hans   40, 155, 169, 172,
   174, 176, 193, *col. pl. 9*
Hausmann, Raoul   158
Hayter, Stanley William   185,
   pl. 139
Heath, Adrian   244
Heckel, Erich   155, 157, 181
Hegedusic, Krsto   127
Heiberg, Jean   256
Heisenberg, Werner   160
Heldt, Werner   178, 180, *pl. 88*
Henriet, Henk   251
Hepworth, Barbara   222, 228,
   230, 243, *pl. 124*
Heramb, Thore   258
Herbin, Auguste   14, 34, 36
Heredia, Pablo Beltrande   122
Heron, Patrick   243
Hessing, Gustav   193
Hill, Anthony   244
Hilton, Roger   244, *col. pl. 118*
Hitchens, Ivon   238, *col. pl. 114*
Hjertén   256
Hoegstraeten, Samuel van   14
Hoehme, Gerhard   188, 190,
   pl. 102
Hölzel, Adolf   174
Hofer, Karl   157, 169
Hoffman, E. T. A.   182, 326
Hofmann, Hans   285, 286, *col.
   pl. 146*
Hooch, Pieter de   14
Hopkins, Gerard Manley   246
Hopper, Edward   283
Horn   251
Hosiasson, Philippe   44
Hülsenbeck, Richard   158
Hull, James   244
Hultén, G. O.   258
Humblot   17
Hundertwasser, Fritz   193,
   pl. 107 b
Hyfte, van   28, 29
Hynckes   251

Imkamp, Wilhelm   157
Ingres   293
Irwin, Gwyther   244

Isakson, Karl 256, 257
Iseli, Rolf 194
Itten, Johannes 184, 193
Iturrino, Francisco 121
Ivancic, Ljubo 126
Ivarson, Ivan 256

Jacobsen, Robert 257
Jaenisch, Hans 182
Jannot 17
Jarema, Maria 128
Jaspers, Karl 284
Jespers, Floris 54
Jawlensky, Alexej von 157
Jensen, Holger J. 257
Jóhannesson, Johannes 255
John, Augustus 236
Jolin, Einar 256
Jones, David 238
Jònssen, Asgrimur 255
Jònsson, Finnur 255
Jorn, Asger 252, *pl. 142*
Junkers, Adja 257

Kadow, Gerhard 157
Kafka, Franz 128, 172
Kallos 44
Kami, Sugai 48
Kandelin, Ole 258
Kandinsky, Wassily 34, 37, 53,
    106, 126, 127, 155-157, 162,
    166, 176, 194, 244, 296
Kanerva, Aimo 256
Kantor, Tadeusz 128, 129, *pl. 74 a*
Kaus, Max 181
Keats, John 321
Kempe, Roland 257
Kennen, Alexis 54
Kerg, Théo 22
Kermadec, E. de 21
Khnopff, Fernand 57
Kinley, Peter 243
Kirchner, Ernst Ludwig 155,
    168, 169, 178, 180
Kjarval, Jòhannes Sveinsson 255
Klee, Paul 22, 42, 47, 57, 106,
    155-157, 166, 168, 172, 176,
    184, 193
Kleint, Boris 174, 196
Kleist, Heinrich von 47
Kline, Franz 316, 326, 328,
    pl. 167

Klomsdorff, Etzel 192
Kluht, Karl 181
Koch 251
Kokoschka, Oskar 157, 181, 182,
    193
Kolos-Vary 44
Kooning, Willem de 236, 292,
    294, 297, 298, 300-302, 304,
    308, 309, 314, 316-318, 320,
    324-326, 328, 330, *col. pl. 149,*
    pl. 161
Kregar, Stane 126
Kreutz, Heinz 188, 190, 192
Krogh, Peer 256
Kvaran, Karl 255
Kulovesi, Erkki 256
Kupka 34
Kuponen, Erkki 256
Kylberg, Carl 256

Labisse, Félix 32
Lacomblez, Jacques 56
Lagage 44
Lagrange, Jacques 26
Lagru 28, 29
Lambert, René 56
Lanskoy, André 40, *col. pl. 10*
Lanyon, Peter 243, *col. pl. 116*
Lapicque, Charles 20
Lapoujade, Robert 48
Lardera, Berto 101, 102
Lautréamont 56
Lebenstein, Jan 128, 129
Leck, van der 58, 251
Le Corbusier 88, 161, 193
Lefrancq, Marcel 56
Léger, Fernand 12, 156, 161, 236,
    286, 294
Legueult 16
Le Moal, Jean 24
Leonardo da Vinci 44, 46, 190
Leoncillo 92, 97, 98, 101, 112,
    116
Leppien, Jean 157
Lepri, Stanislao 30
Lergaard, Niels 257
Leslie, Alfred 328
Lint, Lovis van 59
Leuppi, Leo
Levedag, Fritz 157
Levi, Carlo 93, 104, 112

Lewis, Wyndham 221, 236, 238
Lhote, André 17
Licini, Osvaldo 106, 118, *col. pl. 48*
Limpers, Johan 251
Linnquist, Hilding 256
Lipchitz 236
Lismonde 58, *pl. 36*
Lisitsky, El 158
Ljösne, Halvdan 258
Lohse, Richard 194
Lorjou 17
Lubarda, Petar 125
Luppi, Leo 194
Lyr, René 53

Macbryde, Robert 243
Macke, August 157
MacTaggart 221
Magnelli, Alberto 34, 38, 40, 92,
    100, 106, 118, *pl. 23*
Màkila, Otto 258
Mafai 86, 93, 96, 104, 106, 108,
    119
Maillol 101
Maistre, Roy de 243
Malevich, Casimir 34, 127, 158,
    186
Mallarmé, Stéphane 180, 192,
    317
Mampaso, Manuel 124
Mandyn 59
Manessier, Alfred 24, 25, 26,
    col. pl. 7
Mannucci, Edgardo 100
Man Ray 30, 56
Manzù, Giacomo 90, 96, 102
Marc, Franz 157, 168
Marchand, André 17, 18
Marchiori 110, 112, 114
Margritte, René 30, 54, 57, *pl. 35*
Mariani 102
Marignoli 120
Marinetti 238
Marini, Marino 90, 96, 97, 102
Marlier, François 56
Marstboom, Antoine 58, 59
Martin, Kenneth 242
Martini, Arturo 89, 96-98, 100, 102
Marx, Karl 242
Masaccio 226
Mascherini 97

370

Masson, André   12, 156, 286, 288, 290, 312

Mastroianni, Umberto   101

Mathieu, Georges   46, 47, 188, *pl. 32 a*

Matisse, Henri   12, 25, 53, 161, 221, 256, 286, 305, 313

Matta   33, 286, 289, 296, 297

Maugham, Somerset   246

Mauke, Rudolf   186, *pl. 106*

Maurras, Charles   331

Mazio, F.   93

Mazzacurati   97

McHale, John   244

McWilliam, F. E.   232

Meadows, Bernard   236

Medley, Robert   243

Meistermann, Georg   178, 184, 185, *col. pl. 83*

Meli, Salvatore   102

Melli, Roberto   102

Mendelson, Max   58

Menzio   104

Meyboden, Hans   181, 182

Michotte, Max   56

Mikl, Josef   193, *pl. 107 a*

Middleditch, Edward   250, *pl. 137*

Middleton, Derek   243

Migneco   93

Millares, Manolo   122, 123

Milnes-Smith, J.   244

Milo, Jean   59

Milunovic, Milo   125, 126

Minaux   17

Minguzzi, Luciano   101

Mirko, Basaldella   92, 97, 98, 114, 236

Miró, Juan   121, 122, 164, 176, 288, 290, 294

Mitchell, Joan   328

Modersohn-Becker, Paula   182

Modigliani   226

Moholy-Nagy, Lászlò   37, 115, 156, 158

Moilliet, Louis   193, 194

Molzahn, Johannes   155

Monachesi   108

Mondrian, Piet   34, 36, 58, 126, 127, 157, 186, 193, 240, 251, 286, 288, 302, 308, 313, 314, 318, 320

Monet, Claude   46, 188, 190, 285, 320

Moore, Henry   101, 168, 221, 222, 224, 226-228, 230, 232, 234, 236, 246, *pl. 121, 122, 123*

Morandi, Giorgio   92, 93, 106, 108, *col. pl. 39*

Moreni, Mattia   116, *pl. 61*

Morlotti, Ennio   98, 110, 112, 116, *col. pl. 44*

Mörner, Stellan,   257

Mortensen, Richard   37, 257, *col. pl. 8*

Mortier, Antoine   58

Motherwell, Robert,   285, 288, 304–306, 326, *col. pl. 150*

Muche, Georg   184

Müller, Otto   157, 178

Müller-Kraus   186

Muis   251

Munch, Edvard   169, 176, 180, 182, 256, 258

Murtić, Edo   126, *pl. 72*

Music, Zoran   21 *pl. 65*

Nanninga   254

Nash, Paul   221, 224, 236

Nativi, Gualtiero   120

Nay, Ernst Wilhelm   155, 160, 166, 169, 170, 172, 174, *col. pl. 78*

Nemes, Endre   257, *pl. 143*

Nerval, Gérard de   56

Nervi, P. L.   89

Nesch, Rolf   155, 157, 178, 180, 181, *pl. 89*

Newman, Barnett   309, 310

Nicholson, Ben   222, 240, 242, 243, *col. pl. 111*

Nicholson, William   238, 240

Niederreuther, Thomas   181

Nielsen, Knud   258

Nilsson, Vera   256

Nolde, Emil   155, 181

Nordström, Lars Gunnar   258

Novalis   47, 166

Nowosielski, Jerzy   128, 129

Obermeier   162

Oelze, Richard   158, 184, *pl. 94*

Olofsson, P.   257

Olsson, Erik   257

Orozco   289

Orgeix, Christian d'   *pl. 30*

Osborne, John   250

Ors, Eugenio d'   122

Oteiza, Jorge de   122

Ouborg   251, 252

Oudot, Roland   16

Overstraeten, War van   54

Oteiya   122

Paalen, Wolfgang   33

Pagano, G.   88

Palazuelo   24

Palmer, Samuel   244, 246

Paolozzi, Eduardo   232, 236

Pasmore, Victor   240, 242, 244, *col. pl. 113*

Pasque, Auvin   56

Paulucci, E.   93, 104

Pechstein, Max   157

Peire, Luc   59

Pelayo   16

Pellicer, Cirici   122

Pedersen, Carl Henning   258

Perez, Manuel Gil   122

Peric, Sime   126, 129

Perilli, Achille   108, 110, 120, *pl. 52*

Permeke   53

Persico, E.   88

Peters   251

Petersen, Olle   257

Peturson, Valtyo   257

Pevsner, Antoine   36, 127, 158

Peyronnet   28

Piacentini   86

Piaubert, Jean   44

Picabia   286

Picasso, Pablo   12, 17, 53, 94, 116, 118, 121, 160, 161, 164, 180, 182, 184, 193, 221, 226, 231, 232, 236, 255, 286, 288, 289, 290, 293, 294, 305

Picelj, Ivan   126

Pignon, Edouard   18, 114, *col. pl. 1*

Pillet, Edgar   36, 38, 57

Pirandello, Fausto   119, col. *pl. 50*

Pisis, F. de   92, 193

Pizzinato, Giuseppe   110, 114, 116

Planck, Max 195
Plansdure, Enrique 129, 124
Planson, André 16
Platschek, Hans 122, 186
Poe, Edgar Allan 248
Poliakoff, Serge 22, 176,
  col. pl. 5
Pollock, Jackson 188, 285, 286,
  288-290, 292, 293, 297, 298,
  301, 304, 306, 308, 309, 314,
  316-318, 320, 324, 326, 328,
  330 *col. pl. 147, pl. 158, 159*
Pons, Joan 121
Powys, John Cowper 238
Prachensky, Marcus
Prampolini, Enrico 106, 110,
  118, 122, *pl. 57*
Prassinos, Mario 34, *pl. 20*
Pregelj, Marij 126
Protic, Miodrag 126, 129
Provedano, Antonio 124
Puig, Arnald 121

Quaroni 89
Quiette, René 53

Radice 106
Rainer, Arnulf 193
Rasica, Bozidar 126
Ransy, Jean 56
Raspi 120
Raymond, Marcel 317
Rebeyrolle 18
Redon, Odilon 305
Reggiani, Mauro 106, 118, *pl. 56*
Renoir, Paul 232
Renotte, Paul 56
Resnick, Milton 328, *pl. 168*
Revolt, Axel 256
Richards, Ceri 243, *col. pl. 117*
Richter, Hans 155
Ridolfi 89
Rilke, Rainer Maria 42, 182
Rho 106
Rimbaud, Jean Arthur 56, 180,
  304
Riopelle, Jean-Paul 47, 188, 331,
  col. pl. 13
Rivière, Jacques 322
Roberts, William 238
Rohde, Lennart 257

Rodin, Auguste 232, 235, 285
Rogers 89
Rogers, Claude 238
Rogister, Marie-Luise 174
Rohlfs, Christian 155
Rohner 17
Rolfssen, Alf 256
Rollier, Charles 194
Romiti 120
Ronald, William 331, *pl. 172*
Rooskens 252
Rops, Félicien 57
Rosai 92
Rosenberg, Harold 284
Rosso, Medardo 96, 102
Rothko, Mark 193, 285, 289,
  309, 310, 312-314, 317, 320,
  326, *col. pl. 153, pl. 164*
Rouault 256
Rousseau, Henri 28
Roy, Claude 48
Roy, Pierre 30
Rude, Olaf 257
Ruggeri 120
Rumney, Ralph 244
Russo, Margherita *pl. 96 b*
Ryggen, Hannah 258

Saarinen, Yrjö 256
Sadun 108, 119
Saint-John Perse 172
Sallinen, Tykö 256
Salvatore (Messina) 101
Sandel, Gösta 256
Sanfilippo, Antonio 110, 120
Santomaso, Giuseppe 110, 116,
  col. pl. 46
Saroni 120
Sartre, Jean Paul, 172, 236, 248,
  302, 304
Saura, Antonio 123, *pl. 68*
Scarpa, P. 89
Scauflaire, Edgar 53
Schapiro, Meyer 314
Scharff, William 257
Scheving, Gunnlauger 255
Schiöler, Inge 256
Schlemmer, Oskar 155, 160, 161
Schmidt-Rottluff, Karl 155, 157,
  186
Schneider, Gérard 42, *col pl. 11*

Schnubel 28
Schöffer 36
Scholz, Werner 178, 181, *pl. 91*
Schrimpff, Georg 158
Schulz, Alexander 258
Schultze, Bernhard 160, 186,
  190, 192, *col. pl. 82*
Schulze, Wolfgang, *see* Wols
Schumacher, Emil 160, 188,
  190, 192, *pl. 103*
Schwitters, Kurt 56, 127, 155,
  158, 174, 236, 305
Scialoja 108, 119
Scipione 86, 93, 104, 108
Scordia, Antonio 119
Scott, William 235, 243,
  col. pl. 115
Séaux 53
Seitz, William 302
Serpan, Jaroslaw *pl. 32 b*
Servranckx 53, 58, 60
Severini, Gino 92
Shahn, Ben 283
Shjerfbeck, Helen 256
Sluijters 251, 252
Sibelius 255
Sickert 221, 238
Signori, Carlo 101, 102
Simon, Armand 56
Singier, Camille 24, *pl. 17*
Siquieros 290
Sköld, Otte 256
Skùlason, Thorwaldur 257
Smet, Gustave de 53
Smith, Jack 250, *col. pl. 120*
Smith, Sir Matthew 236
Smith, Richard 244
Soldati, Atanasio 93, 106, 118,
  col. pl. 41
Somaini, Francesco 102
Sommer, Oskar 192
Sörensen, Henrik 256
Sonderborg, K. R. H. 185, 186,
  192, *pl. 100*
Sondergaard, Jens 257
Souverbie 16
Sosset, Louis Léon 59
Soto 37
Soulages, Pierre 42, *col. pl. 12*
Soutine 285, 298
Spazzapan, Luigi 118, *pl. 59*

372

Spencer, Stanley 238
Spiegele, Louis von de 56
Spillaert, Léon 53
Srbinovic, Mladen 126, 129
Srnec, Aleksandar 126
Staël, Nicolaes de 20, 176,
    col. pl. 2
Stancic, Miljenko 125, 129
Staszewski, Henryk 127
Staudacher, Hans 193
Stefànsson, Jòn 255
Stern, Jonasz 128
Stieglitz 286
Still, Clyfford 285, 289, 309, 310,
    317, 318, 326, 328, 330, *col. pl.
    152*
Storstern, Aage 257
Stradone 108
Strzeminski, Wladyslaw 127,
    pl. 74 b
Stupicas, Gabrijel 125
Suarez, Antonio 123
Sutherland, Graham 221, 222,
    224, 244, 246, 248, 250,
    col. pl. 112, pl. 127
Sveinsdòttir, Juliana 255
Swanenburgh 54
Sweeney, James Johnson 294
Szenes, Arpad 26

Täuber-Arp, Sophie 194
Tailleux, Francis 18
Tal Coat, Pierre 24, 25, *pl. 19*
Tanguy 286
Tanning, Dorothea 33
Tapié, Michel 44, 46, 192
Tapies, Antonio 121–123, *pl. 67*
Tchelitchev, Pavel 33
Terragni, G. 88
Tharrats, Juan-José 121–123, *pl. 69*
Thieler, Fred 188, 192, *pl. 104*
Thomas, Dylan 246
Thòrarinson, Karen Agneta 255
Thorleifsson, Jòn 255
Thornton, Leslie 236
Tiepolo, Giambattista 188
Tinguely 37
Tobey, Mark 188, 293,
    col. pl. 145, pl. 160
Tomlin, Bradley Walker 306,
    308, 324, 326, *col. pl. 151*

Toorop, Charley 251
Tosi 92
Toyen 33
Treccani 93
Trier, Hann 174, 184, 185,
    pl. 98
Trökes, Heinz 158, 182, 184, 185
    col. pl. 81
Tryggvadottir, Nina 257
Tunnard, John 243
Turcato, Giulio 108, 110, 112,
    116, *pl. 51*
Turnbull, William 236
Turner, William 221
Tworkov, Jack 325, 326,
    col. pl. 156
Tyszkiewicz, Maria Teresa
    128, 129

Ubac, Raoul 22, 56, *pl. 34*
Uhde, Wilhelm 28, 29
Unger, Carl *pl. 108 a*

Vacchi 120
Vaerten, Jan 59
Valensi, Henri 36
Valéry, Paul 166, 318
Vandercam, Serge 59
Vantongerloo 127
Varlin 193, *pl. 109*
Vasarely, Victor 38, *pl. 22*
Vaughan, Keith 243, *pl. 132*
Vedova, Emilio 104, 106, 110,
    112, 116, *col. pl. 47*
Veen, Gerrit van der 251
Vela, Vicente 123, *pl. 71 b*
Velde, Bram van 40
Velde, Geer van 14
Vénard 17
Venturi, Lionello 104, 116
Vermeer 14
Viani, Alberto 92, 97, 98, 112
Vicente, Esteban 306, 326
Vieira da Silva, Maria Elena 20,
    col. pl. 3
Villeri, Jean 25
Villon, Jacques 12
Vionoja, Veikko 256
Vivin 28
Vordemberge-Gildewart, Fried-
    rich 158

Vozarevic, Lazar 126, 129
Vujaklija, Lazar 127, 129, *pl. 73*
Vulliamy, Gérard 33, 194

Wagemaeker 253
Walters, Max 258
Weichberger, Philipp 192
Wells, John 243
Werkman 251
Werner, Theodor 155, 160, 164,
    165 166, 169, 172, 174,
    col. pl. 76
Werner, Woty 176, 184,
    col. pl. 84
Westerdahl, Eduardo 121
Whistler 221, 238
Whitman, Walt 317
Wiegers 251
Wiemken, Walter Kurt 194
Wiertz, Antoine 57
Wigman, Mary 178
Willink 251
Winckelmann 232
Winter, Bryan 243, *pl. 129*
Winter, Fritz 155, 157, 160, 166,
    168, 169, 172, 178, *col. pl. 77*
Winther, Richard 258
Witte, Emmanuel de 14
Wlodarski, Marek 128
Woestijne, Maxime van de 56
Wolf, Karl Anton *pl. 108 b*
Wolvens, Henri Victor 54
Wols 47, 52, 155, 172, 188,
    col. pl. 79
Wood, Grant 288
Wordsworth, William 246
Worringer, Wilhelm 243
Wright, Frank Lloyd 89
Wyckaert, Maurier de 59

Zabaleta, Rafel 122
Zack, Léon 25
Zangs, Herbert 188
Zao-Wou-Ki 48, *pl. 27*
Zervos, Christian 164
Zevi, Bruno 89
Zimmermann, Mac 182

PHOTO CREDITS

Villand & Galanis, Paris, pl. 16

Galerie Änne Abels, Cologne, pl. 17, 18, 31, 32b, 61

Galerie de France, Paris, pl. 20, 21, 23, 27

Vizzanova, Paris, pl. 25

Paul Facchetti, Paris, pl. 26, 100

Galerie Maeght, Paris, pl. 28, 34

Galerie Springer, Berlin, pl. 30, 88

Robert David, Paris, pl. 33

Jean de Maeyer, Antwerpen, pl. 36

Paul Bijtebier, Brussels, pl. 38, 143

Fototeca A.S.A.C. Biennale, Venice, pl. 51, 58, 62, 66, 67, 68, 69, 70, 71a, 71b, 72, 110b

Oscar Savio, Rome, pl. 52, 53, 57, 60

Gian Sinigardia, Milan, pl. 54

De Antonis, Rome, pl. 55

Galleria La Bussola, Rome, pl. 59

Galleria Blu, Milan, pl. 63

Snimio Toso Dabac, Zagreb, pl. 73

Gnilka, Berlin, pl. 87, 91, 92, 106

Dr. Salchow, Cologne, pl. 90, 95, 98

Landesbildstelle Berlin, pl. 93

Schmitz-Fabri, Cologne, pl. 96a

Manfred Leve, Düsseldorf, pl. 101

Galerie 22, Düsseldorf, pl. 102

Aghot, Hagen i. W., pl. 103

R. Nohr, Munich, pl. 104

Perls, Munich, pl. 105

Karl Koster, pl. 108a

Conzett & Huber, Zurich, pl. 109

Öffentl. Kunstsammlung Basel, pl. 110a

Lidbrooke, pl. 122

Simon Reid, Dumfried, pl. 123

Studio St. Ives, Cornwall, pl. 124, 129

David Farrell, Gloucester, pl. 126

Gimpel Fils Gallery, pl. 130, 131, 134, 135

Alfred Hecht, London, pl. 132

Beaux Arts Gallery, London, pl. 137

Gemeentemusea van Amsterdam, pl. 140, 141

Oliver Baker, New York, pl. 157, 159, 161, 164, 165, 167, 169

The Museum of Modern Art, New York, pl. 158, 162, 163, 171

Adolph Studly, New York, pl. 160

Rudolph Burckhardt, New York, pl. 168

Kootz Gallery, New York, pl. 172